A History of
Uppsala University
1477–1977

Sten Lindroth

A HISTORY OF
UPPSALA
UNIVERSITY
1477–1977

Uppsala University 1976

Distributor
ALMQVIST & WIKSELL INTERNATIONAL
STOCKHOLM, SWEDEN

© 1976 Sten Lindroth

Translated by Neil Tomkinson, B.A., with

the assistance of Jean Gray, B.A., T.K.

The illustrations were chosen by Åke Davidsson

Jacket and binding design by Johan W. Hillbom

ISBN 91-506-0081-8

Printed in Sweden by

Almqvist & Wiksell, Uppsala 1976

Preface

This history of the University of Uppsala was written for publication on the occasion of the University's quincentenary in 1977. I do not claim that it gives a penetrating scholarly survey of this extensive subject. My aim was only to sketch, for the general reader, the main features of the University's history over the past 500 years. The Swedish edition, which is being published simultaneously, concludes with a bibliography of Swedish writings about the University.

I wish to express my cordial thanks to my friend Dr Åke Davidsson, the Principal Librarian in the Manuscripts Department of the University Library, for his invaluable assistance in selecting the illustrations.

Uppsala, June 1976.

Sten Lindroth

Contents

List of Illustrations

CHAPTER I

The Mediaeval University

Towards the end of the Middle Ages, it was only a matter of time before a university was founded in Sweden. The first European universities, headed by Bologna and Paris, were creations of the 12th century and the splendid efflorescence of learning which followed from the renaissance of Roman law and the emergence of the scholastic philosophy. New universities were soon established in the southern European countries and at a very early stage also in England. On the other hand, it was some time before this new type of establishment of higher education was introduced into northern and eastern Europe, i.e. among the Germanic and Slav peoples. Prague came first, in the middle of the 14th century, after which progress was rapid. A number of universities were founded in the German Empire, and early in the next century the movement reached the Baltic coast—the university at Rostock, a busy port in the Hanseatic League, was founded in 1419 and that at Greifswald in Pomerania a good generation later (1456).

The Roman Catholic Church, the mother of all higher education, had not, of course, neglected her educational duty in mediaeval Sweden. The cathedral schools had given boys who intended to become priests the necessary knowledge of Latin ever since the Folkunga period, and the mendicant friars—the Dominicans and Franciscans—kept excellent schools, whose curricula included philosophy and theology. But for more scholarly training, which in time became increasingly necessary for a successful career in the Church, higher education abroad was an unavoidable necessity. Like other Scandinavians, the Swedes resorted to Continental seats of learning. The renowned University of Paris for long exerted an irresistible attraction. From the middle of the 13th century, Swedish students went there to acquire the philosophical learning which was the basis of theology; a few also studied canon law at Bologna or Orléans. However, in course of time the Swedes found other destinations and began to forsake the alleys of the Quartier Latin. When the University of Prague was founded, the Swedish students preferred to attend it, and in the course of the 15th century the number of universities became almost bewilderingly plentiful. There were, at a reasonable geographical

1

distance, several German seats of learning to choose between. To begin with, Leipzig was the most popular but was succeeded in the middle of the century by Rostock, which was so easily accessible by sea. But many students sought out other universities; Greifswald was also well situated and Swedish students might also be met with in Cologne, Vienna and Erfurt; some still went to Paris or travelled the long road to Italy. These study tours, which seem to have reached their maximum about 1450, were still made under the auspices of the Church. Scholarships and other ecclesiastical revenues or offices were granted to these student travellers, who were either young scholars or middle-aged prelates; on returning home with the proper university degrees, they became members of cathedral chapters or received some other ecclesiastical office.

Fifteenth-century Swedish society was seemingly not very favourable to the quiet development of cultural life. The political union with Denmark caused continual friction; revolts, civil wars and *coups d'état* succeeded each other; venerable bishops appeared in the roles of ruthless and fanatical party men and commanded bands of soldiers. A kind of general demoralization was widespread in public life and old ideals mouldered away. The tone of the scanty secular literature was rough and rude; it mostly consisted of crude rhymed chronicles and other political propaganda, full of hatred of the Danes, which gradually became identical with Swedish patriotism. A vulgar bourgeois spirit had replaced the chivalrous courtesy which had set the standard for life and literature during the Folkunga period, the heyday of mediaeval Swedish culture.

However, the picture also presented other features. The late Middle Ages were a period of economic progress in Sweden; foreign trade increased and consequently the towns and the influence of the bourgeoisie increased. The Church and the nobility shared in the new prosperity, great castles were built, monasteries were founded and the churches were embellished with imported treasures and dazzling mural paintings. While the Roman Catholic Church as a spiritual institution was being increasingly divested of its sanctity, its material opportunities of encouraging individual piety and learning were improved. During the 15th century, the monastery founded by St. Bridget at Vadstena constantly grew in wealth and reputation; fervent Christian devotion was cultivated there and its library was the biggest in Scandinavia. In the individual dioceses, men with scholarly qualifications were increasingly in demand. In the cathedral chapters sat canons with masters' degrees acquired abroad; several were doctors of theology or canon law and consequently had the best scholarly training available in that age. In this way, currents of new ideas reached Sweden from the Continent. Kort Rogge, Bishop of Strängnäs, read Petrarch and was influenced by modern Italian humanism, but otherwise the stimuli

2

came chiefly from the German universities, to which the great majority of students went.

Under these circumstances, the idea of establishing in Sweden a seat of higher learning was a natural and inevitable one. There were even financial arguments in its favour. The study tours abroad, which covered long distances and lasted many years, cost large sums of money; it would mean considerable financial reliefs for the dioceses if advanced university training could be given inside the country. According to an unconfirmed report, the matter was first raised in 1417; it was proposed that qualified teachers should be sent for from Germany. Two years later, Erik of Pomerania, who reigned over the united Kingdom of Sweden, Denmark and Norway, took a fresh initiative and obtained a Papal bull authorizing him to establish a university in connection with some cathedral chapter in his kingdom. This initiative, which probably referred to Lund or Roskilde, did not lead to any concrete result.

Not quite twenty years later, the Swedish Privy Council took up the university question. The driving force was undoubtedly Nicolaus Ragvaldi, the newly appointed Archbishop of Uppsala, a learned and eloquent man and a skilful ecclesiastical politician, who had scored diplomatic successes at the Council of Basle. In the autumn of 1438, the Privy Council decided that the tithe which had been granted to the Enköping Leprosy Hospital should instead be paid to Andreas Bondonis, who should lecture at Uppsala Cathedral annually "as a master *in studiis privilegiatis*". As at this period the term *studium privilegiatum* was equivalent to "university", this was a declaration that the modest instruction to be given in Uppsala was to be of an academic character and to be superimposed on that given at the Cathedral School. Nicolaus Ragvaldi's intention was to begin in a small way, with a single teacher. Andreas Bondonis was competent enough; he had taken the degree of Master of Arts at Vienna and had given lectures there before returning to Sweden. However, it is not clear how long he worked in Uppsala as the first university teacher in Sweden or whether he did so at all. As early as 1440, he was back in his home town of Västerås and ten years later died, a well-to-do citizen, in Stockholm.

However, Nicolaus Ragvaldi persevered. At a synod in Söderköping in 1441, it was decided that, somewhere in Sweden, probably at Uppsala, at least one *studium particulare*, i.e. an incomplete course of academic instruction, should be established; bishops and cathedral chapters were to think about students whom they might send there and about providing funds for their maintenance. In the spring of 1444, Archbishop Nicolaus succeeded in obtaining from Christoph of Bavaria, the new king of the united Kingdom, a confirmation that the Enköping Hospital tithe should henceforth be ordered to be paid to "the school which shall continue to be

3

held at Uppsala Cathedral". It has been taken for granted that little or nothing came of these efforts. A wild and stormy period then began; the new Archbishop, Jöns Bengtsson Oxenstierna, threw himself into the violent struggle for political power and would have had little attention to spare for the learned studies being pursued in his archbishopric. However, there are indications that higher education was actually carried on in Uppsala during this period, at least in the 1460s; scholars from the Swedish cathedral schools seem to have found their way here.

Thus, there were stimuli and preparatory work and even a slight academic tradition with which connections could be made when a real university was finally founded in Uppsala. This took place in the autumn of 1477. The man behind this achievement was Jacob Ulvsson, who had been Archbishop for eight years. The situation at the time was propitious. After his victory over the Danes at the Battle of Brunkeberg in 1471, Sten Sture, the Regent, had consolidated his power and a short period of internal calm and national recovery followed. Patriotism was manifested in many different ways: the Germans were excluded from the town magistracies and in the Storkyrka in Stockholm, Bernt Notke, of Lübeck, created in his sculpture of St. George and the Dragon a monumental symbol of the newly awakened feeling of self-esteem among the Swedes. The national kingdom —a prospect which Sten Sture glimpsed from time to time—needed, for reasons of prestige, a university within its borders. The many new academies in the German-speaking countries had been promoted by ambitious princes or bourgeois corporations, who had had regard both to the public utility of the university and to the lustre which the possession of a university of its own shed on the country.

The oldest European universities had come into existence under varying conditions and had been organized on different lines. But, in time a fixed pattern for the founding of a new university had been developed and this became the standard procedure in the German states of the 14th and 15th centuries. The Church and the secular authorities acted in collaboration. In the atmosphere of incipient nationalism, however, the State gained more and more influence. It was now the rule for the prince or—as in prosperous trading towns, such as Cologne and Rostock—the bourgeoisie to take the initiative in founding a university. But, as free institutions at the point of intersection between the ecclesiastical and the governmental spheres of influence, the universities still required Papal authorization. A petition was dispatched to the Curia in Rome, which issued the necessary charter, containing directions as to the structure of the new seat of learning. An archbishop or bishop was usually designated as the chancellor. This established the university in the legal sense, as a corporation divided into the usual faculties and having the right to award valid aca-

4

1. Archbishop Jacob Ulvsson on his porphyry column. This statue, sculptured by Christian Eriksson, was erected in 1927 on the south side of the Cathedral on the occasion of the 450th anniversary of the foundation of the University of Uppsala. Sture-Foto.

demic degrees. The prince or the municipal authorities generally issued secular privileges in addition, but in principle the Papal charter meant that the teachers and students at the university were independent in relation to the government authorities.

The circumstances in which the University of Uppsala came into existence were unusual. There is no indication that the Regent had any part in it from the beginning. The first Swedish university was, from its inception, a purely ecclesiastical affair, and consequently it was naturally located in Uppsala. The previous attempts had been made by the archiepiscopal see and it was the new primate of the Church in Sweden, Jacob Ulvsson, who brought them to a head. The prologue to the action is not known in detail, but the principal part played by the Archbishop is incontrovertible. Jacob Ulvsson's own learning was deep and sound; it had been acquired during prolonged studies on the Continent, first at Rostock and then at Paris, where he took his master's degree, read canon law and probably taught in the Faculty of Arts. In the mid-1460s, he was sent, in the interests of the archdiocese, to Rome, where he gained an intimate knowledge of the labyrinths of Papal policy. In 1469, while still in the Curia, he was appointed Archbishop of Sweden.

The university question was brought up at a general synod of the Church in Sweden, probably in 1475. Jacob Ulvsson and the assembled clergy decided that a university should be established in Uppsala. They aimed to found a complete educational institution with all the usual faculties—a *studium generale,* in the contemporary terminology. There were reasons for urgent action. It was known for certain that the Danes were already busy trying to obtain a university of their own; the Papal bull concerning it was in actual fact made out in the summer of 1475, and it was a matter of getting in ahead of the Danes. The Archbishop seems to have made the first application to the Curia in his own name. When the matter had reached a certain stage, the support of the secular authorities became necessary. The Swedish Church and the Privy Council together drew up a petition (now lost), which was conveyed to Rome by Ragvald Ingemunds-son, a canon at Uppsala. It was finally granted in July 1476, but its formal issue seems to have been delayed by difficulties in producing the large fee for the Papal bull (350 florins). The document in which the Holy Father gave his permission for a university to be established in Uppsala was not dated until 27 February 1477. The Pope was Sixtus IV, who commissioned the Sistine Chapel. This precious document was in Jacob Ulvsson's hands some time at the beginning of the summer.

The bull of Sixtus IV—the real charter of the University of Uppsala—is written in the flowery style of the Papal Chancellery. The Pope takes the new seat of learning under his protection and gives it all the freedoms and privileges which the University of Bologna enjoyed by custom. The traditional four faculties were to be established—theology, canon and Roman law, medicine and philosophy or the liberal arts. The Archbishop of Uppsala was appointed Chancellor of the University, with the right to award the academic degrees (bachelor, master, licentiate and doctor). Moreover, the Archbishop was to see to it that the rights, freedoms and privileges of the academic body (both teachers and students) were preserved.

Once Jacob Ulvsson had received the Papal bull, he acted rapidly. The Privy Council, of which he was the most outstanding member, and the Regent, Sten Sture, met at the beginning of July at Strängnäs. The Archbishop obtained from the Council a special charter for the University of Uppsala, dated 2 July. It is in Swedish and is brief, evidently having been written in a hurry. Since the Pope, "to the continuance, comfort and satis-

6

2. *The charter of the University of Uppsala issued by the Swedish Privy Council on 2 July 1477. University of Uppsala Archives.*

faction of Christendom and the people of the kingdom of Sweden", had founded a *studium privilegiatum* in Uppsala, the Privy Council would protect and defend its Rector (Vice-Chancellor), teachers and students for ever. The Rector was to be the judge in all legal matters, except those concerning the Church's revenues and property; this established the special academic jurisdiction, which was to subsist for centuries. In its haste, the Privy Council did not manage to draw up any further statutes for the University and instead decided that it should be granted the same privileges and freedoms as the King of France had granted to the University of Paris. This may seem contradictory, as the Papal bull had indicated Bologna as the model. But the bull viewed the new seat of learning as a spiritual institution, resting in the arms of the Roman Catholic Church, while the Privy Council's letter was aimed at regulating its external relations in Swedish society. Besides, the difference meant little in actual fact. The Universities of Bologna and Paris—which had once been opposites—had become more and more alike, and reference might be made just as well to the one as to the other. In the late Middle Ages, Papal bulls about universities mentioned Bologna and Paris alternately as models; the University of Bologna was put in as a model for both Copenhagen and Uppsala, but otherwise it was usually laid down that the privileges of the University of Paris were to apply. This was almost formulary. The Privy Council's reference to the University of Paris should also be understood in this sense, though, as a former student at Paris, Jacob Ulvsson could give the formula a living content.

It remained with the Archbishop to complete the work. On 20 July, he issued a letter of invitation, in which he gave an account of the reasons for founding a university in Uppsala and recapitulated what had happened. Divine Omnipotence had caused universities to grow up in many countries, in order that learned men might be trained to feed the Lord's flock with the sacred doctrine. There had, up to then, been no university in Sweden and it was not possible for all students to travel to seats of learning abroad. Talented youths hesitated to do so on account of poverty or timidity and those who actually set off ran great risks to life and property—he mentions both war and pirates. A Swedish university was so much the more urgent in that Sweden was situated at the world's end and was surrounded by heathens and heretics. The Curia and the Privy Council had now granted charters for a university in Uppsala and, as its Chancellor, the Archbishop wished to invite all masters, students and scholars who wished to study and defend their doctoral theses there to come to the town and enjoy the privileges that had been granted. On 21 September, the Pope's bull was to be ceremonially brought into Uppsala, and on St. Bridget's Day (7 October) lectures and exercises in theology, canon law and the liberal arts were to begin. To all appearances, this was also what happened. Sten Sture, the Regent, was in the town at the time and must certainly have attended the opening ceremony.

The new university needed premises, teachers and funds for their subsistence. Premises were no great problem. Around the Cathedral, there were stone-built houses belonging to the Cathedral Chapter and one or more of them was made available for the academic instruction. From the sources, it only appears that a separate hall ("lectorium theologorum") was used for the theological lectures. Probably the University already used as its main building the Chapter House, south of the Cathedral, which was allocated as a lecture hall during Erik XIV's attempt to re-

3. *The mediaeval University building—"Carolina" or "the Caroline Academy"—*
on what is now Riddartorget. It was demolished in 1778. In the background is
the Skytteanum, and on the right, Oxenstierna House, which was used as the
University Hospital in the 18th century. Engraving by F. Akrel in J. B. Busser's
Beskrifning om Upsala *(1769).*

establish the academic instruction and which later, under the name of Academia Carolina or "the Old Academy", was to serve as the University building until it was demolished in the 1770s. In accordance with mediaeval academic practice, the students also demanded their own building (what was called a "community"), where they might live and take their meals. At the beginning of the 14th century, the learned Dean Andreas And had granted to the pupils of the Cathedral School the use of a small island in the River Fyris (probably the island now known as Kvarnholmen); during the 16th century, it is to be met with under the traditional designation of "Studentholmen" and it would therefore seem to be certain that Jacob Ulvsson allowed the University's alumni to be accommodated in the buildings on this island.

It might have been more difficult to obtain qualified teachers. It was

9

always possible to invite them from abroad. This was the procedure adopted at Copenhagen, when after a long delay the university there opened its doors in the summer of 1479, two years after the University of Uppsala had started. Most of the original teaching staff at Copenhagen were fetched, like the University's statutes, from Cologne. But it turned out that Uppsala could rely on its own resources. In the Cathedral Chapter, there were masters and doctors on whom degrees had been conferred abroad and who could be entrusted with the task of giving the lessons. They were, of course, not a distinguished or a numerous body. The Papal bull had permitted the establishment of all four faculties, but the Faculty of Medicine did not materialize during the Middle Ages and the Faculties of Theology and Law had only one teacher each. The teachers in the Faculty of Arts, who gave instruction in the liberal arts (*artes liberales*), would never seem to have numbered more than three or four at any one time. It was no problem to the wealthy Cathedral to maintain from its own resources such a limited number of professors. The University formed a part of the Cathedral—"this *studium* at our church in Uppsala", as Jacob Ulvsson called it—and it was natural that the teachers should be paid with the revenues of the available prebends and prelatures. Thus, the Professor of Theology held the influential office of Dean. According to a letter of 1504, the professors were favoured with a salary increase of altogether 200 marks in cash, mainly from the Cathedral revenues, though a small proportion came from other Swedish dioceses, thus confirming the status of the Uppsala *studium* as a concern of the whole ecclesiastical province of Sweden.

Otherwise, next to nothing is known about the administration and the internal condition of the University during its earliest period. Its archives have long since been lost; one gets only glimpses of light in the darkness. The name of the Rector is mentioned a couple of times and one catches glimpses of the Dean of the Faculty of Arts and the Faculty statutes.

On the other hand, we are, by a fortunate chance, well informed about the teachers and their teaching in the initial period. From the autumn of 1477, when the lectures began, to 1486, a young man from Gotland was a student at Uppsala and faithfully recorded all that he heard the lecturers say. His name was Olaus Johannis and he later became a monk at Vadstena. When he entered the monastery, he took his books with him, including seven volumes of lecture notes from Uppsala, which are now preserved in the University Library at Uppsala, together with other Vadstena manuscripts.

Like all mediaeval students, Olaus Johannis had to begin in the Faculty of Arts, where he took his master's degree after having heard lectures from at least four teachers—Andreas Brusen, Johannes of Mecheln, Petrus

Olai and Peder Galle, who had at this time just returned home with his master's degree after studying at Rostock and Paris. Towards the end of the Middle Ages, instruction in profane subjects became extremely standardized; more or less the same courses were drummed into the students' heads at all European universities. Aristotelian philosophy, which was the nucleus of scholastic thinking, reigned supreme. Logic occupied the central position, as the basis of everything else. Aristotle's writings on logic were gone through one after the other at Uppsala. Olaus Johannis heard lectures on almost all of them. But Aristotle's book on the soul, *De Anima*, was also included and in the spring of 1486, Petrus Olai lectured on the Master's *Physics*. In addition, there were the leading Parisian schoolmen of the high Middle Ages, Albertus Magnus and Thomas Aquinas, whose work "on substance and essence" led the audience up into the highest regions of metaphysics. The instruction given in the Uppsala Faculty of Arts was undoubtedly on the same level as that of a good German university; one could learn one's Aristotle there just as well as at Leipzig or Rostock. But Olaus Johannis's notes show that the mathematical sciences were also in the curriculum; he made notes on Euclid and quoted the text of Sacrobosco's popular astronomical textbook *Sphaera*.

It is uncertain whether he also read canon law. It seems certain that the University's only jurist was assiduous in his teaching of the subject; in 1486, Jacob Ulvsson decided that the Uppsala canons who had not previously studied canon law should learn it by taking a three-year course at the University. Law and theology traditionally constituted higher faculties, in which the final degree (the doctorate) could only be taken after taking a degree in the Faculty of Arts. However, Olaus Johannis attended the theological lectures from the beginning; we know about them only through him. The sole Professor of Theology was Ericus Olai, "holy Doctor Erik", the chief ornament of the newly founded University and perhaps indispensable for its coming into existence. He is now best known for his Latin chronicle of the Swedish nation entitled *Chronica regni gothorum*. He was from first to last a learned and pious theologian; he was Master of Arts and Canon of Uppsala Cathedral as early as the 1450s. As an adult student, he was sent to Siena, where he took the degree of Doctor of Theology in 1475, probably with a view to qualifying for the professorship of theology in his home town. He began his lectures immediately after the University had been inaugurated in 1477 with a series on the elements of theology entitled *Regulae sacrae theologiae* and continued in the course of the years with expositions of New Testament texts and an explanation of the sacrament of confession. In his teaching, he appears to have been a cautious theologian of the old school and uninfluenced by the latest advances of scholastic speculation. To him, the Scripture was the immovable foundation of faith and the Holy Roman Catholic Church the only true interpreter of it.

We have no information as to the number of students at the mediaeval University of Uppsala. They can hardly have numbered more than 40–50. But several of them took the first degree in the Faculty of Arts (Bachelor of Arts), in order to continue their education at some German university; several *baccalaurei Upsalienses* are to be met with at Leipzig from the 1480s onwards. A few took the master's degree. It is not entirely certain whether any Uppsala student completed his studies by taking the doctorate in the Faculty of Theology. But it is known that such training was commenced in some cases, such as that of Kanutus Johannis, the well-known guardian of the Franciscan monastery in Stockholm, in the 1490s. There are also indications that somewhat earlier a regular conferment of a doctorate of theology took place. The doctor concerned was Ericus Nicolai, who later became Archdeacon and well known as a translator of pious writings. He studied for a long time at Leipzig and even became Rector of the University there. After a short stay in Uppsala, he returned in the summer of 1488 to Leipzig as a newly graduated Doctor of Theology, which would seem to imply that the title was conferred on him at the university in his native country.

A single source, preserved by chance, gives a vivid glimpse of an Uppsala student in the late Middle Ages. This is a letter from a worried monk at Vadstena, Clemens Petri, to a young man named Clemens Martini, who in 1482 went to Uppsala to pursue his university studies. It is full of well-intentioned moral maxims and emphasizes that Clemens Martini should stay at the University for at least 2–3 years and avoid bad company; a certain Kristina would write to her uncle Sven and ask him to accommodate Clemens at his house.

So all the activities had pretty well started at Uppsala, the most northerly university in the world. Its sole task was the training of priests and monks for the needs of the Swedish province of the Church. Archbishop Jacob Ulvsson kept unceasing watch over his creation, but for all that it was moving towards extinction. Hardly any information has been preserved about the professors and the instruction at the turn of the century; we do not even know who succeeded Ericus Olai in the chair of theology after he died in 1486. Only the bare names of a couple of Uppsala professors or "collegiati" of this period (Olaus Nicolai and Olaus Kempe, of Bälinge) were preserved on gravestones which were once in the Cathedral but have now disappeared. Some time after 1500, the above-mentioned Peder Galle was once again attached to the University. In the meantime, he had graduated in theology at Siena and would seem to have taken up the professorship of theology. It is not until 1508 that we again catch a

4. This rough woodcut in Olaus Magnus's Historia de gentibus septentrionalibus *(1555) is said to represent the astronomical clock in Uppsala Cathedral, made by Petrus Astronomus, a Vadstena monk, in 1506.*

glimpse of a university teacher. His name was Petrus Astronomus and he was a Vadstena monk of German birth who two years before had built the remarkable astronomical clock in Uppsala Cathedral (this clock was destroyed in the great fire of 1702). Petrus, who compiled some astronomical tables that are still extant, lectured at the University in the autumn of 1508 on "sphaera materialis", i.e. the elements of astronomy. The lectures aroused concern at Vadstena, where the pious monks and nuns feared that Brother Petrus was occupied with forbidden arts, but Jacob Ulvsson sets their minds at rest with the assurance that Brother Petrus had behaved "honestly and reasonably" throughout.

After this, darkness covers the University of Uppsala. During the political storms at the end of the Sture period, learning also suffered harm in Sweden. Owing to age and infirmity, Jacob Ulvsson resigned his office in 1515 and was succeeded as Archbishop by Gustaf Trolle, who threw himself with tremendous energy into the gamble for secular power. The lectures at the University are now stated to have been discontinued for some time; otherwise, the records tell us nothing. It has accordingly been assumed that the University ceased to exist some time between 1515 and 1520. But isolated items of information indicate that it survived in a weakened form for a few years longer. The "Faculty of Theology at Uppsala"—whatever that may mean—is mentioned as late as 1526. Probably old Peder Galle, who was still in good form and was shortly to appear as the opponent of the Lutheran reformer Olaus Petri, lectured in Catholic theology to the young priests. A *baccalaureus Upsaliensis* is mentioned

13

in 1531 as having enrolled at a German university, but by then all university studies must have finished at Uppsala. A new age had set in, the Lutheran Reformation was carried out in Sweden and, as a stronghold of Catholic faith and learning, the *studium generale* licensed by the Pope at the archiepiscopal see was abandoned to its fate.

CHAPTER II

The Reformation Period

1

The establishment of Gustavus Vasa's national monarchy and the reformation of the Church resulted in austere conditions for cultural life in Sweden. It might seem as if the country was threatened with sheer barbarism. The King was concentrating all his energies on building up the Swedish state and had neither time nor inclination to spare for the careful preparation of a policy on cultural matters. The Roman Catholic cultural institutions—chiefly the monasteries and the monastery schools—were abolished in the name of the Lutheran creed and no new ones were established in their place. The Lutheran Church, which was being laboriously organized with the aid of the reformers, was subject to the royal power and its apostolic poverty rendered it unable to find the money for a fuller intellectual life. This was not even regarded as being particularly desirable. The Lutheran minister's office was purely that of a preacher. God's Word, as revealed in the Scriptures, was all he needed; any profounder learning was rather a hindrance and a danger.

Things had looked the same in Germany. As a young man, Luther had stormed at pagan learning as harmful to the tremendous message of the Gospel; schools and studies threatened to decay during the period when the Reformation was emerging. It was Philip Melanchthon, Luther's assistant at Wittenberg, who reconciled Lutheranism and the traditional academic culture and thereby came to play an immeasurably important part in the Lutheran world. He shaped the Lutheran grammar school and made the University of Wittenberg into an abode of the Muses, to which students from other Protestant countries resorted in order to become acquainted with Aristotelian philosophy and the poets of antiquity.

It was some time before Sweden—which the Reformation had made into a province of German culture through and through—could profit from the new educational stimuli. An indescribable poverty characterized Swedish cultural life in the 1530s and 1540s; the few grammar schools were in a very poor way and outcries were raised. The clerical office was said to have become contemptible; things were not as in former times, when lucrative prebends and canonries awaited young men who devoted themselves to study; the schools were therefore deprived of their pupils. As late as 1559, it could be said that there were barely 10 clergymen in

Sweden who deserved to be called learned. Most of the clergy had to manage with the indispensable knowledge of Latin and the Bible acquired at the cathedral schools in their home dioceses. In Uppsala the University was fast asleep and, for the time being, nothing was being done to awaken it. This was something of a national scandal and was also regarded as such in some quarters. A Swedish student in Germany reported in 1538 to Gustavus Vasa that people down there were wondering why he did not, like other princes, have a university established in his kingdom. The King admitted that there was something in this view and declared that he was prepared to remedy the deficiency, but there the matter rested. The following year, no less a person than Melanchthon took up the matter in a letter to Gustavus Vasa; he said that a university in Sweden would redound to God's glory and the King's honour. Worse still, the hereditary Danish enemy began to utter sneers. Hans Svaning, the historian, said that during King Gustavus's reign, when the silver mines had begun to yield a handsome return and Sweden had become more prosperous than ever, the University of Uppsala was being ruined by lack of money. Denmark in particular had been able to give the Swedish King an example to think about. The University of Copenhagen had also been dissolved during the period when the Reformation was emerging but had already, towards the end of the 1530s, been re-established by Kristian III on a splendid scale with 12 professors, taking the University of Wittenberg as its model. In the modern Protestant world, it was the prince alone who was the governor of his university and was responsible for its continued existence.

As things were now, the study tours abroad were the only provision made to prevent learning from dying out in Sweden. But they too had suffered a decline. During the first few years of Gustavus Vasa's reign, the number of students making these tours declined catastrophically (only about 25 during the whole of the 1520s) and it was not until the middle of the century that such tours became approximately as frequent as they had been during the final period of the Middle Ages. The King realized their importance, just as he agreed with the complaints about the decline of the schools, and often maintained Swedish students at the orthodox German universities. As early as 1527, he sent three young Swedes to Wittenberg with letters of introduction to Luther. But the Church's need of capable clergy was not to him a matter of primary importance. During the 16th century, the universities had increasingly begun to prepare their students for other careers. Gustavus Vasa needed competent men for his exchequer, his chancellery and his diplomatic missions. This also affected the Swedish aristocracy. Prelates no longer sat in the Privy Council or performed other duties involving great responsibility; it was therefore important that young nobles should prepare themselves to take their places.

A new aristocratic educational ideal, requiring study and learning, began to develop; individual young nobles were attending German universities. Naturally, the University of Wittenberg was of primary interest to Swedish students. It was the stronghold of Lutheranism in a wicked world and it was there that Melanchthon, the incomparable teacher, worked. In the 1550s, between 10 and 20 Swedes periodically sat at his feet and many of them took masters' degrees. They were all brought up in the spirit of modern humanism, learned Greek and were acquainted with the world of beauty and ethical standards represented in classical literature.

This made things brighter; in the reigns of Gustavus Vasa's sons, the years of austerity were over. As young princes, both Eric XIV and John III had received the best possible education, as regarded learning and aesthetic culture; they purposely wished to appear as Renaissance princes, surrounded by *objets d'art,* fine libraries and eulogistic humanists. The kingdom had been consolidated and the royal succession had been confirmed; there was every reason to think about scholarship and culture and about reviving the somnolent University of Uppsala.

In 1566, Eric XIV took the first step. He had decided to establish in Uppsala "a college or university", where Swedish youth could be trained in the literary arts. To begin with, he would be content with a single teacher, but more would be added later. The King's choice fell on Laurentius Petri Gothus. He had studied at Wittenberg for two periods, had taken his master's degree there and become an enthusiastic admirer of Melanchthon's genius. He had made himself known as a successful Latin poet in the elaborate style of the time and his professorship was significantly to include Greek, the cardinal subject of humanistic culture, together with other suitable *lectiones.* Church tithes and a farm were set aside for his salary. He was to give his lectures in the old Chapter House south of the Cathedral, i.e. the same premises as were probably used for academic instruction during the Middle Ages.

Nothing is known about Laurentius Petri's teaching in the years that followed. But soon he had the colleagues whom he had been promised. Several new "reading masters" were appointed in Uppsala in the initial period of John III's reign (1569–74); their names were Petrus Jonae, Petrus Benedicti Oelandus, Olaus Luth and Henricus Gadolenus. They formed a complete *collegium* of professors, governed by Laurentius Petri as Rector. Their salaries were ordered to be paid in tithe corn, and in other respects also the Crown generously saw to it that the little academy in the shadow of the Cathedral was put into good order. The professors received official residences in the canons' houses round the Cathedral, the University building (Carolina) was repaired and 32 royal scholarships were granted in tithe corn for the students' maintenance, so that they cannot have been altogether few in number. Besides Laurentius Petri, who was soon made Archbishop, only two of the teachers have distinct features. They are Petrus Jonae and Olaus Luth, who were old friends and fellow-students in their early years at German universities. Petrus Jonae, who was to end his days as Bishop of Strängnäs, lectured to his students in 1574 on the Roman Catholic Church's false argument for the primacy of the Apostle Peter and the Pope—a burning subject in an age when theologians hated each other. Luth too was a theologian but also taught the liberal arts and sciences. He wrote a textbook on logic and an account of sundials. His astronomical lectures in 1579 have been preserved and published; they originated from the little manual by Sacrobosco which was already in use at the mediaeval University. The academic teaching at Uppsala in the 1570s was assuredly of good quality and in one instance we see that in the light of memory it could be transfigured: in an epitaph in 1603 on a Södermanland clergyman who had studied at Uppsala in his youth, a tribute is paid to the "exquisite" men who lectured at the University at that time.

John III, who was a learned man and an authority on the Fathers of the Church, felt a genuine interest in the revived University. At some time (probably in 1574–5), he had draft constitutions and privileges drawn up. More definite forms for the University's activities were needed; thus, it was apparently not yet authorized to award academic degrees. The King's draft is incomplete, but its scope is ambitious. A nation's honour and strength were dependent on laws, constitutions and good morals and they in their turn on the existence of flourishing churches and schools, where pure divinity could be preached without senseless disputations and discord. The University of Uppsala should consist of four faculties, each governed by a dean, who would keep the faculty's seal and present reports on its affairs to the Rector. The King would appoint suitable persons to vacant professorships. The theologians should, above all, avoid introducing fanatical views and unnecessary innovations.

But the royal goodwill came to an end. John III was no friend to orthodox Lutheranism; he hankered after the simple doctrine of the oldest Church, combined with a beautiful and solemn liturgy, which he fetched from Catholic worship. When in 1576 he put forward his new order for the Mass, in what was called the "Red Book", a storm broke out. The majority of the Swedish clergy suspected, on good grounds, a popish trap; many of them refused to accept it and preferred to suffer persecution. Among the first to speak out against the King's liturgy were the Uppsala professors, chiefly the uncompromisingly orthodox Petrus Jonae and Olaus Luth. They came to loggerheads with the Archbishop, their former colleague Laurentius Petri Gothus, and at New Year 1577 were summoned to Stock-

5. *King John III, who supported the little academy in Uppsala during the first half of the 1570s and had draft constitutions drawn up for it. Copperplate engraving in the Palmskiöld Collection in the University Library.*

holm to answer for their obstinacy in the King's presence. They were imprisoned for a time and then sent back to Uppsala. But they persisted and in the autumn the King vented his wrath in another outburst of fury. Petrus Jonae and Luth were dismissed from their teaching posts and the position of the sorely tried academy in Uppsala is obscure after this. Yet it continued to exist somehow, for even in 1580 a new professor was appointed. But now the bubonic plague came to Uppsala, Luth was snatched away by death, the students fled and the University was closed.

This suited John III splendidly. As they were subject to the royal power, the universities in the Protestant states were not confined to ecclesiastical centres; it was rather advantageous to locate them in bourgeois towns under the immediate supervision of the secular authority. This was John's policy. As early as 1576, he had founded in Stockholm a school of his own—the college on Gråmunkeholmen—which became an instrument of his zeal for religious reform. Under the direction of Laurentius Nicolai, a Norwegian Jesuit whose nickname was "Larry the Monk", excellent theological teaching was given there in the service of the Catholic Counter-Reformation, to which the King was more and more inclined. Pupils were sent from the college to Rome or to German Jesuit seminaries for further training. As time went on, however, "Larry the Monk" acted with less and less restraint as a Catholic propagandist; this led to violent disturbances and in 1580 the King found it necessary to have him deported.

But the college remained. When the University of Uppsala was closed, it was the only establishment of higher education in Sweden and John concentrated on extending it. He was now a disappointed and disillusioned man, having been compelled to give up all collaboration with the Roman Church, but the liturgical controversy was still raging and it must have seemed important to the King that he should retain his control over higher education. In 1583–4, he re-organized the Stockholm college by appointing several new professors. They were all good Lutherans (it was no longer possible to appoint teachers of any other persuasion) who had recently returned home from Germany, to which the students now went, chiefly to the University of Rostock, in an increasingly rapid stream.

The renovated Lutheran college in Stockholm showed great vigour during the short period for which it existed. The teachers were excellent; three of them became archbishops. Humanistic studies were pursued with particular zeal. Greek was one of the main subjects; it was taught by Jacobus Erici, who published the first Swedish edition of a Greek author (Isocrates). Ericus Jacobi Skinnerus, who was responsible for teaching mathematics, was chiefly known as an excellent Latin poet and orator in the flowing classical style—"a Pericles, a Demosthenes, a Cicero", exclaimed one of his pupils much later, recalling his youthful studies at the Stockholm college. The learned orientalist Nicolaus Olai Botniensis lectured on Hebrew and, together with Petrus Kenicius, on theology. The basic philosophical outlook instilled into the pupils was important. On the Continent, Ramism, the philosophical reformation initiated by the Frenchman Petrus Ramus, had gone into battle against the inherited Aristotelian scholasticism and demanded a simpler and more natural philosophy, orientated towards the requirements of practical life. In Sweden, in the 1580s, the college on Gråmunkeholmen became the gateway to the new philosophy; almost all the teachers would seem to have been Ramists. Their time was not taken up only with lecturing; the instruction included Latin orations and disputations on set theses. But the college was hardly a university in the formal sense; it had no proper charter and obviously did not award any degrees. But the students flocked there and many of the intellectual leaders in the early years of Sweden's period as a great power had laid the foundations of their education at John III's college.

The circumstances in which this college was dissolved are obscure. As late as 1590, teaching was in full swing, but shortly after that it began to decline. John III abandoned the college to its fate, soldiers were quartered in its premises on Gråmunkeholmen and it is possible that some of the professors were imprisoned for a time. As orthodox Lutherans, they probably now openly opposed the King's claims to liturgical authority; hence the unpleasantness. The situation was confused; at any rate, by the summer of 1592 the college was closed and the professors were dismissed from their posts. Some time later, John III died and the field was then open for fresh initiatives in educational policy. Uppsala again came into the limelight.

2

According to unconfirmed reports, John III promised on his death-bed to make amends for his offences by re-establishing the University of Uppsala. As things turned out, it was under quite different conditions that the University was re-born and began its activities, which have continued down to the present day.

Immediately after the King's death, a national movement, led by his brother Duke Charles, was formed. This was a necessity in a situation fraught with danger. Sigismund, the new King, was a Roman Catholic and moreover the King of Poland. John III's semi-popish liturgy had appeared to the indignant clergy to be a deadly threat to the Lutheran faith; now the Roman Anti-Christ seemed to be preparing to take possession of the kingdom. The Duke and the majority of the clergy decided to take rapid action and at New Year 1593 summoned an assembly to meet at Uppsala. This synod met in the old University building by the Cathedral for three weeks in February and March. The controversy about the detested liturgy was the main question to be settled; it was condemned and its supporters were compelled to renounce it. One for all and all for one, the participants in the synod swore, "holding up their hands", to adhere in life and in death to the unchanged Augsburg Confession. The patriotic front was thereby united against Sigismund and Rome; an official confessionist Church of Sweden had at last been created.

The professors from the former college at Stockholm were leading figures at the Uppsala synod. For that reason, it was inevitable that the university question should be raised; Duke Charles and the Privy Council seem to have given binding promises in advance. Nicolaus Olai Botniensis was elected chairman of the synod. The secretary in the proceedings was the young Laurentius Paulinus Gothus, who had previously taught at John III's college. In the "postulates" which the professors and the clergy assembled at the synod presented to the Duke and the Privy Council in the middle of March, definite demands were made concerning the university which was to be established in Uppsala. There should be at least 12 teachers and the revived university should be furnished with proper privileges; a "community" should be founded for poor students, the old library of the Cathedral Chapter should be expanded and the royal printing office in Stockholm should be moved to Uppsala.

Thus, it was taken for granted that the locus of higher education in Sweden would again be Uppsala. This locus could have continued to be Stockholm, where the foundation already laid could have been used for further development. Such a solution would have had drastic consequences for Swedish cultural life in the future, if, as in Denmark, the bourgeois capital had become the centre of the nation's scientific activities, with all that that entailed. But the current situation did not allow of this. The Uppsala synod under whose aegis the university question was decided was a national and ecclesiastical action directed against the Roman Catholic monarch and the university had to be located beyond his reach, close to the Church. It was to be a stronghold of Lutheran orthodoxy, as it had been during the liturgical controversies in the 1570s. This does not mean that this motive alone was decisive; it is only glimpsed here and there in the clergy's "postulates". Lutheran Sweden was, in any case, in urgent need of a seat of higher learning, where profane and sacred knowledge could be imparted in all their fullness and where academic degrees could be acquired.

No formal decision about the university was made at the Uppsala synod. The decision lay with the government authorities, represented by Duke Charles and the Privy Councillors. During the spring or summer of 1593, a fresh petition was presented to them which included some urgent questions: the need of proper salaries for the professors, the importance of having privileges and a chancellor who could look after the university's interests, and a prohibition against Swedish students travelling abroad to study before they had been examined at the university in Uppsala. It is obvious that the main issue had been decided long since; the Duke had the same interest as the clergy in seeing that a university was organized. On 1 August 1593, he and the Privy Council issued the document which re-established the University of Uppsala. It is very brief. It says nothing, for the time being, about the University as a stronghold of the Lutheran faith; it only speaks of the necessity of such a distinguished kingdom as Sweden possessing a school of advanced studies for the training of skilled men for "the sacred and the secular government". To the Duke and the Privy Councillors, the two aims were equally important; the machinery of the state had need of university-trained manpower. Then decisions are made about the professorships and the maintenance of their holders. Seven professorial chairs were to be set up—three in theology and four in the liberal arts and sciences. The theologians, who were to be paid from the tithes and the prebends connected with the Cathedral, were associated, as holders of official posts, with the Cathedral Chapter. Nicolaus Olai Botniensis was appointed Dean and head Professor of Theology, with the duty of lecturing on the Hebrew Old Testament. Petrus Kenicius became

6. *Duke Charles, who, together with the Privy Council, issued the document by which the University was re-established in 1593. Copperplate engraving.*

the Penitentiary and Professor of the Greek New Testament, and Jacobus Erici became Dean of the Faculty, with the responsibility for dogmatics and controversial theology. Only one member of the Faculty of Arts and Sciences is mentioned by name—Ericus Jacobi Skinnerus, who was appointed Rector without his subject field being specified; other chairs in the Faculty were to include astronomy, physics (natural science) and Latin oratory. As we see, all the teachers named were taken over from the dissolved college in Stockholm. It was they, above all others, who carried the matter through to a successful outcome and in their persons John III's college survived under the new conditions in the re-born University.

A few weeks later, a fresh letter came from the Duke and the Privy Council, giving directions as to the establishment of a "community" on Studentholmen. It was intended to accommodate 40 students, who were to receive lodging, food and clothes, and was to be maintained from the tithes.

It remained to obtain a confirmation of the decisions from Sigismund. It could be anticipated that there would be difficulties in this. The University was involved in a political strategy in opposition to Sigismund, the Roman Catholic king, who did everything to delay the making of a decision when he arrived from Poland in the autumn of 1593. However, the Privy Council and the clergy were more than a match for him and in March 1594, after he had been crowned King in Uppsala, he gave an assurance in which he confirmed the clergy's privileges and what had been decided about the University. It is disputed whether this assurance was legally binding; on the other hand, Sigismund soon afterwards returned to Poland, leaving the field free to Duke Charles and the national party. But they were still pursuing a policy of "wait and see" and it was the new Church synod which assembled in Uppsala in February 1595 that first brought the university question to its final consummation. A number of articles were drawn up and presented to the Duke, who delivered a favourable report on them and on 15 March issued, together with the Privy Council, the eagerly awaited charter of the University of Uppsala.

In the formal phraseology of this charter, the secular power took the University into its protection. It was henceforth to enjoy the same privileges and freedoms as previous Swedish rulers and prelates had granted the academy in Uppsala. It was expressly laid down that the University was to act as "an academy of our religion", which might foster men to defend the pure doctrine of Lutheranism and rid it of false ideas. The study of all literary arts and faculties was to be carried on freely, a Chancellor was to be appointed, and bachelors, masters and doctors were to have their degrees conferred on them with the permission of the Chancellor and the Archbishop. The University was to have legal jurisdiction over its own members, except for certain crimes. New professors were to be appointed by the University and the Cathedral Chapter, together with other bishops and the Chancellor, and not by the government. Idle or otherwise negligent professors should be dismissed, after having been given a warning. The University was also assigned, in fairly general terms, responsibility in relation to schools and schoolmasters in the kingdom and certain regulations were issued about the "community". The same day, there came a letter regulating the University's financial establishment. A professor of medicine had been added (for a long time to come, he existed only on paper), which made the full number eight. For their maintenance, they all received tithes and prebends or freehold farms belonging to the Church around Uppsala, assignments of dwelling-houses around the Cathedral and the right to fish with seine nets in the Ekoln creek.

The government's charter founded the University of Uppsala in legal form as an academic corporation. Teaching had begun earlier, probably as early as 1593. The professors, i.e. the former Stockholm professors, were constantly in the town; in the summer of 1594, mention is made of students breaking windows. But Ericus Skinnerus, the Rector, nevertheless wished to celebrate the new charter of foundation with a little ceremony. In April 1595, he summoned the Archbishop, the professors, the Uppsala clergy, the burgomaster and the aldermen and respectable persons of both sexes to the small lecture theatre in the old Chapter House (Carolina), which was now in regular use for instruction. Sixty-four students went through the deposition ceremony and were enrolled in the University register.

The first few years of the re-established University were difficult in many ways. As long as the struggle for power between Duke Charles and Sigismund was undecided, the professors were in an exposed position, especially as the new Archbishop, Abraham Angermannus, unexpectedly established friendly relations with the King and tried by hook or by crook to persuade the professors to do the same; he was not entirely unsuccessful. During these troubled years (1596–8), no new students seem to have come to Uppsala. It was not until after the Battle of Stångebro, when Sigismund had been banished and the Duke had taken over the government, that it was possible to breathe freely and to welcome new alumni. In 1599, 32 students were enrolled, making 150 altogether. They were distributed into four "classes" according to subject, viz. logic, physics, mathematics and astronomy. In addition, all of them doubtless attended the lectures in theology. But there was a lively turnover among the professors and this dislocated the teaching. Of the first set, Skinnerus soon died, as did Nicolaus Olai Botniensis, an excellent theologian who had just been appointed Archbishop when he died in 1600. As the years went by, it became increasingly difficult for the professors to draw their salaries; several of them left their chairs and sought Church appointments in the country. The University was characterized by a shapelessness which restricted the efficiency and orderliness of its work. There was no real division into faculties, as there were still no law or medical students. In addition, there was the University's obscure relationship to the Cathedral and the Cathedral Chapter. Though the secular power, represented by Duke Charles, was ultimately entitled to govern and make decisions for the young Protestant academy, it followed from the circumstances of its creation that it would have a very close relationship to the Church during its first few years. In practice, the University was subject, in the mediaeval fashion, to the Cathedral; thus, the body of professors was almost identical with the Cathedral Chapter, over which the Archbishop presided. There was no University printing office as yet, which was detrimental to the production of theses and other printed matter.

At New Year 1600, however, it was possible to assemble the University for the first conferment of masters' degrees. The credit for this was due to Laurentius Paulinus Gothus, now the leading teacher of the University. After pursuing exhaustive studies in Germany, he had been summoned, as early as 1593, to a professorial chair at Uppsala, where, until the turn of the century, he taught astronomy and other mathematical sciences. He did this in a modern spirit, expounding to his students the new Copernican conception of the world, which was still disputed in Europe. He was an ardent Ramist and an enthusiastic admirer of the philosophical sciences, which were also essential for theology. When on 22 January

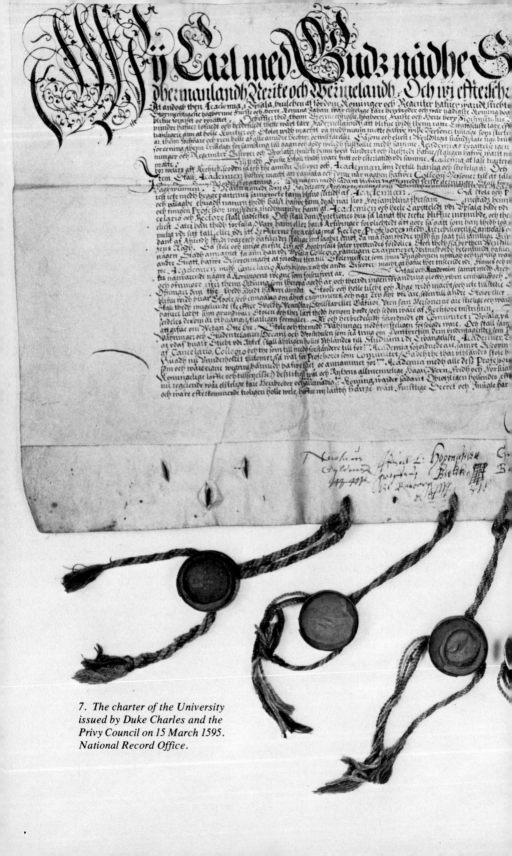

7. *The charter of the University issued by Duke Charles and the Privy Council on 15 March 1595. National Record Office.*

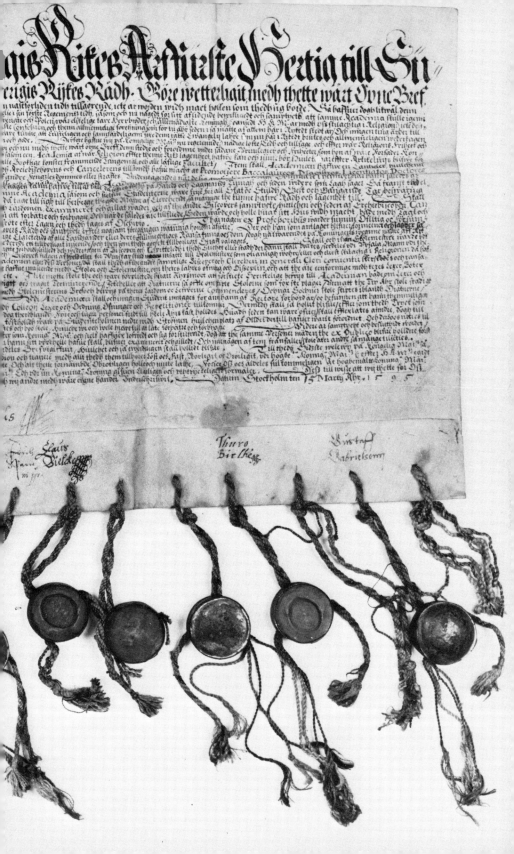

8. *Laurentius Paulinus Gothus, who was successively a professor at Uppsala, Bishop of Strängnäs, and Archbishop and Pro-Chancellor of the University. Oil painting in the Uppsala Cathedral Chapter House.*

1600, as Dean of the Faculty, he went up to the lectern in the great hall of the University to conduct the ceremonial conferment in the presence of the notabilities of the town and the University, he made a brilliant speech about education and about the schools as the workshops of the Holy Spirit, in which the young learned the philosophy of antiquity and the liberal arts for the future good of the Church and the State. He then conferred bachelors' degrees on 15 students; no laurel was obtainable, so they had to be content with wreaths made of rue. Seven of them were immediately awarded the degree of Master of Arts; one by one, they went up to the lectern, a book was opened and closed, the purple hat was placed on the new master's head and the ring on his finger. The symbolic meaning of these actions, which in part survive in the modern ceremony at the conferment of doctoral degrees, was interpreted by the presenter. The ceremony—the happiest hour so far in the history of the regenerated University—concluded with prayer and thanksgiving. When, in the following year, Laurentius Paulinus was Rector, the University received its first seal. It was designed and engraved by Johannes Bureus, the cabbalist and antiquarian, and shows the kingdoms of grace and nature

9. *The University seal, designed by Johannes Bureus, the antiquarian, in 1601. The form shown here is a later design dating from about 1700. After J. Eenberg (1704).*

(Gratiae Veritas Naturae), surrounded by the legend "S(igillum) Academiae Ubsaliensis". In various forms, it has been in use ever since.

The first few years of the following century also exhibited hopeful features in other respects. Duke Charles showed goodwill towards the University. At the Norrköping Riksdag in 1604, at which cultural policy occupied a prominent place on the agenda, he put forward a generous proposal for the expansion of the academy at Uppsala. The number of professors should be increased to 11, including a jurist and a doctor of medicine; new professorial chairs should be established in the subjects of rhetoric, poetics with history, and Greek with Hebrew; the number of places in the students' "community" should be doubled. At this time, two new men of outstanding ability were attached to the University staff. They were Johannes Rudbeckius and Johannes Lenaeus, both of whom had recently returned home after spending several years studying in Germany and were both determined to add some brilliant pages to the history of the Church of Sweden. As Professor of Logic, Lenaeus at once drew a great concourse of hearers. Rudbeckius took over the chair of mathematics with a lofty speech about the indispensability of the sciences and the schools, in which, like Laurentius Paulinus before him, he extolled the power of worldly knowledge; philosophy was a ray of the Divine Being and scientific research was a lodestar in life. At the same time, the appearance of Rudbeckius and Lenaeus on the scene involved complications. They were champions of Aristotle and adherents of the new and intransigent scholasticism which had been adopted by Lutheran orthodoxy in Germany in its controversies with the Catholics, Calvinists and other heretics. But their colleagues in Uppsala, chiefly Laurentius Paulinus, who had now become Professor of Theology, adhered to the Ramist view, which was a legacy from the old college in Stockholm. The ground was prepared for conflicts which were to come to a head in the near future.

It is very likely that the draft constitutions for the University which were written in 1606 were drawn up by the restless Rudbeckius. Although they were never sanctioned or applied, they shed a clear light on the contemporary conditions at the University. They mention daily public lectures from 6 a.m. to 4 p.m., disputations on Saturdays, examinations and requirements for the master's degree, the Senate and the Rector's office, the University's silver wands, and the students' morals. The above-mentioned division of the students into classes was still maintained. In 1605, the classes within which the students were moved were logic, arithmetic, physics, astronomy, geometry and Latin rhetoric, together with a higher theological or catechetical class. The oldest printed theses that have been preserved—written for practice or for the master's degree—date from this period. The master's degree was taken in the Faculty of Arts and Sciences, in which all students were traditionally examined (cf. below, page 80). The great majority of students became clergymen all the same, prepared to curse the Pope and his followers, but it was self-evident that their studies should also prepare them to hold civil posts. To the government authorities, this was a most important matter. "If any good is to come out of the University", growled Duke Charles, "some of them must also be trained for the secular government".

But the University of Uppsala was still not mature enough to brave the current storms. The Duke's goodwill soon turned into suspicion and wrath and Uppsala was made to experience the disadvantages of being dependent on the prince's favour. The Duke's proposal to expand the University was never put into effect. In 1606, Laurentius Paulinus was expelled from his professorship on the ground that he had been collaborating with Sigismund. When in the following year Rudbeckius and Lenaeus returned to Wittenberg, the teaching staff and the instruction were in a wretched state. For some time, there was no Professor of Theology and the "community" had fallen into disorder. The Duke neglected no opportunity of harassing the University; when he was in Uppsala in the spring of 1607 for his coronation as Charles IX, he improved the occasion by appropriating the University's charter, which he never restored. The King, who had reformist leanings, was now engaged in a bitter controversy with the Archbishop and the clergy about the true faith and, as a stronghold of Lutheran orthodoxy, the University was a disagreeable establishment to him. About 1608–9, it might seem that the University was drifting aimlessly; there was neither stability nor peace and quiet in which to work.

Things did not improve when Johannes Rudbeckius returned in 1609 and took up the professorship of Hebrew. At the same time, Johannes Messe-

10. Johannes Messenius, the humanist and historiographer, who was a professor at Uppsala for a few stormy years at the beginning of the 1610s. Copperplate engraving by Johannes Bureus.

nius was appointed Professor of Politics and Law. This precipitated a storm which almost threatened the University's further existence. Two of the most brilliant and strong-willed personalities in early-17th-century Sweden were in opposition to each other. As a young man, Messenius had been trained at the Jesuit seminary at Braunsberg and had then travelled on the Continent before returning home, parading his doctorate and the rank of Imperial poet-laureate, to forswear his popish past and carve out a career for himself. No sooner had he arrived in Uppsala as the University's first Professor of Law than he set about attaching the young students to himself with tremendous energy. He organized a college of his own, where he daily instructed his private pupils, many of whom were of noble families. They were an enthusiastic crowd ("the Messenians") and were often not even enrolled at the University. Messenius's success was a thorn in the flesh to the other professors. The newly appoin-

31

ted Rudbeckius went into action with a speech about the popish bondage, levelled at Messenius's Jesuit background. At New Year 1610, a regular row broke out in the Senate. Rudbeckius brought up Messenius's Catholic past and the Rector accused him of having, with intolerable arrogance, disregarded the University's statutes and ordinances. Sigfrid Forsius, the astronomer and astrologer, who was at that time acting professor, then intervened, "completely drunk", in defence of Messenius.

Rudbeckius then decided to defeat his hated colleague on his own ground; a tug-of-war for the minds of the students began. In the spring of 1610, he opened a rival private college, which immediately attracted many pupils. The teaching was of the highest class, at least as good as the University could offer officially. There were lectures, orations, disputations and examinations in theology and all the subjects taught in the Faculty of Arts and Sciences, the emphasis being on Aristotelian logic and classical studies. Rudbeckius was assisted by his two brothers, Petrus and Jacob, but with his indomitable capacity for work bore the main burden himself. He corrected thousands of translation exercises from Latin and Greek, supervised disputations and guided and exhorted his students. With its fixed organization and strict discipline, Rudbeckius's private school was, even more than Messenius's college, a state within the state. The two antagonists also came into conflict in the field of literary exercises. After Rudbeckius had allowed his pupils to perform a play by the popular Roman dramatist Terence, Messenius replied in the spring of 1611 with a comedy on Queen Disa which he himself had concocted. Then, each in his turn, they appealed to the public with new plays—Rudbeckius with dramas from the humanistic repertoire and Messenius with new historical plays in Swedish, which have procured him a modest place in the annals of Swedish literature.

The struggle continued to surge to and fro and before long assumed scandalous proportions. In the autumn of 1610, Charles IX had appointed a professor, Johannes Raumannus, to act as a kind of royal inspector at the University and to keep the two professorial game-cocks in close check, but he at once fell into Messenius's embrace and made common cause with him. The University was now split into two irreconcilable parties—Rudbeckius and most of the professors, on the one hand, and Messenius with his pupils and Raumannus, on the other. In 1613, the disturbances reached their climax and conclusion. Messenius's students, in their blind devotion to their master, put up libellous posters on the walls, roamed the streets with drawn swords and smashed the windows of members of the opposing party. Messenius refused to comply with any obligations, said that he was responsible only to the King and at a meeting of the Senate abused Rudbeckius as a villain, a traitor and a "base Jute" and challenged him to a duel. That was the last straw and in the summer of 1613, both Messenius and Rudbeckius were summoned to Stockholm to be examined by the bishops and the Privy Council. Order must finally be restored at the University of Uppsala. Both the trouble-makers were ordered to leave the town; Rudbeckius was promoted to the office of chaplain to the King and Messenius became Keeper of the Public Records (in a short time he fell a victim to the intrigues of his opponents and was deported to the prison in the remote fortress of Kajaneborg).

With all its unpleasant features, the quarrel between Rudbeckius and Messenius was, in a way, a sign of health; the minds of men were beginning to awaken at the University of Uppsala. When it was brought to an end, Charles IX had been gathered to his fathers for a couple of years and Gustavus Adolphus had taken over the government. The young King had received from his tutors, Johan Skytte and Bureus, a sound scholarly education, in which the emphasis had been placed on the usefulness of the sciences in politics and practical life. His passion for learning was strong and genuine; no monarch could have a deeper sense of his obligation to make provision for literary studies. At his side he had Axel Oxenstierna, who had been trained in Aristotelian philosophy and Lutheran theology during his student years at German universities.

In Uppsala, passions did not cool down immediately. Raumannus was still there, showering his colleagues with abuse and accusations, but he died in 1614. Step by step, Gustavus Adolphus and Oxenstierna began to restore the decayed University. It was reinstated in its lost privileges; a regulation was issued that a new Rector should be elected annually; in the spring of 1613, a University printer, Eskil Mattsson, was appointed, whose salary was paid by the Crown; a bookseller was brought in somewhat later. Oxenstierna, who in practice acted as the University Chancellor throughout the 1610s, revolved great plans for its improvement, but the difficult times prevented them from being carried out. However, the professors' salaries were improved as a result of letters patent issued in 1613. Now the long-established but vacant professorship of medicine was filled; its first holder was Johannes Chesnecopherus. There was still only a handful of professors—eight on the salary list but often fewer in reality. They were scarcely notable men, but two of them rose above the average—the above-mentioned Lenaeus, who was now Professor of Theology (he became Archbishop in his old age), and Jonas Magni, who in 1614 became Professor of Moral Philosophy with Politics and Jurisprudence. Magni was a combative neo-Aristotelian and on that account became involved in the first and for a long time the bitterest scholarly dispute in Swedish academic history. As we have seen, the first set of teachers at the University were Ramists and detested the intricate

Aristotelian scholasticism, which was again beginning to spread in Europe. Laurentius Paulinus Gothus had already left Uppsala, but even after Rudbeckius and Lenaeus had begun to lecture on Aristotle, Ramism lived on and was considered as late as the 1610s to be good academic form. The fact that Johan Skytte, who had great influence over Gustavus Adolphus, was an ardent believer in the socially oriented Ramist doctrine was of considerable importance in this respect. In the letters of appointment issued to the professors dating from the beginning of the 1610s, it was laid down that the true "Socratic" (i.e. Ramist) method was to be used in teaching. In his quarrel with the other professors, Raumannus also dragged in their philosophical affiliations. He himself was a Ramist and considered that such a person as Lenaeus should be "removed to some country parish", where he might test the value of the Aristotelian logic. But the major encounter came when in some inoffensive theses Jonas Magni made himself the spokesman of the Aristotelian moral philosophy. Laurentius Paulinus, who was now Bishop of Strängnäs, at once attacked him. Although he was still a good Ramist, he had, in the course of time, come to detest the admixture of human reason in religious and ethical matters. For two years (1615–16), Jonas Magni and the Bishop kept up their controversy; Magni's pamphlets were dignified, but the Bishop's were furious and occasionally vulgar. According to Laurentius Paulinus, man was good for nothing after the Fall, Aristotle and the pagan philosophy should be banned from the universities, and ethics, should be learned only from the Ten Commandments. In this controversy, Jonas Magni appeared as a modern unprejudiced man, convinced of the ability of the natural moral law to distinguish between right and wrong and consequently to serve as the foundation of bourgeois society.

This confrontation between Ramus and Aristotle, only half of which took place within the University, foreboded future philosophical wrangles in Uppsala, right down to the present day. It was still to be quite a long time before Aristotelianism became the official university philosophy. The academic calm in Uppsala had not been appreciably disturbed by the unrestrained attacks made by the Bishop of Strängnäs in the name of orthodoxy. The professors and the students were now working under conditions of security; things were going on calmly. In the summer of 1617, the second conferment of masters' degrees in arts and sciences was arranged; after passing the usual examinations, nine masters were created, two of whom were already professors.

An even greater day dawned on 24 October 1617. A week or so previously, Gustavus Adolphus had been crowned King in Uppsala Cathedral, after which knightly tournaments were held in a tilt-yard south of the Castle, in which the King himself appeared as the Gothic warrior

Berik. The conferment of doctorates of theology which then took place —the first in the history of the revived University—may be regarded as part of the festivities. It was a pure act of state, for Gustavus Adolphus himself issued the letters of invitation. He wished to honour four prominent men by conferring on them the degree of Doctor of Theology— Archbishop Petrus Kenicius, Laurentius Paulinus Gothus, and his chaplains, Johannes Rudbeckius and Johannes Bothvidi. At 9 p.m. on 24 October, the procession started for the Cathedral; first the musicians, then the students, clergy and professors, the University beadles with their silver wands, the Rector, the four recipients, and the Privy Council and the Chancellor, Axel Oxenstierna. The conferment was conducted by the Chancellor, who, after a hymn had been sung, went up to the lectern, made a formal speech, declared the recipients to be doctors and handed to them the proper insignia. All then left the Cathedral to the sound of music and marched off to the waiting banquet.

But the University was still living in straitened circumstances. At the 1617 Riksdag, the clergy presented a demand for a substantial increase in the number of professors. The King had already given proof of his affection for the University and, since the wars on the other side of the Baltic had been concluded and circumstances had become favourable, he set to work. The crises and anxieties of the years of growth were over and a new period was beginning in the history of the University of Uppsala.

CHAPTER III

The Seventeenth Century

1

In barely ten years, the University of Uppsala was transformed from an insignificant, out-of-the-way academy into a first-rate European seat of learning. The vigorous and far-seeing zeal for reform which was manifested everywhere in the Swedish public administration during the prosperous 1620s was also concentrated on cultural policy. To Gustavus Adolphus and his assistants, usefulness to the State was the primary consideration. At a time when Sweden was ready to venture the lives and the blood of its soldiers on the Continent, the expanding administration required that officials should have a thorough training, and the same applied to the clergy of the Lutheran Church, which now dominated the lives of the citizens from the cradle to the grave. But the King was also mindful of the nation's honour. It was important that the Swedes should not need to feel ashamed in the presence of the foreigners with whom they were entering into increasingly close relations as Sweden began to emerge as a great power. Learning must be made to feel at home in Sweden; the country must become a cultured nation in a more discriminating sense. For this reason, the government authorities deliberately concentrated—as never before or afterwards in Swedish history—on the schools and colleges. The first Swedish gymnasia came into existence in the cathedral towns of Västerås and Strängnäs and provided a humanistic education of high quality. But hopes were chiefly centred in the University of Uppsala. The royal favour was lavished on the professors and students and soon the University flourished; for nearly two centuries, it stood out as the leading institution for learning and culture in Sweden.

Gustavus Adolphus discussed the University's affairs at the Stockholm Riksdag in 1620. He put to the assembled clergy some arguments concerning the reformation of the Swedish educational system, in which things were in a bad way. It was particularly deplorable that literate government clerks, sheriffs, magistrates and other persons in authority could scarcely be obtained. The schools must therefore be overhauled and the University of Uppsala improved. The clergy agreed and presented in a report their views on the desirable number of professors at Uppsala, their salaries, the need of a chancellor, etc. The royal ordinance was issued in April 1620. At a stroke, the number of professors was increased from eight to 13 (three theologians, two jurists, two doctors of medicine and six teachers of arts and sciences). Instead of receiving Church tithes, which varied from year to year, they were to draw fixed annual salaries in cash (varying between 300 and 600 riksdalers). The theologians were to retain their prebends and to continue to be members of the Cathedral Chapter. Twenty royal scholarships were ordered to be paid to the students from Crown funds, the "community" was enlarged to accommodate 60 students and was repaired, salaries were set down for a University bursar and a secretary, and the newly founded University Library received an annual grant. But Gustavus Adolphus was still not satisfied. Just over a year later, he raised the number of professors to 17 (the newcomers were a theologian and three teachers of arts and sciences), increased the number of scholarships to 30 and augmented the Library grant.

The following year (1622), the University obtained what it had so long desired—a chancellor of its own. The King's choice fell on Johan Skytte. As Chancellor of the Realm, Oxenstierna was fully occupied with matters of state; the restored University needed a man who could devote himself wholeheartedly to its welfare. Skytte, who was at this time a Privy Councillor and President of the Exchequer, had risen to these high offices from a humble bourgeois origin. He had received a most careful education, which he had commenced at John III's college in Stockholm and completed at German universities, chiefly Marburg, where at the turn of the century he had, like a good Ramist, taken up the mathematical and mechanical arts and developed his splendid talent for Latin rhetoric. Gustavus Adolphus had great confidence in his former tutor, employed him on diplomatic missions and took his advice on questions of cultural policy. As the driving force in the work of educational re-organization in the early part of Sweden's period as a great power, Skytte vied with those two fiery spirits, Rudbeckius and Laurentius Paulinus, and shared the latter's philosophical convictions.

Even before Skytte took office as Chancellor, he had wished to set up an everlasting memorial of his connection with the University. At New Year 1622, he donated to the University a number of farms, the profits from which were to accrue to a professorship of politics and rhetoric. The combination of subjects is not as peculiar as it may seem. Ever since antiquity, politics had been an art in which speech played a great part; whether on the rostrum or on diplomatic missions, it was a question of moving people's emotions and stirring up people's minds, of convincing and persuading them by means of speech. To Skytte, an experienced diplomat and humanist, high-sounding Latin rhetoric was almost a means of salvation which was capable of changing the world. He laid it down that the holder of the professorship was to be "a *politicus*, a *historicus* and

11. *King Gustavus II Adolphus, the greatest benefactor of Uppsala University down the ages. Engraving after M. J. van Mierevelt.*

a good orator"; in addition, he was to be a staunch adherent of the Ramist philosophy. Each month, he was to make a public speech in praise of God's infinite goodness; he was moreover to give orations on the achievements of the Vasa dynasty and on the members of the Skytte family. The right of appointment to the new professorship of political science and rhetoric was to be vested in the donor and his descendants in the male or female line, and that rule is still applied today. Skytte soon rounded off his donation by presenting a stone-built house east of the Cathedral as an official residence for the professor—the house which was later to be called the Skytteanum with its vaulted passage, where the professor still lives.

Gustavus Adolphus, who was indefatigable in his good works on behalf of the University, soon took a further step. On 31 August 1624, he signed letters patent in which he presented to the "royal academia" in Uppsala his private hereditary estates in Uppland and Västmanland. He had always had a sympathetic feeling for schools and studies; "without them", he said, "barbarism itself arises in a country". His donation was a magnificent one. The University received "as its eternal, inalienable property" altogether

12. *The Skytteanum and its vaulted passage—the official residence of the Professor of Political Science and Rhetoric, which Johan Skytte donated to the University. Sture-Foto.*

264 complete freehold farms, half-shares in 74 farms and quarter-shares in 40 farms in these two provinces, as well as flour-mills and Church tithes from eight parishes in Hälsingland and Västmanland. This meant annual receipts of over 14,000 riksdalers to be spent on the University's needs. This put the University on a secure financial footing; the sum not only covered the salaries and other expenditure but also left a handsome annual surplus. The possession of the Gustavian hereditary estates made the University self-supporting, but it also involved obligations. The University had itself to take care of the administration of the estates through its bursar. From this time onwards, the Senate records are full of cases concerning refractory farmers who had not paid their dues, and the system afforded the bursar tempting opportunities for peculation. However, it worked for centuries. The Gustavus Adolphus donation is unparalleled in Swedish cultural history and gave the University a unique position and a degree of security which formed the indispensable basis for the zestful optimism which characterized it during the following period.

The new financial system did not mean that the University had its income entirely at its own disposal. It was still subject to the Crown, which issued instructions as to how the income was to be used. Thus, at the same time as he made the donation, Gustavus Adolphus decided that the number of scholarship-holders should be increased to 64, of whom four should be assistant teachers in the Faculty of Arts and Sciences receiving 100 riksdalers for their annual maintenance. The "community" was to accommodate 100 students, of whom 60 were expected to become clergymen and the rest to take up secular careers in the royal administration. It is uncertain where the "community" was now located—probably not on Studentholmen. A menu that has been preserved gives an idea of what was served on the long tables under the steward's supervision. The members of the "community" (who themselves contributed 8 öre per week to the cost) received two main meals a day, at which beef, pork, herring, cabbage, porridge, peas and beer—an ample diet, to all appearances—were served.

It remained to complete the reform work with a new charter and constitutions regulating academic life in detail. The charter, which replaced that of 1595, was mainly the work of Oxenstierna. It was issued in June 1625 and prescribed the rules concerning the Chancellor, the Pro-Chancellor and the appointments of professors but discussed in particular the University's jurisdiction over its own members. This was what distinguished them from the rest of Uppsala society and was traditionally regarded as their inalienable right. The eagerly awaited University constitutions, drawn up by Johan Skytte, were also completed at this time. However, they were found to be imperfect and were improved, on the

King's orders, by Skytte and Oxenstierna working together. The definitive constitutions were signed in the summer of 1626, though not by Gustavus Adolphus himself.They were therefore regarded as provisional, though they were applied in practice for 30 years.

The University constitutions of 1626 were carefully prepared. They dealt with all the University's activities, point by point. The Chancellor, who was appointed by the King, was the head of the University. In addition, there was the Pro-Chancellor, who was always the Archbishop; he was always on the spot and could supervise more closely the professors and the teaching. The direct administration of the University was in the hands of the Senate (*Consistorium*), which consisted of the assembled professors and was the real administrative and judicial body, and the Council, which consisted of 10 persons and dealt with routine business (it was not established for the time being). The Rector was elected by the Senate every six months, but the procedure was mostly a formality, since the professors took turns to hold the office. The installation of a new Rector was an imposing ceremony, which took place in the Cathedral and included a procession, the presentation of insignia, speeches and music, followed by a banquet. In the appointment of professors, the faculty nominated the candidates and the Senate then expressed its opinion of them, before the matter was passed on to the Chancellor and by him to the King, who made the appointment. There were four faculties —theology, law, medicine, and liberal arts and sciences. Each faculty had a dean, who was elected afresh every six months by turns. Precise instructions were given as to the order of precedence in academic processions—a tremendously important matter in an age when a man's honour was determined by the precedence which he enjoyed over other citizens. The bursar, who had to have university training, was appointed by the King. The University's humblest servants—the two beadles—had charge of the student prison (what was called the *proba*) and one of them was present at mealtimes in the "community". This is followed by detailed regulations about examinations, disputations and the conferment of degrees, the professors' teaching of the different subjects, and the students' morals.

The expansion of the University was manifested for all to see in its new main building, the Gustavianum, which was greatly needed. The old University building, Carolina, was still standing but was cramped and in poor condition. The new age, with its influx of teachers and students, required a spacious building—the grander the better—in which all the functions of the University could be gathered together. It was erected between 1622 and 1625 by the Dutch builder Casper Panten on the site of the old Archbishop's House west of the Cathedral. Uppsala, a little town of 3,000 inhabitants living in houses with turf roofs, was not spoilt as regarded monumental buildings; previously there had been only the Cathedral and the Castle on the crest of the ridge. The "new academy", as it was long known, was an impressive building with thick stone walls—a plain and dignified stronghold of the Uppsala Muses. The original building was lower than it is now, the top floor containing 26 rooms for students. On the main or intermediate floor, there were, on the south side, the great lecture theatre, the "Auditorium majus", and, on the north side, first the "community's" refectory, later the University printing office and, finally, a Senate hall with benches upholstered with scarlet fabric. The ground floor contained the University bursar's office and the "community's" kitchen. From the walled courtyard, on the west side, a double, free-standing staircase led into this "royal stronghold of the sun", as an enthusiastic poet called it in the words of Ovid. But it was not sufficient for all everyday needs. Alongside the new building (which became known in course of time as the "Gustavianum"), the "old" or Caroline building was used for lectures and disputations for another 150 years.

The University of Uppsala had been regenerated as the inalienable property of the Crown. Sweden's intellectual welfare was dependent on its prosperity, just as Sweden's material welfare was dependent on the copper-mines at Falun. Both the University and the mines were national treasures and, as such, attracted the most solicitous care and superintendence.

After the expansion, the number of professors at the University increased to 19, including the Skyttean professorship. In addition, there were the four lowly-paid assistants (*adjuncti*), who slaved away at private teaching. There were four Professors of Theology—two for the Old Testament, one for the New Testament and one for dogmatics and controversial theology. There were to be two jurists, one of whom was to lecture on Swedish and Roman law and the other on Roman law with its foundations in moral philosophy and politics. One of the two Professors of Medicine was professor of the practice of medicine, while the other was responsible for the auxiliary sciences—physics, botany and anatomy. Three of the chairs in the Faculty of Arts and Sciences were devoted to the mathematical sciences; the "Euclidean" professor took charge of arithmetic, geometry and algebra, the "Archimedean" professor lectured on optics, mechanics and musical theory and the "Ptolemaic" professor on astronomy. Two professors—one of Hebrew and one of Greek—were responsible for teaching the biblical languages. The Professor of Political Science or *philosophia civilis* lectured on ethics and politics from the writers of antiquity and modern authors; he partly duplicated the work of his Skyttean colleague. The Professor of History was supposed to follow Melanch-

13. The main University building up to 1887, which was erected in the 1620s and became known in course of time as the Gustavianum. Sture-Foto.

thon's world chronicle or some other approved account. Two chairs were dedicated to humanistic aesthetics—one of Latin rhetoric and the other of poetry, with the aim of teaching the students to imitate the poets of antiquity. Finally, there was the Professor of Logic, who had strict instructions to avoid scholastic complications.

It was difficult to find worthy holders of the new professorships. They were hand-picked by the King and added to the earlier set, of whom the foremost were still Lenaeus, the theologian, and Jonas Magni. Several of the younger generation of professors who took up their posts from 1620 onwards were very competent and were to set their stamp on the academic teaching for a long time to come. This applied to Olaus Laurelius, who was first Professor of Logic and then Professor of Theology (he eventually became an energetic Bishop of Västerås), to Sveno Jonae, the real founder of Hebrew studies in Uppsala, and to Martinus Erici Gestrinius,

43

the Professor of Mathematics. A second Professor of Medicine was added in 1624, when Johannes Franck, of Stockholm, was appointed to the post; he served throughout the middle of the century, a "dry and stern" man, who always wore boots and is famous as the first Swedish academic botanist. The following year, Benedictus Crusius, who had just returned home from his studies abroad, was appointed Professor of Law. But the domestic supply of scholars was not sufficient. Oxenstierna and Skytte clearly realized that the University's expansion required that teachers should be called in from abroad. There was nothing unusual in this; the academic international had operated in this way since the Middle Ages. The beginning was rather unsuccessful. Two obscure German jurists appeared in 1622 and 1623 but soon disappeared. Skytte was more successful in filling his own, newly established professorship. In 1625, Johannes Simonius, an old, learned, hard-working and eloquent man, was sent for from Rostock and when he died after a couple of years, he was succeeded by Johannes Loccenius, from Holstein, who had previously been appointed to the professorship of history but now also took over the Skyttean chair. Loccenius became firmly rooted in his new country and during his long life was one of the most inspiring teachers at the University; as humanist, historian and jurist, he was one of the leading scholars in 17th-century Sweden. In 1627, the Faculty of Medicine was enlarged by the appointment of a third professor, Johannes Raicus, a Bohemian, who was a convinced advocate of Paracelsus's doctrines and a capable man, but he soon moved to Dorpat to found the new gymnasium there. It is quite obvious what this immigration of scholars, which reached its climax in Queen Christina's reign, meant for the University of Uppsala and Swedish culture; in this way, fresh intellectual stimuli reached Sweden from the Continent.

The University's progress was reflected in the influx of students. The number of freshmen increased greatly, reached a peak of 302 in 1625, and then remained at about 160 per year. Altogether about 1,000 students would seem to have attended the University by the early 1630s. This is a high figure, even by European standards; however, many of them, chiefly the sons of noble families with their tutors, were under age. These years of the University's emergence were pervaded by a spirit of enterprise and spring-like confidence, which one would like to think was also shared by the students. At least, this was the hope expressed in the new constitutions, which included the following, lofty, patriotic exhortation, probably from the pen of Oxenstierna:

But, above all, the young men should learn not to entertain low and pusillanimous ideas about themselves and the present state of the nation, which commonly en-

44

The text within the image reads:

LIBER
ACTORUM PU
BLICORUM CONSI.
STORII ACADEMICI
Upsalien...

RECTORE
Admodum Reverendo & Clariss
viro .
D. JOHANNE CAN:
LENÆO / SS. Theol D.
eiusdemque Prof primario, & Fa-
cultatis Senat ut ac Civit. Pastore.

NOTARIO
ERICO PET. NORÆO
Nericiensi..

14. These portraits are to be found on a leaf of parchment in the Senate records for 1641. They represent, from the top downwards, Gustavus II Adolphus, Johan Skytte, the University Chancellor (on the left), Johannes Lenaeus, the Rector that year (on the right) and, at the bottom, Ericus Noraeus, the clerk.

45

gender complaints and lamentation, admiration for everything foreign and distrust of one's own ability to perform great deeds, which is the greatest obstacle to the government of a state. This should be corrected by upbringing and instruction, so that the minds of the young men may early achieve that elevation which gives the sure hope of doing great deeds.

The new splendour did not mean that all the reasons for uneasiness and conflict in academic life had disappeared. Laurentius Wallius, the Professor of Theology, was a great trouble-maker; like another Messenius, he led his colleagues a dog's life in the 1620s. The philosophical controversies were by no means settled but rather increased in intensity (cf. below) and the many changes in the professorships prevented the quiet growth of scholarship, both now and later. In accordance with old custom, the professors in the Faculty of Arts and Sciences endeavoured to gain promotion to the better-paid chairs of theology; once they had secured one, they began to dream of obtaining a bishopric. The "community", the University's welfare institution, was the subject of continual anxiety. At times, open warfare prevailed between the students and the steward, whom they accused of dishonesty and of supplying poor food and drink—the beer was "as thick as pigswill" and the cooking vessels were dirty. The complaints reached such a pitch that in 1637 the government decided to close the "community" and instead to devote its funds to the granting of scholarships, which thereby numbered 150 in all.

It was primarily the business of the Senate to remedy defects, to mediate in controversies, and to superintend everyday activities. The Senate met frequently under the chairmanship of the Rector and the series of Senate records preserved ever since 1624 forms the main source material for the University's history for a long time to come. Under the Senate came the four faculties with their deans, but the two smallest—those of law and medicine—sometimes had only one permanent member each and so existed chiefly on paper. About 1640, the faculties procured their own seals, bearing suitable emblems: the theologians an open book with a biblical quotation, the keys of the Kingdom of Heaven, Noah's dove and a serpent; the jurists a scale beam in balance, together with a sword crossed with a spray of laurel; the medical men the pool at Bethesda with the angel stirring the water; the arts and sciences men a cube with Apollo's lyre and a doctoral hat.

But the University belonged to the Crown and had only limited self-government. The Chancellor and the government decided all matters of importance. Johan Skytte carried out his duties as Chancellor with the utmost zeal. He often went to Uppsala on visitations, sometimes with Oxenstierna, and these visitations were carried out with scrupulous care. The professors had to answer for their domains almost like delinquent school-

15. *The seals made about 1640 for the four faculties of the University. From the left, the seals of the Faculties of Theology, Law, Medicine and Arts. After the reproductions in Eenberg (1704).*

boys, severe admonitions were given and unsatisfactory conditions were put right. In later years, Skytte was assisted by the aged Laurentius Paulinus Gothus, who in 1637 was restored to Uppsala as Archbishop and Pro-Chancellor; in that role, he was zealous and stubborn and was soon on bad terms with the whole body of professors. However, such discordant notes should not be allowed to lead us astray. Everything seemed to be developing well at the University and Skytte was the first to acknowledge this. After an inquisition in the autumn of 1639, he expressed cheerful confidence by writing that "we have reason to thank God for the felicity which it [i.e. the University] now enjoys". A year later, Skytte was again in Uppsala and made a brilliant speech to the students, full of paternal exhortations and appeals to their ambition to serve their country. By now, other universities had come into existence in the kingdom, one at Dorpat in Estonia (1632) and another at Åbo in Finland (1640), both modelled on Uppsala and constituting expressive testimony to the liberal and far-sighted cultural policy of the government authorities. But they could not disturb the position of the University of Uppsala as the cradle and chief seat of learning in 17th-century Sweden.

When Queen Christina acceded to the throne, the Crown's solicitude for the University, if anything, increased. It is true that Skytte died in 1645 and that the aged Axel Oxenstierna, who had been persuaded to succeed him as Chancellor, had his hands full of political problems. But the Queen herself was indefatigable. With her ardent desire for knowledge and her passion for learned men—a Minerva on the throne of Sweden—she was, as it were, created to be the mistress of a great and brilliant university. She was active in demonstrating her goodwill to the University, individual professors and selected scholars. In December 1646, she improved the University's privileges and in the following year granted the professors a substantial increase in their salaries. She visited Uppsala over and over again, listened to the Senate's requests and received the University's homage, expressed in high-sounding Latin orations. One memorable day in April 1652, the Queen and her attendants watched the young Olof Rudbeck demonstrate in Uppsala Castle his discovery of the lymphatic system. She was especially anxious that the body of professors should be increased by the inclusion of famous foreign humanists. The European gateway was opened wide; the years around 1650 were the peak period for foreign scholars and men of letters at her court in Stockholm; they came and went and some breakers of this cultural tide also reached Uppsala. As early as 1642, Johannes Freinshemius, the classical philologist and orator from Strasburg, had been appointed to the Skyttean professorship; later, as the Queen's librarian and learned adviser, he rose high in her favour. But other Strasburg men were also attracted to Uppsala. In 1649, the Queen persuaded Joh. Henr. Boeclerus, a well-known Latin scholar at Strasburg, to accept the chair of rhetoric at Uppsala. This appointment ended badly. Boeclerus was full of the pride of learning, the students gave him a good hiding, and he returned home. The next man from Strasburg was a much greater success; he was Johannes Schefferus, who in 1648 succeeded Freinshemius in the Skyttean professorship. He was not only loyal to Uppsala; as a modern classical philologist, he was active far into the Caroline period, acquired a European reputation and also critically investigated the annals of Swedish history. With his rare capacity for work, he practically lived in his study; his professorial residence was on St Erik's Square, where the little museum, in which he kept his books and collections, may still be seen. Two years after Schefferus, another foreigner came to Uppsala at the invitation of Queen Christina. This was Christian Ravius, who had, by the Queen's favour, been made a supernumerary Professor of Oriental Languages—a peculiar man, from whom the University received little pleasure.

The Queen's exuberant goodwill and constant interference in the life of the University aroused mixed feelings, on the whole. She both warmed men's hearts and frightened them. Paying no regard to financial realities, she appointed temporary professors not included in the budget, in spite of the Senate's vociferous protests. In 1654, the full number of professors was 25 and it was incumbent on the University to find salaries for them all from the receipts of its estates. The financial disorder became even worse when in 1652 it was discovered that Bo Chruzelius, the University bursar, had during his long period of office reduced the University's accounts to hopeless confusion; he had neither kept books nor had an audit made and was found to be in debt to the University to an amount which was stated to reach the enormous sum of 124,000 silver riksdalers. The

16. *Professor Johannes Schefferus's little library and museum, erected in the 1670s in what is now St. Erik's Square. Sture-Foto.*

situation would probably have been even more depressing if the Queen's plans for a new University building had been realized. This was a grandiose project—in every way worthy of the extravagant Queen—the total cost being calculated to be 100,000 riksdalers. The architectural drawings, which were probably made by Nicodemus Tessin the Elder, show us what Christina had in mind. The building was to be erected on the hill behind the Gustavianum and was to consist of a main block of six floors, containing lecture halls and library rooms, and four wings filled with two-room apartments, which were certainly intended for noble students and their tutors. The work actually started in 1648 and building materials began to be delivered. But the cost was found to be exorbitant and the undertaking soon came to a standstill. It was intended that the Crown should defray most of the cost, but the University was also required to make sacrifices, which may have exceeded its powers.

During Queen Christina's reign, new constitutions were drawn up for the University. As will be recalled, the previous constitutions drawn up in 1626 had never been officially confirmed and were also imperfect in some respects. From the end of the 1640s, new and definitive statutes were therefore prepared under Oxenstierna's direction. This took a long time; the Chancellor was dead and the Queen had left the country before they were finished. Mattias Biörneklou, a diplomat and under-secretary of state, who in his youth had been a professor at Uppsala and was well acquainted with the ins and outs of academic life, made a considerable contribution to the final draft. The new constitutions, signed by Charles X on 27 June 1655, are remarkable chiefly on account of their prolonged influence; they were soon applied also at other Swedish universities and remained in force for two centuries. Otherwise, they did not present any startling innovations but may be regarded as an improved version of the 1626 statutes. The forms for taking the master's degree were clarified and the students' way of life was regulated with a strictness which heralded the authoritarian barrack-square spirit of the Caroline period.

As the century advanced, the number of students at Uppsala increased. Exact figures are given only of those who matriculated annually: about 170, on the average, during the period 1632–43 and about 180 during the period 1644–54. It is still uncertain what this meant as regarded the total number of students attending the University. In 1636, a total of altogether nearly 1,100 students (54 of whom were noblemen) is reported and for the 1650s there are estimates of up to 1,300–1,500, though they would seem to be on the high side. Not all of them were Swedes or Finns; one of the results of Sweden's expansion as a great power was that a good many students from the conquered provinces on the other side of the Baltic made their way to Uppsala. They were mostly Balts from Estonia and Latvia (45 in all up to 1660); two stray Russians turned up in 1649. Sweden's position as a power that protected Protestants meant that students from the German Lutheran states also found it natural, during the hardships of the Thirty Years' War, to study at Uppsala; during the period 1620–60, there were 60 of them altogether.

In the middle of the century, the Uppsala professors—who were as numerous as at a first-class seat of learning abroad—were a motley crowd. Many did not rise above the level of industrious mediocrity. The Faculty of Law left much to be desired, and things were not much better in the Faculty of Medicine. Franck was old and weary and his colleague Olaus Stenius was not very active; besides, his subject was really astronomy. Among the theologians, there were at least two forceful personalities— Lars Stigzelius, who had much influence on ecclesiastical policy and finally became Archbishop, and Johannes Terserus, a pugnacious and disputatious man who had previously been a professor at Åbo. Among the teachers in the Faculty of Arts and Sciences, Loccenius and his son-in-law, Schefferus, were the bright stars. Henrik Ausius made an important contribution to the study of the Greek language, while Edmund Figrelius

(Gripenhielm), who was later famous as a statesman, became, while he was Professor of History, a pioneer of Swedish research into the history of art with his book on Roman sculpture (*De statuis illustrium romanorum*, 1656). The most distinguished of the mathematicians was Bengt Hedraeus, who was a skilled instrument-maker and built a small astronomical observatory, the first in Sweden.

Two establishments which we have so far only glimpsed now and again —the printing office and the library—were indispensable for academic life and the expansion of scholarship. Eskil Mattsson, the University's first printer, gave his assistance over a long period. In his simple office, he produced the plain printed matter required in the academic routine— theses, orations, the Rector's programmes, etc. In the 1650s, when he was succeeded by Johannes Pauli, a Dutchman, the printing office was moved to a separate building in the courtyard of the Gustavianum. As learning progressed, the printer had to see to it that he had Hebrew, Arabic and other exotic founts in stock.

From the beginning, the University had no library of its own. In Uppsala, there was only the old Cathedral library, which, as the years went by, became increasingly dilapidated. It was Gustavus Adolphus who first laid the foundations of a real university library with his letters patent of April 1620. He now donated to the University all the books which had been collected at the Franciscan monastery in Stockholm. They included some priceless treasures—the old manuscripts from the Vadstena monastery, the remains of the libraries of the Stockholm monasteries, and the large collection of books made by Hogenskild Bielke. But they were insufficient as a basis for scholarly studies and it was not until the spoils of war began to pour in that the Uppsala library increased in size. In accordance with the custom of the time, the victorious Swedish armies on the Continent laid their hands on captured treasures of all kinds. Splendid Baltic, German, Polish and Bohemian libraries fell into the Swedish generals' hands and were packed into chests and sent to Sweden. Most of them went to Uppsala. As early as 1622, Gustavus Adolphus presented the Jesuits' library in captured Riga to the University; somewhat later, there followed the Jesuits' library at Braunsberg and the precious books belonging to the Ermeland bishops in Frauenburg (including several volumes that had belonged to Copernicus). In 1636, the library of the Prince Bishop of Würzburg arrived in Uppsala. In a short time, this rather unscrupulous traffic converted the University Library into an important institution, even by Continental standards. About 1640, the book stock amounted to 8,600 printed books and about 1,165 manuscripts. But Swedish works were lamentably few (only five) and honest purchases were rare. This meant that the most recent literature was poorly represented and that the Library could scarcely serve as an adequate scholarly armoury. The professors were mostly compelled to rely on their own collections of books, some of which were very well stocked; this was true of Schefferus and the above-mentioned Figrelius-Gripenhielm, who possessed one of the largest private libraries in the country.

The University Library was intended for teachers and students, but only the former were allowed to borrow books to take home, which they sometimes kept all their lives. The Library was housed for the time being in cramped, unheated and damp premises in a turf-roofed, stone-walled house west of the Cathedral. A librarian was responsible for the lending and care of the books. He was, as a rule, a professor working part-time; from the end of the 1640s, this work was done by Loccenius.

2

By the middle of the 17th century, the University of Uppsala had gained stability and reputation; there was every reason to hope for the best in the future. During the Caroline period (1654–1718), the University's activities were to continue unchanged in their external forms and with a general liveliness which sometimes found expression in tumult and uproar.

The Chancellor now was Magnus Gabriel De la Gardie, who succeeded to the office in 1654 after Oxenstierna's death the same year. De la Gardie had qualities which made him very suitable for this office. He had received the finest aristocratic upbringing, including thorough academic studies at Uppsala and on the Continent. As an accomplished courtier of the French school, he had basked in Queen Christina's favour and advanced to higher and higher offices, until, after the death of his brother-in-law Charles X, he became, as Chancellor of the Realm in the regency government, the real director of Swedish policy. If ever a Swede lived and worked as a cultivated nobleman in the grand style, it was De la Gardie. He lavished enormous sums on building splendid castles, but he also had a genuine passion for learned studies; he built up the largest private library in the kingdom and encouraged research into the country's antiquities with magnificent liberality, both officially and in his private capacity. He realized the genuine importance of his office as University Chancellor and during his long tenure of it, he devoted his attention with almost pathetic zeal to both great and small matters at the University. But with all his inspiriting and brilliant qualities, he was not entirely blameless as regarded the disturbances which now affected the University. His achievements as an administrator were marked by the same weaknesses as contributed

17. Magnus Gabriel De la Gardie, who was both Chancellor of the Realm and Chancellor of the University. Copperplate engraving.

to his poor posthumous reputation as a statesman; he lacked firmness and consistency and his judgement in financial matters was poor.

The professors began to quarrel with each other even during De la Gardie's first year as Chancellor. The vigorous Professor Terserus was particularly active; he led the theologians in their struggle for the introduction of the preliminary examination in theology, which all masters were to undergo. At the same time, he carried on a rancorous personal feud with Ravius, the eccentric orientalist. More prolonged and more trying was the quarrel which raged for several years (1656–61) between Schefferus and the young temporary Professor of Law, Petrus Gavelius. Gavelius had attacked a thesis by Schefferus and called him a misleader of youth and his thesis a scandal. Naturally, Schefferus was irritated, paid Gavelius back in the same coin and reported him to the Senate, where the case against him came up year after year, prolonged by the defendant's ingenious legal quibbles. It was not until 1661 that De la Gardie succeeded in putting things right during his visitation of the University.

However, more serious conflicts were to come. In the autumn of 1661, Olof Rudbeck was elected Rector and this ushered in what may justly be called "the Rudbeck epoch", a short period of scarcely 10 years, created by a brilliant man who loved power and authority and whose appetite for action was boundless.

After he had discovered and described the lymphatic vessels—the first independent achievement by a Swede in the history of science—Rudbeck completed his medical studies at Leyden. On his return home, he worked for two years as a non-established Professor of Medicine, before being appointed in 1660 to be the established holder of the chair of theoretical medicine, including anatomy and botany. He tackled with tremendous energy the task of lifting medical studies at Uppsala out of their decline. This was manifested most spectacularly in the new buildings which he had erected for the requirements of medical instruction—the botanical garden and the anatomical theatre (see page 74 below). But Rudbeck could not begin to work on a large scale, for the good of the whole University, until after he had secured greater power in 1661 on his election as Rector. He was seething with reforming zeal and new ideas; he wanted to re-mould the University—the town of Uppsala as well, for that matter—in his own way. In all this, he had the Chancellor's whole-hearted support. De la Gardie admired Rudbeck's genius; as long as he lived, he supported him and endeavoured to implement his plans; the abundant correspondence between the two of them forms an important source material for the history of the University in the Caroline period. No sooner had Rudbeck left his Rectorship than De la Gardie forced through, in the face of the Senate's protests, the establishment at the University of a new office, that of *Curator* (1663). This office was specially designed for Rudbeck; it is true that he was given two fellow-curators, of whom Stigzelius, the theologian, was one, but they could not hold out against his inexhaustible vitality. As the University *Curator,* he had the royal authority to act, under the Chancellor, as the chief supervisor of the University and to see that the professors fulfilled their obligations. By this means, Rudbeck secured a powerful position which was a challenge to his colleagues and intensified the passions felt by the University. He was cautious enough to refer seldom to his new authority, which soon quietly disappeared, but it was a weapon against those who opposed him and it authorized everything that he undertook.

To begin with, Rudbeck wished to renovate the University in the external sense. He was a Jack-of-all-trades and one of his passions was to design and erect buildings. The anatomical theatre was only a beginning; during the 1660s and afterwards, there came into existence down the years a series of buildings in the rustic, classicizing style which was the distinctive feature of Rudbeck's work as an architect. Some were private buildings or structures designed for municipal purposes. He built a dwelling-house for his friend Verelius and, probably, the Schefferian Museum already mentioned, constructed a suspension bridge over the River Fyris and produced a design for a new Castle garden. Other buildings or technical arrangements were connected with Rudbeck's increasingly restless and comprehensive work as a teacher. After he was appointed "commissioner for rural culture" (a kind of teaching post in economics and technology) in 1665, he built a factory with moving machinery on a reduced scale on the island in the River Fyris formerly known as Studentholmen or Kvarnholmen. From a tank in the Castle courtyard, he had water conveyed in wooden pipes to the botanical garden, where, towards the end of his life, he built the prefect's house for the professor which Linnaeus was to take over half a century later. Rudbeck himself died there.

The plans for a new University building which Rudbeck drew up in the 1660s were intended to be his finest work as an architect. Like Queen Christina's plans, which would seem to have inspired him, they were on too large a scale and were never executed; we know of them only from his own illustrations. He imagined a central block of two floors, with two wings, ornamented with antique pilasters; he added to one of the plans, clearly at a later date, an equestrian statue in the courtyard and two gigantic pairs of entwined dolphins on the gables. However, something came of these grandiose plans—they were implemented, on a greatly reduced scale, in the "exercise house" which he built in 1663–64 behind the Gustavianum and to which we shall return.

Another of the fine arts for which Rudbeck was an enthusiast was music. It was thanks to him that it flourished in Uppsala. He had a bass voice of overwhelming range and wrote music himself; from 1662 onwards, he began to ginger up the dormant musical life of the University. He bought music by modern German composers, as well as violins, flutes, dulcimers and shawms. At the coronation of Charles XI, he had performed a work for 12 trumpets and 4 drums which he had composed himself. He also patronized Harald Vallerius, the young man who in 1675 became *director musices* (he later became Professor of Mathematics), and induced Uppsala music to flower for the first time.

No one could have any objections to this, but in other connections there were conflicts. The first of these concerned the abandoned "community", which Rudbeck, supported by De la Gardie, wished to re-establish. The royal scholarships, for which the funds of the old "community" had been appropriated, led, in his opinion, to serious abuses; amongst other things, they were often granted to wealthy, noble students. A "community" would more effectively provide the poor students with lodgings and food. In 1661–2, despite the furious resistance of the majority of the Senate, Rudbeck succeeded in forcing through a decision that this utilitarian establishment should be revived under his supervision. However, it never paid its way and was again closed down after a time.

The storm clouds soon gathered; Rudbeck's autocratic behaviour was increasingly felt to be unbearable. His numerous building projects cost large sums of money and during the second half of the 1660s the University was experiencing a financial crisis. This was probably due to the external conditions, for which no one could be blamed. After a long period of good harvests and high prices for corn, several lean years followed, the price of corn declined and the University, which lived on the yields of its farms, got into a difficult situation. Things were not improved by the fact that De la Gardie, like Queen Christina before him, had, with misdirected generosity, blessed the University with a number of professors not included in the salary list, which made inroads on the salaries account. He and Rudbeck carried out these and other actions between them, usually without consulting the Senate. Rudbeck took the initiative, as a rule; he held De la Gardie in the palm of his hand and plied him continuously with academic gossip, suggestions and schemes behind his colleagues' backs. Verelius, the University Bursar, was a close friend of Rudbeck's and willingly opened the coffers for him. All this increased the animosity towards Rudbeck and when the deficit in the University's finances increased and the salaries of the professors were endangered, this animosity grew into a storm of indignation. A vigorous anti-Rudbeck party was formed, led by Schefferus, Claes Arrhenius-Örnhielm, the historian, and Erik Benzelius the Elder, the theologian, under the protection of Stigzelius, who had just become Archbishop and Pro-Chancellor. When, at New Year 1669, Rudbeck retired at the end of his second term as Rector he took the opportunity to defend what he had done for the University and to settle accounts with his opponents. In the spring of 1670, Schefferus and Arrhenius accused Rudbeck in the Senate of having set aside the legal forms in his despotic career. At a subsequent meeting, there were chaotic scenes, with much shouting and bawling. Finally, the Chancellor, who was just as responsible as Rudbeck for the University's tight financial position, had to intervene. During the summer, he attended a meeting of the Senate, at which he sought, by using all kinds of evasions, to exonerate himself from blame and to restore order. Rudbeck—alone against practically the whole body of professors—stuck to his guns, as always,

18. *Olof Rudbeck, dressed in the simple garb of a scholar. On the table, there are a few instruments and an anatomical illustration and on the bookshelves stand the thick volumes of his* Atlantica. *Oil painting by Martin Mijtens the Elder (1696). University of Uppsala.*

and in a pathetic address reckoned up all that he had done for the University's benefit; envy and slander, he said, had now made him sick and tired of it all.

However, Rudbeck's period of greatness as the University's man of action was now at an end. This did not mean that the 1670s were a period of calm at Uppsala. The disputes about the University's staff and expenditure continued, the question whether there should be a "community" or not still aroused passionate feeling, and Rudbeck, who was quite imperturbable and always prepared to defend with sparkling humour the steps he had taken, neglected no opportunity to punish old and new antagonists. He was vindictive and small-minded and never forgot an injury. In 1670–71, he and De la Gardie, who still had every confidence in him, took action against Jonas Fornelius, the eccentric Professor of Astronomy, who was notorious for his disorderly life and had made disparaging remarks about the King, the Chancellor and Rudbeck, and compelled him to apologize. Rudbeck made his contempt for his colleagues and the Senate increasingly obvious; he never set foot in the Senate for seven years.

In a final, furious outburst, Rudbeck tried to settle accounts with his opponents and to disgrace the Senate. This took place in connection with a law-suit which was brought in 1674 against Henrik Curio, the University printer, who had neglected his duties. What followed almost defies description. Curio was related to Rudbeck by marriage. Animated by passionate family feeling, Rudbeck flung himself into the conflict and, when the Senate sentenced the wretched printer to lose his post, took the astounding step of registering himself under the Uppsala municipal law, in order to bring an action in the Court of Appeal as an independent citizen against the University. He brought his influence to bear on De la Gardie, who came to his aid. The situation became more and more confused, full-scale war soon raged between the Chancellor and the Senate, slanderous aspersions were cast, and De la Gardie completely lost his head. The Curio affair dragged on indefinitely and, when judgement was given ten years later, the original sentence was confirmed and Curio had to leave his mismanaged office.

As the years went by, Rudbeck's behaviour became calmer; he was absorbed in his enormous literary works, *Atlantica* and *Campus Elysii*. Almost everybody acknowledged his greatness, whether reluctantly or not. But the reverberations of the storm were to last for a long time; Rudbeck's monumental self-esteem could still give offence. In the middle of the 1680s, the storm broke out again at Uppsala. Rudbeck himself was fairly innocent, being involved rather against his will in a struggle for power which lasted several years.

This struggle was over the Schütz affair. In 1679, Henrik Schütz had, in an unfortunate hour, been attached to the University as Professor of Theology. For some unknown reason, he enjoyed the favour of Charles XI and, when the King appointed him University Librarian, his ambitions had full scope. Schütz was a trouble-maker of unequalled proportions even for that quarrelsome age; he was always excited and angry and was constantly running about. "He lives on quarrels", sighed De la Gardie, whom he reduced to extreme despondency. Schütz used his undeserved position as Librarian to persecute Rudbeck, who had many of the Library's books on life-long loan. The usual quarrels broke out in the Senate, but on this occasion Rudbeck was not alone. Schütz had made himself generally unpopular, even among the students, who played funeral music outside his house, and when it was his turn to be Rector, the Senate refused to elect him. The King then intervened, forced Schütz on the University as Rector and later (1684) appointed him and Jacob Arrhenius, the University Bursar and another staunch anti-Rudbeckian, members of a special committee of inquiry which was to examine the University's finances. The Chancellor and the Senate were rendered powerless; Schütz became for a while—with the support of Arrhenius and with the King behind him—a kind of Grand Inquisitor at the University. He at once tackled Rudbeck and called him to account for his administration of University funds right from the beginning. Extravagant and cogent, as always, Rudbeck defended himself in long memorials, which give invaluable glimpses of the University's history during the previous 25 years. Actually, De la Gardie got into more trouble. Irresolute and impotent, he did not really know what to do. He made an unsuccessful attempt to bring a law-suit against Schütz and was induced to take other injudicious steps, which weakened his already tarnished authority and embittered his last few years as the University Chancellor.

However, the disturbances in the 1660s, 1670s and 1680s, which also infected the students, should not be allowed to lead us astray. Everyday academic life, with its lectures and disputations, went on just as usual. Nor were the passions and the conflicts always prompted by commonplace lust for power or personal aggressiveness. During this period, currents of new ideas, chiefly the Cartesian philosophy (see below, p. 72), reached Uppsala from the Continent and provoked some of the worst storms. Academic Uppsala was intellectually more vigorous than ever and in many subjects the studies flourished under outstanding teachers. Rudbeck and, even more, his colleague, the popular Petrus Hoffvenius, put new life into the medical instruction. The theologians, who formulated the Lutheran faith in an inexorably orthodox spirit, included the above-mentioned Erik Benzelius the Elder, who in time became Archbishop. Considerable efforts were made to put fresh life into the Faculty of Law. A prominent German jurist and philosopher named Daniel Lipstorpius was called in in 1662 but stayed only a few years. A good ten years later, the University had an erudite Professor of Law in Carl Lundius—Rudbeck's brother-in-law—who trained generations of students in Swedish law well into the next century. Loccenius and Schefferus continued to shine in the Faculty of

Arts until they departed this life towards the end of the 1670s. The Faculty received its first and for a long time its only chair of archaeology (antiquities) in 1662, when the famous Olof Verelius was appointed to it. Among the humanists, there were otherwise Andreas Norcopensis and Johannes Columbus as the faithful guardians of the classical heritage. The orientalist Gustaf Peringer-Lillieblad made a name for himself as a scholar in Jewish literature, and the implacable anti-Rudbeckian Claes Arrhenius-Örnhielm was an experienced historian who specialized in Swedish mediaeval church history. There were now only two professors of mathematics—one of astronomy and the other of mathematics proper. In 1679, Anders Spole came from Lund to discharge the duties of the professorship of astronomy with great credit and to build an observatory in Svartbäcken. At the same time, the talented Johan Bilberg was appointed Professor of Mathematics.

The number of students seems to have declined at the beginning of the Caroline period. During the first half of the 1670s, according to official reports, there were, on the average, only about 730 students in Uppsala, but later the number increased and towards the end of the century seems to have been stabilized at about 1,000. The competition from other Swedish seats of learning had gradually increased. It is true that Dorpat in Estonia was, for the time being, out of the running, but Åbo in Finland still attracted Swedish students and in 1668 the new Caroline university at Lund came into existence; students from the southern Swedish provinces especially attended it. The foreign universities were also still in the picture. They had never lost their attraction and the flow of study tours to the Continent continued throughout the 17th century and beyond. Almost without exception, the student now laid the foundation of his education by studying for a few years at Uppsala, Åbo or Lund, before going off to Germany, Holland or France. The clergy were anxious to have a system like this. At Reformed or Roman Catholic universities abroad, the student might pick up ruinous false doctrines and therefore it was important that he should be well grounded in the Lutheran faith before he went abroad. The clergy succeeded in inserting into the 1655 constitutions a regulation that every student who was thinking of travelling abroad must first pass a minor examination in theology. However, it remained for the most part a dead letter and in practice the Swedish students travelled wherever and whenever they wished, in order to sit at the feet of famous teachers and to imbibe draughts from the stream of modern European culture.

At the end of the 17th century, the University Library was moved into more appropriate premises. It had then been enlarged by fresh donations. Its most precious treasure, the Silver Bible (Codex Argenteus), written in

19. The Linnaeanum, the prefect's house built by Rudbeck in the old Botanical Garden. Aquarelle painted in 1933 by Hugo Alfvén, the composer and director *musices at the University from 1910 to 1939. University of Uppsala.*

Gothic, had been presented to the University by De la Gardie in 1669, together with some priceless Icelandic manuscripts, and in time they were followed by De la Gardie's own private library of 4,700 volumes, which had been confiscated by the Crown. At Rudbeck's suggestion, the Gustavianum was reconstructed, in order to accommodate the University Library also. The height of the upper floor was increased and there two large library rooms were fitted up in the 1690s, with stucco ceilings, pilasters, portraits of the Chancellors and reading desks. The books were arranged by faculties along the walls on shelves with green curtains. Between the two rooms was a gallery containing globes, mathematical instruments and curiosities of natural history. The famous art cabinet from Augsburg, presented to Gustavus Adolphus and given to the University in 1694, was placed in the northern library room.

61

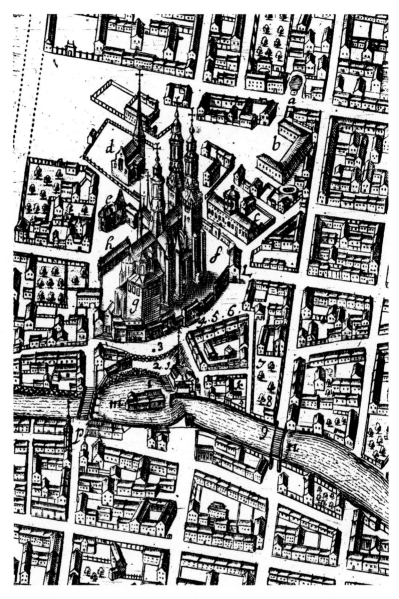

20. *"Nova Upsala", a map of Uppsala drawn by Dionysius Padt-Brügge at the end of the 17th century. From Peringskiöld's* Monumenta Ullerakerensia *(1719).*

21. A leaf from Petrus Aurivillius's stud-book in the summer of 1633. On the eve of Aurivillius's departure on a study tour to the Continent, Professor Johannes Loccenius entered his good wishes for the tour. University Library.

The Library remained at the Gustavianum for a century and a half, until the Carolina Rediviva was brought into use in the 1840s. About 1700, it would seem to have contained about 20–25,000 volumes. At this time, a new young University Librarian took up his duties and with him the Library entered upon a new phase. This was Erik Benzelius the Younger, who had recently returned from his travels abroad. He was a fully fledged orientalist, a classical philologist and an expert on the writings of Philo, the Graeco-Jewish philosopher, but, being a polymath, he was also active in other fields, chiefly the sources for the history of mediaeval Sweden and the Gothic text of the Silver Bible. Benzelius brought the University Library into a flourishing state. He had new catalogues compiled, made systematic purchases of literature abroad, subscribed to learned journals, took advantage of book auctions and acquired a multitude of manuscripts. He had his agents in Paris and elsewhere, and assiduously corresponded with learned bibliophiles on the Continent. Benzelius lectured to the students on the history of learning and on Swedish history. When, after a good twenty years, he changed over to theology, Uppsala possessed a large scholarly library run on modern principles.

On the whole, peace and order descended on the University of Uppsala towards the close of the 17th century. The era of passion and intrigue was past; in this respect, the Caroline autocracy had a salutary effect. Bengt Oxenstierna, the new Chancellor from 1686 onwards, was a states-man of experience and firm principle, and under him the University's finances and administration were set in good order. For this, a price had to be paid. The all-supervising monarchy "by God's grace" required an unyielding orthodoxy in questions of theology and politics; the University and the Church were government departments under the King's immediate supervision, firmly placed in the Caroline social hierarchy. At length (1705), the professors received their due place in the official list of precedence as the equals of cavalry captains and assistant judges; they had contended for a long time over this matter, complaining that "con-stables and gardeners" had higher social status. Over and over again, in orations and at disputations, professors and students willingly expressed their loyalty to the interests of the State. They did so in particularly im-pressive forms in the spring of 1693, when the University celebrated, in the presence of Charles XI, the centenary of the Uppsala assembly. The festivities lasted for a whole week, and Jesper Svedberg, the Rector, did the honours. Speeches were made in fluent Latin and Greek, disputations and banquets were held at which cannon salutes roared, and a ceremonial conferment of doctoral degrees in theology took place in the Cathedral —all in all, a brilliant demonstration of the unshakeable alliance between the secular power and the Lutheran Church.

The body of professors had gradually changed. Outspoken and self-assured, Svedberg infused life and pith into the Faculty of Theology. Olof Rudbeck the Younger, who succeeded his father during his lifetime, was not inferior to him as a natural historian, and his colleague, the eccen-tric Lars Roberg, covered the whole field of medicine and natural history. Even more versatile was Harald Vallerius, the musician and mathemati-cian, whose pupils argued about "everything knowable", as it was once called. About 1700, classical studies reached an unequalled level under the two aesthetes and Latin orators Petrus Lagerlöf and Johan Upmarck (Rosenadler); alongside them worked the legendary Laurentius Norrman-nus, a paragon of Greek learning. The oriental languages (Hebrew and Arabic) also flourished at this time, the principal teachers being Johan Palmroot, Daniel Lundius and the remarkably learned and long-lived Olof Celsius. In their Protestant zeal, the Uppsala scholars were particularly fascinated by the Jewish antiquities, which shed light on the text of the

64

22. *Erik Benzelius the Younger, the University Librarian from 1702 to 1723 and later Bishop and Archbishop. Detail from the drawn title-page of a copy dated 1746 of his lecture notes on Swedish antiquities. University Library.*

Old Testament. The Talmud was studied and about 1700 the University secured its own rabbi, Johan Kemper, a converted Jew, who was an expert on the Cabbala.

Otherwise, the new century brought with it hard conditions for the University. In May 1702, Uppsala was ravaged by a devastating fire, which in a short time reduced the greater part of the town to ashes. Many of the professors, including the aged Rudbeck, lost all their possessions; the Cathedral was badly damaged, but fortunately the Gustavianum was saved. Three days after the disaster, Upmarck spoke on "The peace of the soul", and the work of reconstruction began immediately. In the autumn of 1710, the bubonic plague reached Uppsala and claimed many victims; the students left the town and all instruction was suspended, to the benefit of the professors' scholarly labours. Now the misfortunes of the great war also cast their shadow over the University and in 1714, when the Russians occupied Finland, Benzelius had the Library's treasures packed in large boxes, in order to be able to move them quickly to a place of safety. Charles XII was far away and had neither time nor opportunity to devote any care and attention to the academy in Uppsala. But, in spite of the hardships, the flame of learning was kept burning and when the dream of Sweden as a great power was shattered for ever by the King's death, the University of Uppsala was by no means in bad shape.

During the 17th century the universities were not scholarly institutions in the modern sense. Neither in Sweden nor abroad was it any part of the university teacher's duty to carry on scientific research. Nevertheless, many university teachers did so, and Uppsala's contributions to intellectual progress began with the work of Rudbeck and Schefferus. But the principal task of the universities was still to educate new generations of students in the traditional ways of thinking, which were regarded as a precondition for the continued existence of the State and the national culture. The universities existed to communicate to the students the tried and tested stock of knowledge which was considered necessary for prospective clergymen, teachers and public officials and which gave them at the same time a share of the European cultural heritage common to all educated persons. For this reason, the 17th-century universities were the bulwarks of the established order and were averse to accepting any hazardous, new-fangled ideas. The intellectual landslide of the century—the scientific revolution which created a new heaven and a new earth—took place essentially outside the bounds of the universities; its strongholds were in the independent academies of science. But, in the end, "the new philosophy" gained a footing also in the universities. They did not succeed in maintaining their positions as sanctuaries protected against the storms of time; amid a great uproar, modern ideas forced their way in and found utterance in lectures and disputations.

Academic learning in the Uppsala of that period was based on three foundations—Lutheran theology, classical humanism and scholastic philosophy. The first two might seem to be unshakeable and unchangeable; Luther and Cicero appeared side by side as symbols of a whole epoch.

The theology taught in 17th-century Uppsala was imported from Germany. The professors had studied at orthodox German universities and what went on there in the subject of Lutheran theology was closely followed from the Uppsala horizon. Theological developments during the century largely resulted in Melanchthon's mild and tolerant attitude being superseded by an increasingly implacable orthodoxy. In this connection, the Aristotelian philosophy was used to demonstrate and confirm the Lutheran dogmas; this had created an involved kind of Lutheran scholasticism, whose proponents were prepared to silence heretical opinions of all kinds. This was, in the main, the form which theology took also in Uppsala. The leading professors of theology during the first half of the period—Jonas Magni, Lenaeus, Olaus Laurelius and Stigzelius—were all out-and-out Aristotelians, who would explain the essential lines of thought in the doctrine of salvation with the aid of logic and the scholastic conceptual apparatus. Jonas Magni maintained that theology was an "argumentative" science, which learned from logic how to work out the consequences of the scriptural texts. Laurelius, who was officially responsible for teaching "controversial" theology, expounded Lutheran dogma with all the artifices of the scholastic method in his chief work *Syntagma theologicum* (1641), which was directed against the Papists, the Calvinists and other heretics. Together with Jonas Magni, he struggled to get the Concordia Formula, the bulwark of high German orthodoxy, adopted as the creed of the Church of Sweden.

However, very profound metaphysical theology, such as was pursued in some quarters in Germany, never really gained a foothold in Uppsala. The teachers in the Faculty of Theology were rather moderate; no orthodox dogmatist of any distinction ever made his appearance. There were obvious, external reasons for this, at least from the middle of the century. As the Church of Sweden became set in its rigid, orthodox creed, it became more dangerous to discuss knotty theological questions. Syncretism, i.e. attempts to unite the contending Christian Churches, had caused deep disquiet in responsible quarters and the royal decrees on religious matters issued on this account in the 17th century introduced the strictest theological censorship, hinting that the death penalty would be applied in particularly serious cases of aberration. It was easy, even with the best will in the world, to stray away from the right path. The Lutheran creed was established for all time and therefore there was no reason why theological research should flourish at the University. But the safe subject of Church history could be studied without risk, as could also the exegesis of the Old Testament, to which the above-mentioned Terserus made an important contribution with his commentaries on Genesis and Exodus (1655–60). What the government authorities expected was that the Uppsala Faculty of Theology, which, together with the bishops, represented the most important body of theological expertise in the kingdom, would ensure that the students were well grounded in the Lutheran creed and the basic principles of biblical exegesis. Unity in religion was conceived to be a necessary condition for the continued existence of the kingdom, most of all during the Caroline period, when the teachers and students in Uppsala hailed the absolute monarchy as a manifestation of God's will, on which more detailed instruction could be derived from Luther's writings and the dreary form of political science outlined in the Old Testament.

It was not until after the turn of the century that signs began to appear, indicating that high orthodoxy under the direction of the State would not last for ever. Pietism came to Sweden from Germany and taught sensitive souls to experience religion as something subjective—an affair of the heart —alongside dogmas and symbols. The State and the Church sounded the alarm, but Pietism could not be restrained; students returning home from the University of Halle spread the new piety about the country and in the 1710s it even gained a footing among the Uppsala theologians. The confessional Lutheran Church had been called in question.

Humanism, the study of the ideal world of antiquity, was in a certain sense the antipole of Lutheranism. During this period, the legacy of Greece and Rome lived on more vigorously than ever before or since in Swedish history; at schools and universities, it moulded young men for life. Here everything referred to life on earth; moral examples, splendid quotations and archetypes of beauty were fetched from the ancient poets, philosophers and orators. Both as a general outlook on life and as an aesthetic programme, Renaissance humanism formed the very nucleus of 17th-century academic instruction, in Uppsala as elsewhere in Europe. The aim was to secure a complete mastery of the Greek and Latin languages and an equally complete insight into the emotional world of antiquity.

The constitutions show how classical studies predominated in 17th-century Uppsala. Over half of the professorships in the Faculty of Arts and Sciences were mainly devoted to them and several others partly. The key subjects were poetics and oratory (eloquence, rhetoric), in which the sluggish sons of farmers were to be trained to orate in Latin or to be dexterous writers of verse in imitation of Virgil and Ovid. The professors wrote the necessary textbooks—Laurentius Fornelius a guide to poetics (1643) and Schefferus a clear and precise textbook on Latin style (*De stylo,* 1653). The Uppsala student of this period was surrounded by Greeks and Romans from morning to night; their works became his intellectual viaticum on his journey through life. Young noblemen, who were later to advance to high offices, were not excepted; even an admiral should know his Cicero. Above all, Latin oratory was indispensable. Two chairs were devoted to it—the ordinary professorship of eloquence and the Skyttean professorship (see above, p. 37). In actual fact, in the course of the century and beyond, the Skyttean professor came to represent the finest humanistic training in Sweden. Men like Loccenius, Freinshemius and Schefferus attracted large crowds of students, whom they trained in the appreciation of the classical authors. In the Gustavianum or the old Carolina, both teachers and students frequently gave impressive Latin orations, modelled on the Roman patterns and full of undulating, interwoven sentences, metaphors, climaxes, exclamations and other subtleties. However, the formal skill was not the whole point. The many orations that have been preserved give vivid expression to the lofty attitude to life which the students met with everywhere in the ancient models. They abounded in words of wisdom and heroic figures to be imitated; the Romans were al-

23. *Title-page of* Syntagma theologicum *(1641), a book on dogmatic theology by Olaus Laurelius, Professor of Theology.*

ways talking about Virtue and Honour, which ennobled mankind and secured its immortality. Through humanism, this view of mankind, so remote from the Lutheran doctrine of sin, became a kind of official university philosophy in Uppsala and probably also played a part in the formation of the energetic patriotism of this period. But the world of classical thought also contained other mansions, especially the austere Stoic philosophy, which taught mankind to live healthily under hard conditions and gave grounds for consolation when a man's fortune changed for the worse.

Academic humanism reached its climax in Uppsala during the late Caroline period. The Latin language blossomed, in the Baroque spirit, more exuberantly than ever and some virtuosi appeared who have never been excelled. This applies chiefly to the above-mentioned Upmarck-Rosenadler, the first native Swede to hold the Skyttean chair and a brilliant Latin orator whose majestic periods and sudden transports lifted the minds of his hearers towards the sublime.

Classical philology, as a science, was born from the humanistic passion for antiquity. It was pursued with tremendous enthusiasm during the 17th century, particularly in Holland, and gained recognition in Sweden through Johannes Schefferus. He was also famous among his foreign colleagues and in a long series of published works he showed himself to be a skilful textual critic and an extremely learned authority on the cultural history of antiquity. In the 1660s, Schefferus published excellent editions of the works of late Greek and Roman authors (including the *Satyricon* of Petronius), wrote on Pythagorean philosophy and ancient painting, and in his best-known works discussed essential subjects in military and technological history—the art of naval warfare among the ancients (*De militia navali veterum,* 1654) and their means of land-transport. This was classical archaeology on a high level, though carried on almost wholly with the aid of literary sources. Inspired by Schefferus, the younger scholars tackled the publication and annotation of the works of Greek and Roman writers. They did not achieve any noteworthy results, not even the famous Norrmannus, who stuck to the works of Byzantine Atticists and other, obscure, late-Greek authors. Erik Benzelius the Younger might well have been a brilliant exception, but he never succeeded in completing the great edition of Philo's collected writings which he worked on all his life.

Scholastic philosophy was less safe as one of the corner-stones of the University; before the end of the century, it had collapsed. On the whole, the vicissitudes undergone by philosophy in this period exhibit a variable and dramatic spectacle. As may be recalled, the philosophy of Aristotle or the new scholasticism had to struggle for a long time against the more superficial philosophy of Ramus, inherited from the 16th century. Ramism

70

24. *The industrious Johannes Schefferus also had artistic talent. This is a self-portrait dating from 1679. In private possession.*

defended its positions tenaciously; as Chancellor, Johan Skytte enforced it with all the authority of his office. The University constitutions of 1626 included an energetic defence of the socially useful Ramist philosophy; complicated scholastic metaphysics must be avoided at all costs. During his visitations of the University, Skytte intervened ruthlessly time after time to defend Ramism, supported, as time went on, by Laurentius Paulinus Gothus, the old Archbishop and Pro-Chancellor. As vacant professorships were filled by reliable Aristotelians, Skytte's indignation increased. He harassed his opponents, impressed on them that they were obliged to lecture on Ramus's logic, and in 1640 went so far as to actually propose that scholastic philosophy should be forbidden, as only breeding quarrels and the splitting of hairs. A strict censorship should be introduced and accordingly the University bookseller should be allowed to import only Ramist textbooks.

But their time was now past and by the middle of the century Aristotelian scholasticism was victorious on the battlefield. Regarded by the

Lutheran dogmatists as an indispensable ally, Aristotle—the master of order and clarity—underwent a last autumnal flowering in Uppsala and Åbo. Textbooks in Aristotelian metaphysics and logic were published for grammar schools and universities; the manual of scholastic logic published in 1672 by Petrus Aurivillius, Professor of Logic at Uppsala, was in use for a long time. Natural science also needed the Aristotelian definitions. In Uppsala, as elsewhere, the traditional scholastic natural science or "physics" had reigned uninterruptedly, even during the palmy days of Ramism. Its main concepts (form, matter, substance, etc.) were discussed in innumerable academic theses. A principal feature of this picture of the world, which had been inherited from the Middle Ages, was the geocentric theory, which was based on the evidence of the eyes and on unshakeable authorities, according to whom the earth was in the centre of the universe and the everlasting celestial spheres revolved round it. This theory was dutifully expounded in Uppsala in the early part of the period by the professors of mathematics, one of whom, Martinus Erici Gestrinius, produced in his *Urania* (1647) the first Swedish textbook of astronomy.

However, the intellectual revolution which had broken out in Europe eventually reached Uppsala. In alliance with modern science, Descartes had overthrown Aristotle and the old science collapsed in ruins. The introduction of Cartesianism, leading to the Cartesian controversies, was the most important event at the University of Uppsala during the 17th century.

The heralds of the new philosophy, with its strictly mechanistic conception of the world, were the two Professors of Medicine, Hoffvenius and Rudbeck. They had been won over to the Cartesian doctrine during their studies at Leyden and for a long time fought for it single-handed. The theologians and the philosophers were both frightened and on the alert and were only waiting for a chance to strike; when, in a disputation in the autumn of 1664, Hoffvenius openly came forward as a Cartesian, the storm broke out. In the Senate, Hoffvenius came to loggerheads with the theologians, who succeeded in preventing the discussion of the obnoxious thesis. The academic atmosphere was embittered for some years to come. During the 1670s, calm seemed to prevail and Hoffvenius was able to publish unhindered a brief summary of Cartesian physics (*Synopsis physica*, 1678), which indicates the emergence of the new *Weltanschauung* in Uppsala. But the following year there was a regular accusation of heresy against the young Nils Celsius, who had defended the Copernican heliocentric system in an astronomical thesis and, in doing so, had expressly set aside the authority of the Bible. The Faculty of Theology summoned Celsius to an interrogation in the Cathedral and forbade the disputation. This was followed by a truce which lasted several years, until the second Cartesian controversy broke out in the autumn of 1686—the most violent scholarly feud ever carried on at the University. The orthodox Lutherans, feeling themselves in a powerful position under the protection of the Caroline autocracy, brought up the matter at the Riksdag held that year. The Cartesians had again become active at Uppsala; the new philosophy should therefore be forbidden for all time and the strictest censorship should be introduced at the University. However, at the University the front line had changed. The doctors of medicine, the philosophers and the jurists were now all adherents of Descartes; the theologians, led by the indefatigable Schütz, were alone in the camp of scholasticism. When the King referred the whole question back to the individual faculties, the liveliest scenes took place in Uppsala. Bilberg, the mathematician, and Andreas Drossander, Professor of Medicine, came forward as the leaders of the Cartesians. They were both lively and quickwitted men and extolled in enthusiastic terms the blessings of modern science and the unrestricted freedom of the human reason to seek the truth. To the Faculty of Theology, such ideas were inspired by the Devil. In its letter to the King, the Faculty summarized what made the Cartesians so intolerable to a good Lutheran: they destroyed the Aristotelian concepts, which gave dogma its stability, and asserted that the Bible was not a reliable guide in scientific matters.

It was not until the spring of 1689 that the King's decision with regard to the Cartesian philosophy was promulgated. It was more like a compromise than anything else. The King permitted "the free use and practice of philosophy", provided that the authority of the Bible and the Christian faith remained undisturbed. At any rate, the theologians had not secured their original demands and the Cartesians, chiefly Bilberg, interpreted the outcome as a victory. They considered that it meant that they might preach the new philosophy to their heart's content and so they did. At the turn of the century, Cartesian physics reigned supreme at Uppsala. The painful cultural conflict, from which a new epoch was being born, had been fought to a finish, during a period which had otherwise been characterized by the strictest State control over the University.

Cartesianism was accompanied by modern mathematical and experimental science. The Copernican system, in which the sun was at the centre of the universe, was one of the bases of the Cartesian cosmology and was embraced more or less openly by all Cartesians. Thus, it was also embraced by Anders Spole, who, however, did not venture to take sides in his printed works; it was left to Per Elvius, his successor as Professor of Astronomy, to appear publicly as a convinced Copernican. Drossander made a decisive contribution to the new experimental physics in the 1680s by procuring an air-pump, a barometer, thermometers and other instruments, which he demonstrated to greatly appreciative audiences at private lectures.

Otherwise, the leading scientists in Caroline Uppsala were the two Rudbecks, father and son. Olof Rudbeck the Elder was one of the best anatomists and botanists of his time. The botanical garden which he established in Svartbäcken towards the end of the 1650s (the present Linnaean Garden) was filled with exotic and indigenous species of plants. During the last decades of his life, Rudbeck, assisted by his children and some of his students, worked on the enormous collection of wood-cuts entitled *Campus Elysii,* which was intended to depict all the plants in the world. As a specially commissioned natural historian, Olof Rudbeck the Younger travelled through Lapland in the 1690s, collected and drew plants and animals, and later founded Swedish zoology with his hand-coloured pictures of birds and his lectures on them. On the other hand, the first blossoming of anatomy in Uppsala was of shorter duration. Rudbeck, who became a European celebrity after his description of the lymphatic vessels in 1653, wished to give anatomy a permanent home at the University and in 1662–3 built his remarkable anatomical theatre on the roof of the Gustavianum. It was a unique creation—an amphitheatre in classical style with a suspended cupola and room for 200 spectators round the dissection table. But it was scarcely ever used for the purpose for which it was designed. Rudbeck soon grew tired of anatomy; only three or four public dissections were performed in the theatre during his time, and at the beginning of the new century the premises were quite dilapidated. However, Lars Roberg, who was now Professor of Practical Medicine, did not neglect anatomy. He wrote a textbook on the subject and wanted to perform autopsies on dead patients. But Roberg's most far-sighted achievement was his creation of the *nosocomium academicum,* the University Hospital in Uppsala. It was accommodated in Oxenstierna House in Riddartorget (the present Juridicum) and received its first patients in the plague year of 1710. However, it seemed to stop growing after that; it was still functioning with a few beds about 1720 but then became dormant for the time being.

While the plague afflicted Uppsala and the professors were released from the duty of giving lectures, a society called "Collegium curiosorum" (Society of the Curious) was founded; it is generally regarded as the first academy of science in Sweden. The driving force behind it was Erik Benzelius, but the idea had come from Christopher Polhem, the brilliant engineer and inventor, who corresponded with the Uppsala gentlemen and communicated to them his technical and scientific speculations. The Society's meetings, which were methodically recorded, continued only for a short time, but after an interval of a few years the Society was revived

25. *An interior view of Rudbeck's anatomical theatre, which was erected in 1662–3 on the roof of the Gustavianum. At the bottom is the dissection table and above it the rows of stepped wooden benches decorated with pilasters for the spectators. Sture-Foto.*

in 1719 under the direction of Benzelius as the "Bokwettsgille", from which the Royal Society of Sciences at Uppsala was soon to be developed.

Yet another of the predominant intellectual activities in the 17th century was patriotic historical research or Gothicism. The University of Uppsala was not by any means its stronghold; on the whole, Swedish history was neglected in the academic instruction. The Gothic myth—the belief that Sweden was motherland of the nations at the beginning of time—had a long history; during Sweden's period as a great power, isolated scholars, such as Bureus and Stiernhielm, directed it towards new goals. It was not until after Olof Verelius had been appointed Professor of Scandinavian Antiquities in the 1660s that the University of Uppsala became the stronghold of Gothic research. Verelius and his pupil Rudbeck raised the subject to undreamt-of heights. Icelandic literature—the works of Snorri Sturluson and the sagas—had been added; here Verelius was the undisputed master. He published the Icelandic texts and in his comments squeezed out of them every particle of information about the radiant Scandinavian past. However, when he identified Old Uppsala church with the hyperborean Temple of Apollo, he encountered resistance. Schefferus, who was also an outstanding authority on Swedish history, had already in his book *Upsalia* (1666) denied that the Old Uppsala church was of great age and now a dispute broke out between him and Verelius about the site of the heathen temple. This dispute raged for several years and finally had to be brought to an end by De la Gardie. In the heat of the debate, Verelius was supported by Rudbeck, whose enthusiasm for the dream of Gothic greatness was inspired by his teaching. The result was Rudbeck's immense work *Atlantica* (1679 ff.), a product of genius and madness, which was intended to present to the whole world the evidence that Sweden was once the home of the gods and the cradle of culture. *Atlantica* is the most celebrated work that issued from the University of Uppsala during the 17th century; it attracted attention abroad and in Sweden a little group of faithful adherents gathered round Rudbeck—including his son Olof and Carl Lundius, the jurist—and passed on these ideas. But the future was not favourable to them; soon historical criticism awoke and dispelled the dream world of Atlantis.

Modern natural law was much more durable. During this period, it became characteristic of the instruction and studies at Uppsala, as at other Protestant universities. Its principal field of application was in constitutional law or political science, which at Uppsala were dealt with by several teachers, partly in the Faculty of Law and partly by the Skyttean professor and the Professors of History and Moral Philosophy. Their task was to consolidate the students' political thinking along the lines laid down by the government authorities. Natural law, with its belief in a moral system inherent in human nature, fitted in well in this connection. Its theories as to how the legal relationship between prince and subject should be regulated were applied to Swedish conditions. During the early part of the period, the Uppsala professors lectured about the ruler's contract and the monarch's being bound by the will of the people, but under the Caroline absolutism the situation was different. Grotius and Pufendorf —the latter taught at Lund—had placed the natural-law doctrine about the social contract at the service of absolutism, and after Charles XI had declared himself to be an all-powerful king, the political teaching at Uppsala had to be re-organized in accordance with the new line. Letters patent in 1689 laid it down that no one was to touch upon the principles of autocracy or otherwise to express "heterodox opinions in political science", which was subject to the same inexorable constraint as religion. As the King's henchman, Lundius saw to it that this ordinance was obeyed. Pufendorf, who at this time became the great legal authority at

76

the University, was considered to be the surest guarantor of Caroline autocracy. As soon as anyone drew erroneous conclusions from his works, Lundius stepped in. In 1691, a disputant was accused of political heresy and his thesis, which asserted that no man was born to rule over another, was confiscated.

But the explosive material contained in Pufendorf's works and in natural law could not be neutralized. The theory of the ruler's contract concealed from the beginning a democratic point: the original power actually belonged to the people. With the overthrow of the autocracy and the introduction of the constitution of the Age of Freedom, this application of natural law was to become the only acceptable one, even at Uppsala.

4

Academic education continued during the 17th century and afterwards in forms which were still, in the main, mediaeval. The instruction was dominated by lectures. The professors were obliged to go to the lecturer's desk no less than four times a day on four days in the week. They dictated their lectures slowly in the traditional manner, while the students wrote them down word for word. Usually, the works of only a single approved author, classical or modern, were gone through for one or more terms and were extensively commented on. The audiences varied a great deal in numbers. The Professor of Dogmatics, whose lectures all the students seem to have been obliged to attend, might have up to 300 of them sitting on the benches, and a celebrated figure like Schefferus might now and then have as many. But others—even Schefferus sometimes—had only a handful of listeners, if even so many; this was the case for a long time with the professors of medicine. Lecture catalogues printed in single sheets—the oldest date from the 1630s—gave the syllabus for the coming term. Until the middle of the century, the old division into classes was retained, i.e. every student was obliged to attend the classes in a certain subject; this was omitted from the 1655 constitutions.

In addition, private lectures—what were called *collegia*—were given to a large extent. Fees were charged for them and in favourable cases these fees yielded the professors a large part of their incomes. The assistants (*adjuncti*)—there were eight of them altogether during the Caroline period—lived almost entirely on fees for *collegia*; they toiled in the academic dust in the hope that a regular chair might become available. Some professors were extremely diligent in giving tuition in *collegia*, for example, Schefferus, whose main clientele was among the noble students, and later Lundius, the jurist, who claimed that he gave up to six of them every day. It is scarcely possible to over-estimate the importance of this form of instruction in Swedish educational history. In their private *collegia,* which were held in their homes, the professors felt freer; they could discuss complicated scientific questions or new ideas which they did not venture to put forward publicly.

Orations and disputations also formed part of the routine academic education. The orations have already been mentioned. The disputations were a heritage, for good and ill, from mediaeval scholasticism, and in the Swedish universities in the 17th and 18th centuries they were to flower more abundantly than in any other country. There was an enormous number of disputations in Uppsala during this period. The writing and defence of Latin theses on selected subjects were skills that all students had to acquire. It was not required that the theses should be original. Academic dissertations kept, as a rule, to the approved syllabus; the important thing was the actual disputation ceremony, when the student (the respondent) defended himself against the attacks of his opponents and thereby demonstrated his gifts in Latin oratory and his dialectical skill. In accordance with the constitutions, disputations were held either for practice (*pro exercitio*) or for the master's degree (*pro gradu*), in both cases with a graduate university teacher acting as the president. The disputations took place on Wednesdays and Saturdays in one of the university lecture-rooms, beginning at 7 or 8 a.m. The presiding professor opened the ceremony from the lecturer's desk and then the opponents began their speeches; they were allowed to speak for at most 4 hours. A disputation could be a quite expensive affair for the respondent; he had to bear not only the cost of printing his dissertation but also that of a party after his task had been successfully carried out. Friends and acquaintances used to decorate the dissertation with encouraging congratulatory verses in Latin or Greek. The question of authorship, i.e. who actually wrote the dissertation—the president or the respondent?—has been much discussed. The matter has to be decided from case to case, but, as regards the 17th century, it may be assumed, as a rule of thumb, that the respondent was also the author —obviously always in a disputation *pro gradu* and usually also in disputations *pro exercitio.* Hence, it was by no means essential that the subject of a dissertation should be within a professor's subject field; with the work he had written, a student could approach any professor in the faculty and ask him to act as president. Nevertheless, what he had to offer was only exceptionally his own work; it was based on the handbooks and his teachers' instruction.

The thesis-writers did not have unlimited freedom of expression. The State and the Church saw to it that only commendable ways of thinking were taught at the University; as we have already seen, it was no part

26. *Disputation ceremony in the large auditorium in the Gustavianum on 14 April 1709. At the lectern is the president—probably Professor Johan Arent Bellman, the grandfather of the poet—and on his right are the opponents and the respondent. Aquarelle in Carl Fredrik Piper's exercise book. Engsö Library.*

of the University's task to arouse an unseemly and dangerous curiosity in the students. However, during Gustavus Adolphus's reign and the regency period, when the intellectual climate was less restrictive, it was seldom that any respondent or president got into trouble. It was only when the orthodox restrictions were introduced after the middle of the century that the censorship of opinion became a constant, statutory threat at the University. The 1655 constitutions forbade disputations on any thesis which defended "an absurd or impious opinion" or disputations which caused a din, and non-theologians were not permitted to introduce theological questions into their theses. This prepared the ground for future conflicts. The Faculty of Theology had got weapons in its hands and used them ruthlessly in the Cartesian controversies; any new-fangled scientific idea could, with a little goodwill, be squeezed until it came within the scope of the constitutions and could then be condemned as being dangerous to society.

The disputation *pro gradu* was the final aim of university studies. But the majority of students never reached as far as this; many of them contented themselves with studying at Uppsala for one or two terms. They were almost all in the Faculty of Arts and Sciences, which was still, in the mediaeval fashion, the basic Faculty, through which all students had to pass. After six years, it was possible, under the 1626 constitutions, to take the master's degree in the Faculty of Arts and Sciences; to graduate in one of the higher Faculties, a further three years was required. But in Sweden at this period, hardly anyone took the doctorate in a higher faculty. At the few conferments of doctorates in theology, only bishops and other established prelates were honoured with the title; the doctors of medicine and the jurists defended their doctoral theses abroad. The only academic degree that really mattered—in short, *the* contemporary university degree—was the master's degree in the Faculty of Arts and Sciences. It is true that in 1655 the Estate of the Clergy succeeded in getting a separate bachelor's degree in theology introduced, but hardly anyone took it. However, there were no barriers between the faculties. All students had to attend at least a few lectures in theology. After tough resistance from the artists and the scientists, the theologians were able to insert into the 1655 constitutions the requirement that all who wished to take degrees in arts or sciences must take a short preliminary examination in theology.

Studies in the Faculty of Arts were characterized by a certain formlessness that was typical of the period. The students went through the subjects one by one; a complete degree required that they should all have been studied. But the knowledge tests were not very rigorous. To begin with, the professors examined the students every six months on the course held during the preceding term, after which they were examined only once a year; during the Caroline period, the students seem normally to have been excused from any kind of test. The requirements were so much the harder for those who persevered to take the master's degree. In its final form, this degree required that, after translating a text into Latin, the can-

JUVA יהוה

Diſputatio Phyſica
D E
PRINCIPIIS RERUM
NATURALIUM,
QVAM
Ex conſenſu Ampliſſimæ Fa-
cultatis Medicæ,

In Athenæo, quod ad Salam eſt celeberrimo,
Guſtaviano Maj: die Iun.27 Anni Præſentis 1668.

SUB PRÆSIDIO
D. OLAI RUDBECKII.
Ventilandam reverenter offert

MAGNUS A. CAROLINVS Vermel.
Sereniſſ. R. M. Stipendi:

UPSALIÆ.

Excudit HENRICUS CURIO S R· M. & Academiæ
Upſalienſis Bibliopola.

---

27. Title-page of a medical dissertation in 1668. Rudbeck acted as president at the disputation. The dissertation was printed by Henrik Curio, the University Printer.

didate should be publicly cross-questioned for four hours by all the professors of all the subjects taught in the Faculty. This part of the examination (which was equivalent to the examination for the bachelor's degree) was followed by the defence of the master's thesis and finally by two lectures on a subject selected by the candidate himself. After these feats, the

81

young man was considered mature enough to ascend Parnassus and to receive the coveted tokens of his academic rank. However, conferments of master's degrees in the Faculty of Arts and Sciences were not arranged every year. The authorities were afraid of creating an academic proletariat and therefore deliberately sought to restrict the number of recipients. Towards the end of the 17th century, new masters were created approximately every three years, about 25–40 on each occasion. The actual ceremony took place with all the pomp of which the contemporary University was capable. At 8 a.m. on the day of the conferment, the participants went in procession, while the bells were rung, from the house of the conferrer to the Gustavianum, where they took their seats in the large lecture hall. The highest place among the prospective masters was occupied by the cleverest (*primus*), who answered what was known as "the master's question", and the last place by the next best (*ultimus*); immediately next to him was placed the wretched *penultimus*, the occupant of the little-coveted "donkey's place". The conferrer made a speech and solemn music was performed, after which the recipients rose one by one and received the insignia—the ring ornamented with precious stones and the laurel wreath or the purple hat (the custom seems to have varied in this particular). For poor masters, the conferment might be an expensive business—in addition to the fixed fee, there was the cost of the inevitable black-silk gown and a substantial dinner. But it was probably worth the cost to be initiated into a life-long alliance with the Muses under the protection of Phoebus Apollo.

5

The Uppsala students of the century represented a cross-section through contemporary Swedish society. All social classes were represented, from the swaggering, spoiled, young nobleman to the poverty-stricken crofter's son. The contemporary expansion of schools and universities had opened up opportunities of study for new categories of the Swedish people and therefore the question of the social recruitment of the students is of special interest. More and more young men could now make their way by university studies from humble origins to ecclesiastical and civil offices; the universities consequently became the principal instruments of social change.

The available information about the social origins of the Uppsala students during this period is not particularly complete, but it gives a general picture of the situation. The largest group always consisted of the sons of the clergy. Of the altogether 740 students investigated during the decade around 1650, 262 were the sons of clergymen, 66 the sons of farmers and 57 the sons of burghers; in addition, 33 were the sons of officials who were commoners, 10 were the sons of officers in the armed forces, and 9 were the sons of nobles (there is no information about the father's profession for no less than 39%). The distribution was approximately the same in the Caroline period. During the years 1680–1719, the sons of the clergy seem to have constituted 36–42% of the total number of students at Uppsala, the sons of untitled persons of rank 14–18%, the sons of burghers 12–15% and the sons of farmers 12–19%. The figures show that the poor peasant's son in his little room, with his sack of food from home to last him the whole term, was not so common as has sometimes been imagined. The results of the 17th-century expansion of education must not be over-estimated; the great majority of the students came from more or less educated middle-class homes, primarily those of the clergy.

However simply the students lived—often in twos in the same lodging—the financing of university studies was difficult for the majority. But even those who were completely destitute usually managed to get along. Those who had a gift for study were favoured with generous royal scholarships and all students could resort to private tutoring in time of need. As a tutor in a middle-class or a noble family, it was possible to save money for a period of study at Uppsala, but it was far more advantageous to obtain what were called "academic conditions", when the student acted as a teacher and both he and his pupil attended the University.

A great deal has been written about the Uppsala student's way of life during this period and later; no part of the University's history is as well known as this. The sources are abundant, but they give a one-sided picture of the reality—literally, its aspect by night. We learn next to nothing about the hard-working model student bent over his lecture notes; he is glimpsed only in school plays and congratulatory writings. Instead it is the students' bad habits, in the atmosphere of boisterous academic freedom, that have been primarily preserved to posterity. In virtue of the University's jurisdiction and the directions in the constitutions, students who transgressed the rules were brought before the University Senate, whose records consequently abound in racy stories. The period was coarse and uncouth, there were no public amusements in the little university town, and the students had therefore to provide their own. The townsmen kept taverns and beer-houses, where there was a cheerful atmosphere in the evenings. Crowds of drunken students marched through the streets with drawn rapiers, "bellowing and making trouble", firing off live ammunition and smashing windows. Large-scale fighting, sometimes partly organized, took place and a few cases of manslaughter occurred. Things were particularly bad in the 1660s and 1670s; it was as if the general disquiet among the professors had infected the students. Venus also claimed her tribute; in the districts of Fjärdingen and Svartbäcken, there were girls who were willing, in return for a promise of marriage or a cash payment, to grant a man their favours. The Senate did what it was empowered to do and the guilty were interrogated and punished. For serious offences, the students were sentenced to varying periods of expulsion from the University, but the commonest punishment was a few days' wholesome sojourn in the University lock-up (the *carcer* or *proba*) in the courtyard of the Gustavianum.

Towards the end of the 17th century, the Uppsala student began to display a certain amount of refinement in his public behaviour, refinement which was stigmatized by Jesper Svedberg and other earnest Lutherans. It is true that the remarkably foppish *academicus Upsaliensis* depicted in Leopold's copperplate engraving of about 1700 would never seem to have stalked about in the real world. But many students—and not only the young nobles—yielded to the temptations of the new French fashion and wore a powdered, full-bottomed wig, together with "a long, lace neckerchief with a red rosette", as it was indignantly observed.

The student nations, which developed in the course of the 17th century and are still flourishing today, were of profound significance, as regarded daily life at the University. They originated in the four nations at the mediaeval University of Paris, but the immediate model was provided by the *societates nationales,* which came into existence spontaneously at the German Lutheran universities, such as Rostock, which was well known to Swedish students. It was natural enough that such associations should be formed; students from the same part of the country or from the same cathedral school came together at the University for mutual help and amusement. At Uppsala, the nations developed from the ceremony known as the "deposition", which was introduced when the University was reestablished in 1595. The "deposition" (from *cornua deponere,* to shed the horns) was the official ceremony at which the boorish schoolboy was received into the academic fellowship before being enrolled in the University register. A "depositor" chosen by the Senate directed this high-spirited show, which was held in a special "deposition" room in the Gustavianum, as long as it was carried on under the auspices of the University (up to 1691). The "depositor", who was terrifyingly dressed and armed with a long wooden axe, drove in the freshmen, who were decorated with motley patches, horns, asses' ears and pigs' tusks, all alluding to their beastly condition. After making all kinds of coarse jests, he rid them of their attributes with suitable tools (fortunately still preserved)—a pair of wooden tongs, a saw and a plane; salt was then placed on their tongues and wine was poured on their heads, whereupon they were declared to be

84

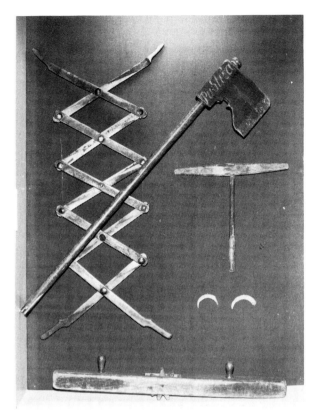

*28. The tools—axe, wooden tongs, pig's tusks, plane and au-
ger—used in the University "deposition" ceremony in the 17th
century are still preserved. Museum of Nordic Antiquities.*

free students. This hilarious ceremony was followed by a lavish drinking-
bout (what was called "a *cornutus* party"), when older students took
charge of their newly arrived fellow-countrymen and initiated them into
the mysteries of student life. In time, these clamorous groups with a common provincial background were organized on an increasingly permanent
basis, until in the 1640s the first real student nations or "provinces"
were formed, each with its officials, rules and cash-box. The Västman-
land-Dala nation is probably the oldest (founded about 1642); the Småland
and Östergötland students formed their nations somewhat later and after
them came the others.

This development was long regarded with aversion by the Senate. The

85

student nations were accused, not without reason, of encouraging excesses, including heavy-handed bullying; strict prohibitions were issued against them and they were compelled to exist in secret. However, it was finally decided to make a virtue of necessity: in 1663, the Senate made the nations legal and appointed a professor to act as inspector in each of them; somewhat later, membership of a nation was made compulsory for all students. These spontaneously developed associations of fellow-countrymen were thereby fitted into the academic system; within the framework of these associations, student life was lived in fairly restrained forms. The comradeship within the circle of his fellow-countrymen gave the student security and a feeling of being at home; the nation's funds were drawn on in cases of sickness and death, and now and then boisterous parties were arranged. Otherwise, the students met in the home of the inspector, who helped his fellow-countrymen in every possible way, chiefly by assisting them to get advantageous posts as tutors or a more settled livelihood in the future. Towards the end of the 17th century, the nations also began to take over some of the University's tasks and to arrange learned exercises (disputations and orations) for the edification of their members; these learned exercises were kept going for nearly two centuries.

The noble students presented special problems. Aristocratic education was one of the burning cultural questions of the time. In the expansion of the Swedish government administration, the nobility were given new and extremely important tasks. It became more and more a nobility based on service, with a legal and exclusive right to the higher offices in the Privy Council and the administrative departments; during the regencies, it achieved a powerful position such as it had never had before nor has had since in Swedish history. But this also made increasing demands on the upbringing of the young nobles in good breeding and book-learning, to fit them for their future official functions. In addition, the art of war had lately become more and more a kind of applied science and required a good knowledge of fortification, ballistics and other mathematical subjects. The young Swedish aristocrats therefore made their way in increasingly large numbers to the sources of learning, and we meet with the well-read nobleman, equally versed in intellectual matters and in knightly exercises, as an ideal figure in the literature of the period.

It was not taken for granted that he should be educated at the University. The nobility were unwilling to allow their children to mix with the common people; they learned the elements at home under tutors and abroad—in Germany, France and Denmark—there were special colleges for the further education of young nobles, which were often attended by Swedes. In the 1620s, an attempt was made to found an indigenous gram-

*29. The leather-clad coffer of the Uppland nation (*fiscus nationis Uplandicae*), dating from the beginning of the 18th century. The Uppland nation.*

mar school for noble pupils in Stockholm in what was known as the "Collegium illustre". It failed and instead the University of Uppsala took over the responsibility for the higher education of the young nobles. There were already quite a number of young noble students at Uppsala at the beginning of the century, when Messenius recruited them for his private college, but the breakthrough did not come until the 1630s, as the fruit primarily of Axel Oxenstierna's endeavours. He saw clearly that, if Uppsala was to be made attractive to the offspring of the aristocracy, it must offer them, over and above the ordinary subjects, opportunities for what were known as "noble exercises". These included modern languages —essential in diplomatic intercourse now that Sweden was a great power—and various physical accomplishments. In 1637, the University secured its first teacher of the French language, a Swiss by the name of Isaac Cujacius, and in the following year a teacher of dancing and fencing. In the 1640s, teachers of Italian and Spanish were periodically available. However, these foreign experts were birds of passage and the instruction was at times sporadic. But the efforts bore fruit; during the first regency, at least 50 young nobles would seem to have been studying at Uppsala each year and members of the principal families in the country—the Oxenstiernas, Sparres, Gyllenstiernas and Bielkes—sent their sons there. They were usually quite young—aged 10–12 or so—and were tenderly watched over by the tutors who accompanied them. But they were full of the self-esteem of their rank; in the academic processions, the sons of counts and barons took precedence over the professors. Now and then, as late as the 18th century, some brilliant young noble was elected as the University's *rector illustris,* which meant that, in honour of the University, he nominally took over the office of Rector, as De la Gardie did as a young man. The noble students did not work for any degrees. They attended lectures and *collegia* pretty much as they pleased, preferably those on the indispensable subject of political science, which they usually learned from the Skyttean professor, who, during Schefferus's time, could almost be regarded as a kind of tutor to the young nobles.

After a period of decline, the noble exercises were organized in the 1660s in more permanent forms. The moment was a favourable one. De la Gardie was the University Chancellor and no one could have more sympathy for the modern aristocratic culture; with his colleagues in the Privy Council, he himself was the ruler of Sweden. Obviously on De la Gardie's initiative, Rudbeck set to work and built on the hill behind the Gustavianum a building which was designed for instruction in the "noble exercises" and was completed in 1663. The main block and the two wings housed stables, a fencing hall, a riding school and living accommodation for the five masters: two language teachers (one for French and one for Spanish and Italian), a fencing master, a riding master and a dancing master. The new establishment was a kind of "Collegium illustre" incorporated in the University and designed in order that the young Caroline noblemen might receive an upbringing in accordance with their station in life. Soon 55 noble students became proficient in courtly exercises and the languages of the elegant world in this building; there were 22 horses in the stables. The language teachers, who were sometimes cultivated men driven to Sweden by the winds of chance, included the temperamental Italian Antonio Papi, who taught French from 1705 until well into the Age of Freedom. Otherwise, the initial enthusiasm began to peter out. The stables were abolished at the end of the century. However, under varying conditions, Rudbeck's building was to continue to serve its original purpose until it was demolished in 1879 to make way for the new University building.

The careers that the Uppsala students of this period chose are fairly well known. As might have been expected, the majority became clergymen. At the beginning of the 17th century, about 65% entered the service of the Church; in the middle of the century, the corresponding figure was 40% and about 1700 about 55%. In this connection, it should be noted that by no means all the Church's servants had studied at the University. Even far into the 17th century, the greater number of clergymen and school-teachers had attended only the cathedral schools or the grammar schools and it was not until the late Caroline period that it became

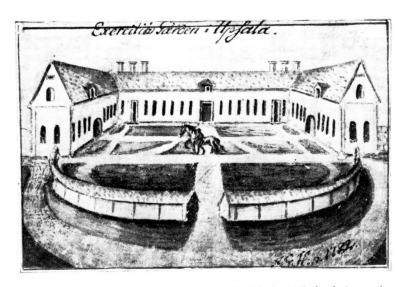

30. The building (exercitiehuset) *erected by Rudbeck in the 1660s for the instruction of students from aristocratic families in the "noble exercises", i.e. modern languages, dancing, riding and fencing. It occupied the site of the present University building. Aquarelle by J. G. Härstedt (1782). University Library.*

the rule for all ordained clergymen to have studied for some time at a university.

Next after the Church in order of attractiveness came the government administration and the judicature. A large group of students always made its way to the government departments in Stockholm or became district judges and chief magistrates in the provinces. In Queen Christina's reign, there was about one prospective official or government employee to every three candidates for holy orders in Uppsala and the proportion was approximately the same 50 years later. It was in the nature of things, as already indicated, that the government authorities should particularly encourage this category. These students pursued "political" studies, and the division of the royal scholarships into "theological" and "political" ones was intended to guarantee that the growing state machinery would secure a supply of capable recruits. Gustavus Adolphus emphasized this energetically: learning must be adapted to ordinary life and, whatever they did, they should see to it that the University of Uppsala did not become just a seminary for Lutheran preachers. But this educational policy was not entirely free from problems. It contained the germs of other conflicts, besides the clash between the Church's and the State's demands on the Univer-

89

sity. In the middle of the century, the power-hungry nobles began to regard the endeavours made by the commoner students to secure careers as public servants, perhaps crowned by their being raised to the nobility, as a danger to their own status. This view was particularly urged by De la Gardie, who wished to persuade the great majority of students to stick to theology and not to aim at the stars.

Thus the 17th-century University of Uppsala was by no means, as has often been stated, a purely ecclesiastical training establishment. Academic learning could be employed in many connections; it was meant to serve the whole of Swedish society. But also in another way theology played a far smaller part at the University than is commonly imagined. It did not by any means dominate the training of the young prospective clergymen. The situation was almost paradoxical. The State required that the universities should train people for the Church, the schools, the public administration and the government departments, but little was done to give them the proper specialist knowledge. All the students were gathered into the Faculty of Arts and Sciences and read roughly the same subjects, independently of their future careers; in practice, the only degree that was awarded was the master's degree. What the students of this period imbibed was an academic curriculum that was common to all. In this training, logic, astronomy, Cicero and Vergil were more important than the doctrine of salvation. It is true that the government and the University authorities were aware of the problem and that complaints were raised. They came primarily from the clergy. There were few or none, they said in 1655, who "*ex professo* devoted themselves to *studia theologica*". The majority studied "without any system and with no certain aim". Prospective clergymen often displayed a shocking ignorance of theology.

All this was connected with the University's structure, which was still largely mediaeval. The Cartesians and the pioneers of modern science in the Caroline period took up the struggle against the antiquated academic system from other starting-points. Rudbeck was very active and, as always, was supported by De la Gardie. All students could not be "thrown into a heap"; each science and profession made distinct demands on its practitioners. Encyclopaedic general training was no longer sufficient. For this reason, Rudbeck, as a man of the new era, demanded radical reforms. The scholarships should be firmly linked to the subject; each student should be made "perfect in his science" and not dabble in them all. Towards the end of the 17th century, not only Rudbeck but also other professors sought, by holding private *collegia,* to increase the supply of modern and topical courses that were suitable for all professions and careers. About 1710, Israel Nesselius, who later became Professor of Greek at Uppsala, put forward a radical proposal for reformed studies at the University. The students should be bound from the beginning to follow certain lines of training—one-third should read theology, one-sixth law, one-sixth technical subjects and economics, and so on.

However, officially nothing was done. About 1720, the Swedish universities in Uppsala, Åbo and Lund were still safeguarding the conservative educational tradition. The seven liberal arts, in the scholastic sense, gave the mental pabulum which all students were considered to need on their journey through life. The academic instruction served the purposes of an authoritarian culture, in which, on principle, nothing new should happen and in which the requirements of society were only incompletely satisfied.

CHAPTER IV

The Eighteenth Century

1

The new epoch which set in after Sweden ceased to be a great power—the Age of Freedom (1718–1772)—did not bring with it any substantial changes in the University's circumstances. Its structure and methods of working remained essentially the same, as long as the 1655 constitutions continued in force, i.e. until the middle of the 19th century. The organization which had been built up by the politicians and university officials of the preceding period proved to be quite durable. It is true that minor reforms were made and discussions about the University became increasingly animated during the 18th century, but the foundations were not disturbed. The situation is quite different if we consider the intellectual and scholarly life which gave everyday academic activities their real meaning. Radical changes took place in this sphere. At the end of the century, students and teachers thought along different lines from those of their predecessors in 1700 or 1750. The intellectual climate was transformed, the aims of education and training were changed, and naturally we must adjust the narrative of the University's fortunes accordingly.

Thus, a new stage in the University's history began with the Age of Freedom. It was of a quite distinctive character. After a breathing space or a period of decline in the 1720s—this applied to Swedish cultural life in general—an age of scientific greatness began at the University which has never since been surpassed. It coincided with the characteristic economic policy of the period, which was pursued by the Swedish Estates in the name of mercantilism. Public utility, industry and trade—in a word, the "economy"—had the highest priority and therefore it was the natural sciences which flourished. They could be applied in agriculture, mining, manufacturing industry and navigation and were continuously encouraged by the State, especially after the reformist Hats party came to power in 1738–9. Contemporary Swedish research in the natural sciences had two centres, one at the Royal Academy of Sciences in Stockholm, which was founded at this time, and the other at the University of Uppsala. Around the middle of the century, there were working at the University a number of professors who gave Swedish natural science a European reputation. Incomparably the greatest of them was Linnaeus (Carl von Linné), the dictator and legislator to botanists all over the world. Anders Celsius was the shining light in astronomy and Klingenstierna in mathematics and physics; Rosén von Rosenstein was the first Swedish doctor of medicine to attain international fame and Johan Gottschalk Wallerius was one of the leading mineralogists of the period; the young chemist Torbern Bergman was on his way to the stars, as was, in a more literal sense, the astronomer Daniel Melander-Melanderhjelm. But this edifying spectacle was not to last for ever. New signal flags were hoisted after Gustav III's national revolution in 1772. The utilitarian culture of the Age of Freedom no longer attracted university students; a new stage in Sweden's intellectual history and in the development of the University was at hand.

The University's progress during the Age of Freedom came about in fruitful collaboration with the State. But the relationship between the University and the State was far from being clear-cut. During the Caroline autocracy, the Crown had exercised full control over the University. It could be expected that its grip would slacken once the new constitution was introduced and the Senate and the faculties in Uppsala had been given more influence on the University's affairs. But this did not prove to be the case; indeed the situation was rather the opposite. Party-political passions blossomed forth and the Estates or the Riksdag, in which the Hats were in the majority for the greater part of the Age of Freedom, neglected no opportunity to apply the principles underlying their university policy. It was part of the Hats' programme that civil society, with all its ramifications and institutions, should be subordinated to the all-powerful Riksdag. The University was subjected, at least spasmodically when the Estates were assembled, to the most impertinent kind of supervision. Right ways of thinking were regarded as being as essential now as in Charles XI's reign and proposals for reforms and improvements followed each other in quick succession. There was not much peace and quiet at the University; the rigid Caroline discipline had been replaced by a state of hectic unrest. The professors—especially Linnaeus—complained. But at the same time scientific research blossomed in a way that was a joy to behold, and in other respects the University was in excellent trim. The ruling Hats party—led by cultivated noblemen such as Tessin and A. J. von Höpken—honestly desired to improve it and the status of the natural sciences at Uppsala was in essence a result of their initiative and encouragement in the sacred name of public utility.

During the period of transition in the 1720s, the University, on the whole, retained its Caroline character. The old professors were still there and instruction and learning were still dominated by Lutheran theology and Roman eloquence. The University Chancellor (until 1737) was the generally respected Privy Councillor Gustaf Cronhielm, the man responsible for the Legal Code of 1734. However, the new spirit began to break

93

through. Towards the end of the decade, the young Samuel Klingenstierna was appointed Professor of Mathematics and soon afterwards Anders Celsius was established in the chair of astronomy. Abraham Sahlstedt, who later became a lexicographer, has left us a picture of the conditions at the University at the beginning of the 1730s. He speaks with contempt of the traditional instruction in scholastic logic, Latin poetry and history. Professor Hermansson, the occupant of the Skyttean chair, gave an account of "the English royal regalia and a description of Edward's sceptre". But breezes of fresher air were also blowing, thanks especially to two young men who were still on the threshold of fame—Linnaeus, who demonstrated plants in the Botanical Garden, and Nils Rosén, who lectured on anatomy.

The wise and cautious Arvid Horn was now at the helm of State and the Riksdag and the government left the University to its own devices for the time being. It was not until the 1734 Riksdag, when political antagonisms were accentuated, that the Estates were impelled to scrutinize its activities and to propose improvements in keeping with the times. The somewhat unpopular "Records Deputation" which was now set up (it was comparable with a modern Public Accounts Committee) interfered in matters great and small at the University. It urged that the time-honoured academic jurisdiction should be abolished, as being too onerous for the Senate, where the professors wore themselves out examining unimportant cases. This proposal met with bitter opposition in Uppsala. To exercise jurisdiction over their own members had been regarded since the Middle Ages as the universities' inalienable right, the very seal of their status as independent corporations, and the Senate succeeded in fending off the attack. But it was a portent of what was to come. After the overthrow of Horn and the Hats' accession to power in 1739, the reforming zeal of the Estates hung like the sword of Damocles over the University, which was, as a rule, hostile to all radical changes and found it difficult to tolerate the bureaucratic tutelage of the party politicians in Stockholm.

The Riksdag and the government (formally the King-in-Council) repeatedly interfered during the 1740s in the University's activities, often against its will. The University Chancellor at this time (1739–47) was none other than Carl Gyllenborg, the President of the Chancery and the powerful leader of the Hats, a self-important and intractable man, not very popular in Uppsala. He demanded that the Hats' intentions with regard to the University should be carried into effect. He took a hard line and at times a state of war existed between him and the Senate, where the political dichotomy—the division into Hats and Caps—played the same part as in national politics. Gyllenborg and the ruling Hats had a body of reliable supporters among the professors and not among the worst of

31. *Carl Gyllenborg, the*
University Chancellor in
the 1740s. Copperplate
engraving.

them—chiefly the natural scientists, who benefited from the Estates' investment in economic management and the utilitarian sciences. The Hats had the whole-hearted support of the influential Celsius family and also that of Klingenstierna. Linnaeus, who was unsophisticated and little acquainted with the ins and outs of politics, was the darling of the Hats; he was favoured in every possible way and responded by supporting their leaders. In the Senate the Caps were, however, more numerous and became very active whenever the University was threatened by political interference from above. After the Hats had waged an unsuccessful war with Russia and after the 1742–3 Riksdag, when the Caps increased their pressure on the government, they prospered for a time. Passions ran high in the Senate and there were bitter conflicts between the professors who supported the Hats and those who supported the Caps; party affiliation even played a role in the appointment of inspectors to the nations. The professors who supported the Caps advocated, as a rule, a somewhat more old-fashioned, humanistic type of education. Petrus Ullén, the Professor of Philosophy, was something of a leader among them; Johan Ihre, the

Skyttean professor and philologist, who was the shining light among the Uppsala humanists, was also reckoned to be a supporter of the Caps. Those who were undecided followed whatever happened to be the public opinion at the moment or accepted only positive arguments.

The Hats in the Riksdag were especially eager to make decisions in the appointments of professors and to create new chairs, which might serve their purposes. They proceeded with no great respect for the University's statutory rights, brushing aside the idea of academic freedom, which was guaranteed by the constitutions. They began with the new chair of economics or economic management (*oeconomia publica*), which was the fruit of their enthusiasm for public utility. The initiative had been taken at the 1738–9 Riksdag, where the decision was forced through against the opposition of the Estate of the Clergy. From the first, Anders Berch, a young junior officer in the Chancery, was designated for the post, which, oddly enough, was included in the Faculty of Law. Normally, the Senate would propose three candidates for each vacant professorship, from whom the Crown would make its choice after consultation with the Chancellor. But now the University was eliminated from the transaction. A number of candidates had applied and their qualifications were being pondered in Uppsala when it was learned in September 1741 that Berch had already been appointed to the post, after pressure had been exerted by the Riksdag. Fortunately, he proved himself worthy of it.

At this time, party-political passions played a part in an even more critical appointment. This concerned no less a person than Linnaeus. In 1740, the aging and infirm Lars Roberg had been induced to resign his professorship of medicine and Linnaeus, together with Johan Gottschalk Wallerius, an assistant lecturer in medicine, had applied for the post. Having recently returned from Holland and already basking in his European fame, Linnaeus appeared to be the obvious choice and indeed he probably was. This was Gyllenborg's view, but relations between him and the Caps in the Senate were, as usual, irritated and they created difficulties. In accordance with the regulations in the constitutions, Linnaeus, like other candidates, had to establish his eligibility for the post by holding a public disputation. But the Celsius family (Olof Celsius, the theologian, Anders Celsius and his cousin Magnus Beronius), who were attached to the Hats, regarded Linnaeus as being superior to such petty regulations and followed the University Chancellor's lead, which won the day. Linnaeus was released by the King from the necessity of taking any examination, but his fellow-candidate was not. The result was a scandalous disputation unparalleled in the history of the University. In the theses which the embittered Wallerius was forced to compile to prove his eligibility, he took the opportunity to deliver a scathing criticism of Linnaeus's rather mediocre doctoral thesis on the causes of ague. There were stormy scenes when Wallerius's theses were publicly debated in February 1741. Beronius took a hard line against Wallerius, Rosén, the Dean of the Faculty, lost his head and Wallerius himself became quite enraged, shouting, stamping his feet and banging on the lecturer's desk, while the student audience yelled, climbed up on the benches and tore up copies of the objectionable thesis. Linnaeus stayed away but was awarded the professorship.

The Hats also looked after their own in other respects; party loyalty had become an academic qualification. It caused a sensation in the spring of 1741 when Gyllenborg appointed one of the Celsius family, Olof Celsius the Younger, to the post of temporary Deputy Librarian without consulting either the University Librarian or the Senate. In the following year, he was commissioned by the Chancellor to lecture on the history of learning (*historia litteraria*), also without consulting the Senate. This was only the beginning. Celsius was striving to get a professorship; after carrying on a well-thought-out intrigue, he succeeded. He appealed directly to the government and in 1747 was appointed Professor of History, after promising to make an annual payment to his successor as Deputy Librarian.

The ruling Hats were keeping watch lest any heterodox political opinions should creep into the University. Johan Ihre got into trouble in this connection. He was always independent, fearless and sarcastic and often behaved provocatively; he had already incurred the wrath of the Faculty of Theology (cf. below). He was not a fanatical party man, but he had no sympathy for the Hats, who were often the butt of his gibes. As the Skyttean professor, he dealt with delicate political questions in his disputations and his criticisms were directed more or less at the Hats' policy. In December 1747, the authorities pounced. Official proceedings were instituted against Ihre; they were occasioned by two disputations —one on the rebellion of the Dala peasantry in 1598 and the other on the State's right to sacrifice an individual citizen to save itself. A special Chancery court was appointed and began its deliberations. Three years later, Ihre was proclaimed to have been a misleader of youth and was sentenced to pay a fine equivalent to one year's salary and to receive a severe reprimand. "The self-assumed and punishable freedom" which existed at the University had been stifled; the situation was as serious as that.

But the great question during the troubled year of 1747 was the election of a new University Chancellor. This caused party-political passions to run higher than ever and events quickly took an unpleasant turn. Old Gyllenborg had died and it was obvious that the election of his successor would take the form of a trial of strength between the Hats and the Caps in the Senate. The parties were more or less evenly matched, but there was an uncertain intermediate group to be considered. Petrus Ullén, the leader of the Caps mentioned above, took the matter in hand. After conducting reckless intrigues, he succeeded in getting the election postponed. When it took place in February 1747, the Caps won a victory which was both unexpected and overwhelming; their candidate, Samuel Åkerhielm, a Privy Councillor and a Cap, received 12 votes, as against 7 for Prince Adolf Fredrik, the heir to the throne, who had been proposed by the Hats. The outcome of the election made a great stir in Stockholm and the Hats in the Privy Council (where they were in the majority) were enraged. But Åkerhielm gave way and relinquished the appointment and the Privy Council forced through the election of the Crown Prince, concerning which letters patent were immediately issued. But this was not the end of the matter. The Hats on the Privy Council clamoured for revenge; the wretched majority in the Uppsala Senate had wellnigh committed *lèse-majesté* and should be disciplined. Some of them called for immediate action by the Public Prosecutor, but instead the matter was remitted to the "Secret Committee", which demanded that the Cap professors should explain their lack of respect for the Crown. The professors humbled themselves and the King was finally content to give them a stern warning, accompanied by threats that severer measures would be taken in future cases of misdemeanour.

But the Hats also pursued university policies in a larger context. They regarded as out-of-date the old academic learning, with its emphasis on theology and dead languages. Taking public utility as their yardstick, they sought, as we have already seen, to renovate the Swedish universities. Berch's chair of economics was the first step and soon they went further. Their policy of educational reform reached its peak with what was called the "Educational Commission" of 1745–50. The proposal put forward by the Commission's Committee on the "University Education Department" in 1750 was not merely the first in the long series of reports on Swedish universities. It was so revolutionary in its bold freedom from prejudice that only today can we evaluate it dispassionately. No university teachers sat on the Commission; it was wholly a political body, with leading Hats, such as Tessin, Claes Ekeblad and, as long as he lived, Carl Gyllenborg among its 15 members. Its terms of reference were quite specific; it was to see that the youth of Sweden were "guided to economics and other practical sciences".

The proposal that was put forward after prolonged discussions stressed that university studies were to be strictly vocational. Rudbeck had already been thinking along these lines (see above, p. 90), and now his ideas gained a hearing. The purpose of the University would be to produce competent officials for the service of the State. Scientific research and its

32. "Prospect of the town of Uppsala, looking north-east from the cemetery and over the wall of the Senate House". In the foreground is the University Mill and in the distance the "watchtower" of the observatory built by Anders Celsius. Aquarelle by J. G. Härstedt. University Library.

diffusion should be linked with the universities only as "side-lines". It was thought that the Royal Academy of Sciences in Stockholm could take care of this matter. If this idea had been carried into effect, a radical distinction would have been drawn between research and education. Before the universities could be transformed into vocational colleges, it was necessary that they should be completely re-organized. In this respect, the Commission took drastic measures and broke down the mediaeval division into faculties. Instead, studies should be oriented towards the public sector or the government departments. The proposal envisaged what was called a "basic faculty", common to all students, in which the general training necessary for holding each post would be obtained from the Professors of Logic and Metaphysics, Ethics, Latin Rhetoric and Poetics. Thus equipped, the individual student would then "choose his genius", as it was called in contemporary parlance, and select one of the four lines of study or faculties which would then be open to him. Prospective clergymen and teachers would apply to the Faculty of Theology. A Faculty of Public Service would take care of the training of students for legal and financial posts, a Faculty of "Mathematics" would be responsible for recruitment to the officer corps, the land-surveying department, etc. and the fourth and last Faculty ("Physics") would be devoted to training in medicine and mining engineering. Thus, the separate Faculty of Medicine would disappear. The Commission observed regretfully that

99

the number of students in each vocational faculty could not be exactly determined for the time being, because of the lack of a reliable forecast of the needs of the labour market. The students should be passed through the basic faculty and the chosen vocational faculty under constant examination and supervision. The Commission, which was reluctant to leave one stone of the old structure in place, also suggested that the student nations should be abolished and replaced by faculty associations.

The Education Commission's scheme represented a triumph for the Hats in their endeavours, inspired by mercantilist theory, to regulate society by bureaucratic methods and to mark out the paths by which the citizens should achieve happiness. The comparison with our own times, i.e. with the university reforms of the 1960s and 1970s, is inescapable. The spirit is the same—the belief that restricting the students to certain lines of training guarantees that university studies will be adapted to working life. The reformers of the Age of Freedom also wished to turn the universities into vocational schools, in which scientific research would, it is true, be tolerated but no more than tolerated. All this was primarily aimed at Uppsala, the largest university in Sweden. It is not surprising that the University of Uppsala declined the scheme. The University was in its most fertile period of scientific research and now the professors were being told that such research was not part of their real task. The long reply to the Commission's report which the Senate finally despatched in the summer of 1751 was in fact a crushing one. The idea that the training of manpower for "the country's civil service" was the University's main task was indignantly rejected. There were other groups in society, besides the "young men seeking jobs", who derived benefit from university studies. The universities' chief endeavour must be to promote the sciences; otherwise it was to be feared that Sweden would relapse into its ancient barbarism. The Senate rejected the Commission's scheme for the University as unreasonable in all respects; everything should, on the whole, remain as it was before. In the Senate's reaction, we may perceive an interpretation of the professors' duties and the University's role in society which originated in the enlightened 18th century; it would have been inconceivable during the 17th century. Scientific research had come to the universities to stay; the promotion of natural science by performing experiments and making observations was just as important as lecturing and giving *collegia*. No one was more insistent on this point than Linnaeus. Though otherwise loyal to the authorities, he shuddered at the thought of what would happen if the Education Commission's programme was carried out. There would be compulsion, restraint, drill and slipshod knowledge of the elements everywhere; the universities would be turned into grammar schools and the sciences would be exter-

100

minated in Sweden. Linnaeus was exaggerating, as was his wont, but he hit the target—bureaucracy and short-term considerations of public utility were threatening to stifle the "noble freedom" which was the breath of life to research.

The general reform of the universities proposed by the Educational Commission came to nothing, but some of its more limited suggestions bore fruit.

Acting on a suggestion from Lund, the Commission succeeded in forcing through a measure which gave the examination system a more vocational emphasis. Alongside the existing master's degree in the Faculty of Arts and Sciences, a new type of degree, intended for aspirants to the civil service, was established by letters patent in 1749 and 1750. Students who wished to enter the civil service had only to prove their knowledge of selected subjects which were suitable for their future careers. These degrees were called "civil-service degrees" and were of several kinds. For entry into the courts of justice, the candidate had to undergo a public examination in law and moral philosophy; entry to the Military Board required the passing of tests in arithmetic, physics, chemistry and economics; candidates for the Chancery had to have a knowledge of politics, oratory and history; the Board of Mines required candidates to have a knowledge of chemistry, physics, geometry, economics, mining law, etc. These civil-service degrees, which survived into the present century in the form of the Chancery degree, probably increased the competence of candidates for the public service. However, they cut down the range of the student's all-round vision and general knowledge. Many students hurried through their courses with the greatest possible despatch, in order to begin earning their bread and butter as soon as possible.

On the other hand, there could be no doubt about the benefits conferred by the two new professorial chairs established on the initiative of the Education Commission. They covered the fashionable natural sciences —physics and chemistry—which in contemporary parlance were "practical sciences" and were necessary for the newly established civil-service degrees. Both traditionally came under the Faculty of Medicine and their separation from it bore witness to the progress of experimental research in natural science. In Uppsala, Anders Celsius had been urging the need of a chair in experimental physics since the end of the 1720s; he would willingly have sacrificed the useless professorship of Latin poetry to this end. After the Riksdag had discussed the question in 1747, the Education Commission pursued it to a successful conclusion and even beyond. A chair of chemistry was added, there being room for both posts if the superfluous professorships of oriental languages and poetics were combined with other professorships. With typical effrontery, the Senate was never asked for its opinion but was nevertheless compelled to draw up nomination lists for the two new chairs, which were established in February 1750. The outcome was self-evident. Klingenstierna, who, as Professor of Mathematics, had also dealt with physics, was transferred to the chair of experimental physics. Johan Gottschalk Wallerius was equally the obvious candidate for the chair of chemistry, the first of its kind in Sweden.

With all their turbulence and despite the party-political intrigues, the 1740s marked the beginning of the University's brief high summer. The Estates' incessant interference in the University's affairs must also be regarded as expressing a sincere concern for the University and for the introduction of a modern cultural and educational policy. The leading natural scientists of the Age of Freedom, together with Anders Berch and Johan Ihre, the humanist, were now in their prime and Uppsala's fame was spreading throughout the world. In a certain sense, the University's position was an unusual and remarkable one. The old and renowned seats of learning abroad had steadily declined. Once famous universities, such as Oxford and the Sorbonne, were regarded in the 18th century as foci of conservatism, remote from the intellectual currents of the time. But the Uppsala of the Age of Freedom was in touch with these currents, like the recently founded German universities at Halle and Göttingen. The natural sciences and utilitarianism had been wholeheartedly accepted and it is significant that the antagonism between the academies of natural science and the universities, which was almost taken for granted in Europe, played no part in the Sweden of the 18th century. There was a propitious harmony between Uppsala and Stockholm, which gave the scientific culture of the time its distinctive character and strength.

The external environment of the University was also transformed. In a short time, a number of new institutes were built and older ones were re-equipped. The work began with the erection of Celsius's astronomical observatory in Svartbäcken, which was followed by Linnaeus's restoration of the Botanical Gardens. Rosén revived the dormant University Hospital, in which a special room was fitted up for Klingenstierna's physics apparatus. Wallerius had no sooner entered upon the duties of his professorship in 1750 than he began the building of a chemical laboratory. Somewhat later, Berch fitted up his *theatrum oeconomico-mechanicum*.

Carl Hårleman played a decisive part in this building activity (cf. below, p. 130). He was the leading architect of the Age of Freedom and was closely associated with the Hats; in the 1740s and 1750s, he acted in practice as the official architect to the University, the Cathedral and the Castle in Uppsala. He designed both Celsius's observatory and Linnaeus's orangery. He then set to work on the buildings for the University's central institutes, rebuilding the Gustavianum and erecting a new building for the

ASTRONOMISKA OBSERVATORIUM

33. The astronomical observatory built by Anders Celsius in Svartbäcken. Engraving by F. Akrel in Busser (1769).

Senate. The Gustavianum was given the appearance which it has today. The external staircase in the courtyard was demolished, another entrance was made from the street, and the monumental staircase in the entrance hall was erected. On the main floor, which the Senate had already quitted in the 1690s, Hårleman renovated the *auditorium majus* with its double lectern and rows of benches and fitted up, directly opposite to it, a new *auditorium minus*, together with a small library room for manuscripts and rarities. The two library rooms on the upper floor were decorated in accordance with the requirements of fastidious taste; the bookcases along the walls were decked with pink curtains, and portrait medallions surrounded by stucco work were placed above the windows. But the overcrowding of the books was intolerable and shelves had also to be put up in the free floor space. Hårleman was dead when the restored Gustavianum was finished in 1757. Before his death, he had presented rococo lecterns (which are still in use) to each of the University's four lecture rooms—the two in the Gustavianum and the two in the old Carolina, where the major academic ceremonies were usually held.

Since it left the Gustavianum, the Senate had been accommodated in the old library on the Cathedral terrace. At the beginning of 1749, Hårleman set about erecting a more stately building and in 1755 the new Senate House was inaugurated. It was situated close to the earlier premises, north-west of the Cathedral. Its main floor contained an assembly room for the Senate, with a long table for the professors, an armchair beneath a red-velvet canopy for the Rector and royal portraits on the walls. There were also a room for the Council ("Consistorium minus") and other administrative offices. The rooms for the faculties were on the top floor. The University had acquired a new focus, alongside the Gustavianum and the Carolina. For generations, Hårleman's Senate House (now occupied by the Institute of Art History) was the centre of University life. Its splendour was to some extent a sign of the increasing self-confidence of the professorial body in a bureaucratic age; when assembled in the Senate, it became a counterpart to the government and the Riksdag and zealously guarded its rights.

The work of the Senate had become increasingly heavy and many people complained. The Senate met once or twice a week, often for 3–4 hours at a time. The many trifling financial matters took up much time. Particular problems arose from the uneasy relations between the University, with its separate jurisdiction, and the town of Uppsala, whose magistrates got themselves involved in a large number of disputes over questions of competence with the Senate, which usually won the day. The Council, which had been established during the previous century, did not begin working properly until the 18th century. It consisted of the Rector or the Pro-Rector, together with four professors chosen for six-monthly periods, and was in practice only a subordinate body which prepared the agenda for discussion in the larger assembly.

As we have already seen, the professorial body had been enlarged by new appointments—those of Berch, Wallerius and Klingenstierna as experimental physicists. They had been forced on the University, for what proved to be its own good. Other new chairs came into existence under less controversial circumstances. At the beginning of the period, the

*34. The new Senate building erected by Carl Hårleman in the 1750s in St. Erik's
Square (it now houses the Institute of Art History). Sture-Foto.*

Faculty of Theology acquired a fifth professorship and in 1754 a sixth
was created as a result of a private bequest by Andreas Kalsenius, the
recently deceased Bishop of Västerås, who had previously given Sätra
Spa to the University. This "Kalsenian" chair was to be devoted to pole-
mic theology, i.e. to the defence of the Lutheran faith against atheists,
deists, naturalists and other heretics. Its first occupant was the irascible
and intolerant Nils Wallerius, an adherent of Wolff and a man after the

105

Bishop's own heart. Periodically, the Faculty of Law possessed an additional chair of practical law, which towards the end of the Age of Freedom was held by Olof Rabenius, a teacher of excellent repute. Moreover, the Hats succeeded in enforcing the establishment of a chair of Swedish constitutional law. Complaints had long been raised in Stockholm about the diffusion of politically disquieting doctrines among the students (cf. p. 97 above on Ihre). They should therefore be encouraged as energetically as possible to learn about the happy constitution, whose safest guarantor was the Hats party. It was decided that all students who took degrees in the Faculty of Arts and Sciences should be examined in Swedish constitutional law by the Professor of Law; at the same time, the Senate was ordered to subscribe to the Hats' journal, *Ärlig svensk*. The establishment of the new chair of constitutional law in 1761 gave the government a henchman in Uppsala who was even ordered to follow the instructions of the Chancery Office. The University was never asked for its opinion. The Estates forced the matter through on their own authority and appointed the mediocre Nils Risell as the first occupant of the chair. None of the new professors devoted themselves to fundamental theoretical studies in law. This burden was borne, far into the Gustavian era, by Daniel Solander, the zealous occupant of the now combined chairs of Swedish and Roman law.

Yet another professorship was created as a result of a private donation in 1759, when Erik Borgström, a foundry owner, provided the funds —probably on Linnaeus's advice—to establish a chair of practical economics. This professorship was assigned to the Faculty of Arts and Sciences and was to be devoted to the applications of natural history to agriculture and other industries. The first fortunate occupant of the Borgström chair (which still exists) was Johan Lostbom, who is best known for having planted the avenues of trees in Odinslund, derisively described by the students as Lostbom's *Opera omnia*. His colleagues in the established sciences regarded with some contempt an activity which served, in a way so typical of the period, the purposes of utilitarianism in the most trivial sense. Melanderhjelm, the astronomer, thought that such a "professorship of manure" was "not particularly academic". All these new chairs brought the number of permanent professors at Uppsala to 24 at the beginning of the 1770s.

The appointments of professors in the Uppsala of the Age of Freedom often developed into confused affairs, whether the government intervened in them or not. This was partly due to the prevailing idea that a public office was a kind of personal possession, which could be purchased or given away. The purchase of offices or agreements involving such purchases did not occur openly at the University; they were camouflaged

35. One of the four rococo lecterns (that for the Faculty of Law) which Carl Hårle-man presented to the University.

in the most complex fashion. Olof Celsius the Younger's acquisition of the chair of history has already been mentioned. The terms dictated to poor Melanderhjelm in 1761, when he applied to succeed Mårten Strömer, who was always on leave, as Professor of Astronomy, were wellnigh astounding. He was told that he could have the chair, provided that he paid 15,000 copper riksdalers to a fund, the interest on which would be used to supplement the salary of Mallet, the observatory officer. Furthermore, the aforesaid Strömer had been appointed professor in 1745 after sundry obscure transactions in which Klingenstierna played a less than honourable part. From time to time, the appointments were decided by shameless nepotism; the contemporary public saw nothing objectionable in this. A father handed down his office to his son, with the King's blessing; this was what Linnaeus and Anders Berch did. Berch succeeded in getting his son Christer appointed first *adjunctus* and then Professor of Economics. Rosén von Rosenstein, the famous Professor of Medicine, performed the feat of exchanging posts with his son-in-law, Samuel Aurivillius, the University

107

Librarian. Aurivillius became Professor of Medicine, for which he was fully qualified, while for a short time Rosén took over the Librarianship, although he had no qualifications for it. The Riksdag, its committees and secret contacts with Privy Councillors and other patrons were available to any man who wished to pursue an academic career or to assist a protégé, unbeknown to the Senate.

Not all the worries were dispelled when the letter of appointment as professor was received. Many new appointees had to wait for years to draw their salary, because some frail retired professor was entitled to it until his death. At times, the confusion over salaries reached serious proportions and to a considerable number of holders of academic posts a secure livelihood appeared to be only a far-off prospect. In 1759, two *emeritus* salaries were established for retired professors; this was an improvement but by no means sufficient.

During the 18th century, the *adjunkter* (assistants) were responsible for an increasing proportion of the instruction; now the *docenter* (assistant professors) also appeared on the scene. The assistants, who numbered 14 towards the end of the century, included the new officials who had been attached to the staffs of the institutes of natural science and medicine —the assistant astronomer, the demonstrator in anatomy, the demonstrator in botany and the associate professor of chemistry. The assistants' salaries were still low, but the *docenter* formed the real academic proletariat.They had no salaries at all. The title *docent* meant only that the faculty or the Chancellor had conferred on a master the right to lecture and to give private *collegia* (the *venia docendi*). The first *docent* appears to have been appointed in 1728; by the middle of the century there were five or six of them, all in the Faculty of Arts and Sciences. "I have no desire", it could be said, "to be a *docent* for 10 years and then an assistant without pay for 10 years and at last get with difficulty a professorship, in which one can scarcely make a living." Nevertheless, as entrances to an academic career, the *docent* posts were desirable ones in a society in which seniority was regarded as a ground for promotion and their number increased during the Gustavian period.

The finances of the University were usually in good order throughout the 18th century. Gustavus Adolphus's donation was still the basis of its existence. The income from it had to suffice for all the University's needs, chiefly the increasingly large salary list, new buildings and repairs; the government made grants only in exceptional cases. The new professorships which the Estates blithely established without asking the Senate's opinion were especially burdensome; the situation resembled that which had prevailed in Queen Christina's time. It fell to the University to fit them into the normal budget or at least to promise the holders salaries in reversion. The lively building activity in the 1740s and 1750s—the Observatory, the Hospital, the Botanical Garden and the Senate House—cost large sums. But the yield from the Gustavian hereditary estate sufficed and periodically there was even an annual surplus. With a little exaggeration, we may say that the University's glory at this time was dependent on the outcome of the harvest and the price of corn. Most of the annual rents paid by the University's tenant farmers were paid, as before, in corn, which was delivered *in natura* and sold by the University on contract, mostly to Stockholm and Västerås and the foundry owners of Bergslagen. The ultimate responsibility for these transactions lay with the Senate, in which the professors acted as grain dealers to the best of their ability and discussed prices and contracts. The total annual deliveries of University corn increased as the century went on and in addition the sales prices were sometimes high, the initial peak coming in the 1740s, when the University's resources were more strained than ever.

The expanding University made great demands on the Bursar and the Bursary, who were responsible for the financial administration and who carried out the decisions. The accounts were kept by the book-keeper, who was raised in 1759 to the dignity of University Accountant. Out in the country, five University bailiffs saw to it that the University's revenues from the hereditary estate were correctly delivered. But there were always opportunities for peculation and a heavy blow fell in 1768, when Peter Julinskiöld, the Bursar, was declared bankrupt after having embezzled 120,000 silver riksdalers from the University's funds. He lived in splendid style and was involved in extensive private business transactions; in Uppsala he built the imposing mansion which is known today as Dekanhuset. Professors and other private persons who had invested their savings with Julinskiöld also suffered heavy losses, perhaps more than the University, which succeeded in coming to a kind of composition and more or less cleared up the situation with the aid of the able Anders Berch.

It did not follow from the general prosperity of the University that the professors lived luxuriously. Their salaries declined in real value, in spite of the nominal increases; in the 1760s, a professor in Lund received twice as much as one in Uppsala. Many a university professor lived in straitened circumstances all his life and had to resort to taking in lodgers and giving private tuition to earn a living. Now as formerly, there were teachers who gave enormous numbers of *collegia* (Linnaeus was one of them), but academic life also offered other opportunities of increasing one's income. Examination fees and charges for acting as president at disputations could yield a pretty penny, at least to those who knew how to attract the young. In the middle of the 18th century, the charge for acting as president is said to have been 100–150 copper riksdalers and this sum had to be paid by the respondent. The theologians with their prebends were still better off, so that professors in the Faculty of Arts and Sciences persisted in seeking promotion to vacant chairs of theology. However, during the Gustavian period, the differences began to be evened out, owing to the fact that prebends were granted to certain professors in the Faculty of Arts and Sciences after ordination. In any case, by making use of the available expedients, diligent and popular professors could attain a considerable degree of prosperity and live elegantly in spacious houses. In addition to the prefect's house in the Botanical Garden, Linnaeus acquired his beloved house at Hammarby outside Uppsala. The wealthy Johan Ihre, the aristocrat among the Uppsala professors of his time, resided in the fine house on Övre Slottsgatan which is now called Geijersgården and erected close by a counterpart to it (the present Ihregården), where he accommodated his noble students. Petrus Ekerman, the Professor of Latin Rhetoric, set a noteworthy example; during his long life, he presided over a total of 516 disputations (an unbeatable record) and managed to supplement the fees for doing so by writing the theses himself ("Give me 200 riksdalers, my boy, and I'll write the thesis myself"). With his savings, he built Ekerman House, next door to the Gustavianum, which, after various vicissitudes, is now leased to the Institute of History.

The University Library and its renovated quarters at the Gustavianum have already been mentioned. As the century went on, it increased in size through purchases and gifts. Benzelius had seen to it that the invaluable Palmskiöld collection of manuscripts came into the Library's possession, but it was not until 1788 that Georgii, the Professor of History, arranged and catalogued it. Other noteworthy acquisitions were the collection of musicalia donated by Anders von Düben, the Lord Chamberlain (1732), and Jacob Cronstedt's exceptionally rich collection of Swedish books, which had been bought by the Estates and passed on to the University Library in 1767. A large number of oriental manuscripts were received in different ways. The Library's treasures were scarcely easy of access. For a long period, the Library was open for only two hours on two days each week, but the University lecturers were still permitted to borrow books and in 1790 the collections were at last opened each day. At this time, the first heating stove was installed in the ice-cold room between the book-rooms where the Librarian and his assistant had previously shivered throughout the winter; the book-rooms were still not heated. The Librarian at this time and right up to 1829 was Pehr Fabian Aurivillius, an unusually able man and a tremendously hard worker, who in the middle of the 1790s began to prepare the printed alphabetical catalogue of the Library's book stock which is an indispensable tool even today. It then included 42,000 volumes.

36. *"Geijer House" and "Ihre House" on Övre Slottsgatan. In actual fact, they both belonged to Johan Ihre, the Skyttean Professor. He lived in "Geijer House" all his time as professor and he built "Ihre House", to the north of it, in 1754 as accommodation for his noble students.*

The University printing works, which was now housed in the *exercitie-hus* (see above, p. 88), was managed during the greater part of the 18th century by the Höjer company and later by Johan Edman. Their printing charges were promulgated by the Senate. The University printer seldom undertook large-scale scientific works. Linnaeus, Wallerius and other famous authors required greater resources, above all, a publisher who would introduce their books on the European market and preferably one who would pay a fee. They therefore went to the enterprising Lars Salvius in Stockholm, who was both printer and publisher. A University bookshop had been in existence since the beginning of the century, to the great benefit of the teachers and students, at least after Magnus Swederus, an energetic former student, took charge of it in 1780.

The University Chancellors during the last decade of the Age of Free-

111

dom were, in turn, the wise and popular Carl Ehrenpreus, the brilliant but capricious Anders Johan von Höpken and, from 1764, Crown Prince Gustav. Of these, von Höpken certainly performed his duties amidst the greatest personal pomp and circumstance; on his last visit to Uppsala, he had the great Cathedral bell rung for his entrance into and exit from the Senate. Otherwise, particular splendour was naturally displayed on the visits of the Crown Prince as Chancellor. In the autumn of 1767, when he came to Uppsala with the King and Queen, the Court and several Privy Councillors, two public disputations were held, at Queen Lovisa Ulrika's request, on subjects chosen by her, one being on Rousseau. The young Prince took his duties as Chancellor very seriously, making detailed inquiries into the University's affairs and proposing reforms. Uppsala was the national university; the fact that the heir to the throne was chosen as Chancellor marked its status.

The disquiet arising from political interference and antagonisms at the University had gradually died down. But the Estates still hung like a threatening cloud over the professors and the Senate, even during the brief period when the Caps were in power, and from time to time the lightning struck. The politically motivated heresy hunt after Peter Forsskål created a great sensation. This young Finn was talented and fearless, an academic fighting cock if ever there was one. He had made a name for himself during his studies in Göttingen as a furious opponent of the Wolffian philosophy. On his return to Uppsala in 1759, he submitted a thesis in public law on the subject of civil freedom (*De libertate civili*). This thesis was found to contain dangerous propositions on the freedom of the press and the like, directed against the paternalistic policy of the Hats, and the Faculty of Arts and Sciences forbade the disputation. But Forsskål took up the cudgels. He applied to the Chancery Office and when the Office confirmed the Faculty's ban, he boldly had his thesis printed and published in Swedish. The Chancery Office at once intervened, confiscated the remaining copies of the book on the ground that it disseminated "obnoxious ideas on the way in which the country was governed" and imposed a fine of 1,000 silver riksdalers on anyone who sold or bought it. Forsskål was already on the point of leaving with the great Danish–German expedition to Arabia, where he died, but was summoned before the Senate, which condemned his anti-social behaviour.

The number of students remained more or less unchanged during the first few decades of the Age of Freedom. No reliable figures are available as yet, but in the 1730s they appear to have numbered over 1,000, i.e. only slightly fewer than during the Caroline period. Some people considered that there were too many and feared the coming into being of a student proletariat which would be a burden on the State. This problem was particularly topical during the intensive debates on the public utility of education in the 1740s. The Universities of Uppsala, Lund and Åbo were said to be hatching "a brood of useless mouths"; it would not be possible to provide for them all. In order to put a stop to the over-production of scholars, the much-discussed "choice of genius" should be strictly applied, so that young men who were unsuitable as students could be directed to handicrafts, agriculture and other industries. Anders Berch, the leading Swedish expert in the utilitarian science known as political arithmetic, thought that the universities were producing each year twice as many graduates as there were vacant posts and, on retiring from the Rectorship in 1749, he spoke on "the necessary proportion of the graduates to the vacant posts in the kingdom" (cf. above, p. 99, on the proposed vocational faculties).

But by this time the situation had already changed. The number of students at the Swedish universities declined, strangely enough, especially at Uppsala. In the middle of the great Linnaean period in the 1750s, the number evidently did not reach 800 and the decline continued. Exact statistical data are available from 1761 onwards in what are called the "general tables" drawn up by Berch. During the latter half of the 1760s and the 1770s, the number of students at Uppsala remained stable at 500–600; in the 1780s, it fell to its lowest level, with, at times, only just over 400 students attending the lectures; the situation was not much better at the end of the century. The total number of those who matriculated was always much higher, but this figure also showed the same trend, with a steep drop after the middle of the century. This decline, in an age when the population of Sweden was rapidly increasing and the people's ways of thinking were increasingly enlightened, may seem puzzling and probably cannot be fully explained. But the increasing tempo of study certainly played an important part. The system of promotion by seniority which was the rule in the civil-service departments prompted the students to complete their university courses as quickly as possible, in order that they might take up their careers and get on the salary scale without delay; the civil-service degrees introduced in 1749–50 and required for posts in the administrative and legal departments had been devised primarily for this purpose. The large number of students who held posts as tutors also probably contributed to the decline in the number of students attending the University. But other, less comprehensible reasons must also have played a part. During the closing years of the Age of Freedom and the Gustavian period, university studies were not as attractive as they had formerly been. The fact that, in enlightened and aristocratic circles, the universities were despised as old-fashioned and out-of-date (cf. below, p. 119) was perhaps of less importance. Probably the slow change in the

113

structure of Swedish society that went on in the 18th century had greater effects; fewer and fewer students became clergymen and the sons of citizens and gentlemen who now made their ways to Uppsala or Lund with a view to taking up careers in the civil service were still too few to keep up the number of students.

2

The accession of Gustav III to the throne in 1771 and the proclamation of the new national constitution in the following year inaugurated an era in which the intellectual atmosphere of Uppsala slowly changed. The golden age of the natural sciences and economic utilitarianism was on the wane. Linnaeus died in 1778 and more or less simultaneously one after another of the great generation of scientists of the Age of Freedom disappeared. The centre of gravity shifted, and the tone changed. Belles lettres, aesthetics, the elevated emotions of the theatrical world and the radical humanism of the French Enlightenment formed the core of the culture which we call Gustavian and which spread out across the country from the Court and the literary circles of the capital. The universities could not really keep up with these developments; they defended the old thoroughness. But in the long run the new aesthetic and humanistic educational ideal could not be excluded; it began to leave its mark on teaching and research without any concessions being made to licence. As far as Uppsala was concerned, this meant that the University sank into national obscurity. The natural sciences were oriented towards the international community and Linnaeus and his colleagues had been the voices of Sweden in the outside world, but towards the end of the 18th century few people outside Sweden's borders or even in Lund bothered about what was happening in Uppsala.

The relationship between the University and the government authorities underwent a complete transformation in the reign of Gustav III. The contending political parties no longer existed and the Estates had lost all their influence in educational matters. The King had taken over their powers; he gave the Senate its orders and had no hesitation in appointing professors at his own discretion. There can be no doubt that, despite his fashionable French education, Gustav III really had the University's welfare at heart and often saw clearly in questions concerning the staff. He showed this even when he was Chancellor, when in 1767 he insisted that Torbern Bergman, the most brilliant scientific genius of the new generation, should be appointed Professor of Chemistry. When, 10 years later, Bergman received an invitation to move to Berlin and was greatly

37. When he was Crown Prince, King Gustav III was the University Chancellor. This illustration shows a picture and a description of the medal struck in 1764 in his honour. Engraving by Jacob Gillberg after a drawing by Louis Masreliez in Skåde-penningar öfver de förnämsta händelser som tillhöra konung Gustaf III:s historia (1858).

115

tempted to do so, the King again intervened and induced him to remain in return for the grant of a pension to his widow. In 1774, without consulting the Senate, the King established a much-needed third medical chair in anatomy and surgery and appointed the young and zealous Adolf Murray to be its occupant; as usual, the task of finding the money to pay his salary was left to the Senate. An equally worthy object of the King's benevolence was Jacob Fredrik Neikter, perhaps the most talented of the Uppsala humanists in the Gustavian period. After having approached the University Chancellor on his own account, he was favoured in 1785 by being made Professor of Aesthetics and Modern Literature—a subject befitting contemporary taste. However, professorships were sometimes withdrawn in an equally dictatorial fashion. This was what happened to the time-honoured chair of Latin Rhetoric (combined in 1779 with the chair of poetry) and to no less than two professorships of theology. When the second of these was abolished in 1786, the Faculty of Theology consisted of only three members, which was probably a source of satisfaction to enthusiasts for the Enlightenment in Stockholm. In his university policy, Gustav III tried to comply with the wishes of such men. Under a different sign, the self-government of the University of Uppsala was as restricted as it had been during the Age of Freedom.

The new situation meant that the Chancellor lost the authority which he had formerly had. He became primarily a kind of rapporteur on University matters in relation to the Crown. This did not prevent the Chancellors of the Gustavian period from being of use to the University. This statement applies chiefly to Carl Rudenschiöld, an engaging and highly cultivated man, who was Chancellor from 1771 to 1783. At the suggestion of Gustav III, he was succeeded by Gustaf Philip Creutz, the poet and Chancery President, who was the most outstanding representative of French rococo sensualism in Sweden. He died in a short time and Gustaf Adolf, the young Crown Prince, was elected Chancellor, following what had now become a tradition. This gave the King an even freer hand as the head of the University. But he listened to advice, above all, from a man whom he trusted—Nils von Rosenstein, who was in practice his Minister of Culture and whom he appointed to report on questions concerning Uppsala. Rosenstein was also the tutor of the young Crown Prince and the secretary of the Swedish Academy and was always present whenever the cause of the Enlightenment was in jeopardy.

During these years, Gustav III made increasingly frequent visits to Uppsala. He ostentatiously showed his goodwill to the University, charming the professors and trying to win their support for his interests. He gladly listened to disputations, inspected the University institutes and attended lectures, particularly those given by Fant, the historian. These royal visits

116

38. The students paying their respects to Gustav III outside the Gustavianum during a royal visit in the middle of the 1780s. Aquarelle by Louis Jean Desprez (1792). National Museum of Fine Arts, Stockholm.

occasionally took the form of shows, more or less directed by the monarch himself, that were as brilliant as they were superficial. However, the courtiers and the *blasé* favourites sometimes groaned. Gustav Mauritz Armfelt complained that Uppsala was "the cave of boredom". At that time, in the autumn of 1786, the King, accompanied by a splendid retinue, was spending a full six weeks in the town, where his arrival was greeted with a 160-gun salute. The climax of the visit was a disputation—in Swedish, to please the exalted guest—on 17 theses put forward by the witty Neikter, for which no less than 15 opponents entered their names. On other occasions, the courtiers joined in the discussion. An even more remarkable disputation was held in the spring of 1788, when Gustav III visited Uppsala in the company of several members of the Swedish Academy. Thomas Thorild, a fiery genius, had for some time been studying

117

at the University (which he greatly despised), in order to take a doctorate in law and to reform the world. He had some violent battles with Kellgren and good taste behind him and Gustav III was anxious to see so strange a bird in action. His wish was granted. When, on 22 March in the Gustavianum, Thorild defended his theses on Montesquieu ("scribbled down in a few hours") and gave the great Frenchman a thorough drubbing, the King was sitting with his retinue in the crowded auditorium. Roars of laughter alternated with rounds of applause, for Thorild was in his most extravagant mood and overflowed with witticisms, paradoxes and impudent remarks, showing no respect for persons or facts. For one concentrated Gustavian moment, scholarship had been transformed into a high-class show.

From time to time, Gustav III personally intervened in affairs for the University's benefit. As Chancellor, he had suggested that the Library should be moved from the Gustavianum, where the overcrowding on the shelves had become worse and worse, to a new building near the Academia Carolina. The project remained dormant until 1778, when it was changed; Adelcrantz, the Chief Surveyor, whose help the King had enlisted, submitted designs for a fine new library, which would extend along the southern side of the Cathedral in Riddartorget. This meant that the old Carolina would have to be demolished and this was immediately done, so that then the University had only two auditoria for lectures and disputations. But soon the plans were again changed; the site near the Cathedral was found to be too cramped and Gustav III commanded that the new Library building should be erected at the foot of the hill in Drottninggatan (the site now occupied by the Stockholm nation). Work on the foundations began and was completed in 1783, but then the authorities tired and the University's library problem was not to be finally solved until the following century, by the intervention of a new king. Gustav III initiated another scheme in the spring of 1787. He donated to the University the large garden below Uppsala Castle for the creation of a new botanical garden and promised to defray the cost of erecting a building to house the Institute of Botany. The old Linnaeus Garden in Svartbäcken, which was marshy and exposed to frosts, had long been considered to be unsuitable; something new and better was needed. The King himself laid the foundation stone, cannon were fired and music was played. But afterwards progress was slow (cf. below, p. 174). In addition, Gustav III donated his invaluable private records (the "Gustavian Papers") to the University, to be opened 50 years after his death. No Swedish ruler, except perhaps Queen Christina, has ever had a closer personal relationship to the University of Uppsala and its professors. A well-managed and renowned University was not the smallest jewel in the crown of an enlightened monarch.

Nevertheless, there was now an unmistakable antagonism between the University and the culture of the Court or the capital. This was in itself nothing new. Even in the early part of the Age of Freedom, the spokesmen of the middle class and the advocates of the Enlightenment, which was then in its infancy, had tried to invest what they called "pedantic academic learning" with an air of ridicule. The modern scientists, gathered together in the newly founded Academy of Sciences, were inspired by the same spirit. But they hardly directed their attacks against the University of Uppsala, for the simple reason that it had got into step with the times and was pursuing the natural sciences and the public weal with a success which rather excited amazement. It was only when the times changed once more and even research in natural science, which had been Sweden's pride, began to be regarded with indifference that the attacks were renewed. It was impossible to learn about modern currents of ideas in Uppsala; neither Locke nor Montesquieu was in the curriculum there. The leading critic of the Gustavian University was Johan Henrik Kellgren, who was sometimes seconded by his colleague, Carl Gustaf Leopold, the poet. The *Stockholmsposten* newspaper was his forum and in it one satire on the University followed another. Kellgren showed equal readiness in attacking both theological disputations and moss-grown Latin learning and the claims of the natural scientists to be contributing by their meaningless observations and experiments to the happiness of mankind. The professors at Uppsala and Lund were quarrelsome fellows and old fogeys unworthy of the attention of enlightened citizens; the object of all their endeavours was to arrange things in "systems" and "to bore people" (the reference was to Linnaeus). About the only things that mattered —society and human nature—they taught nothing; for such teaching, one had to go to Voltaire, Hume, Rousseau and other heroes of the new age.

In some respects, Kellgren's views could also be accepted by University people. The natural scientists of the Age of Freedom, from Klingenstierna and Celsius onwards, had likewise attacked the still-surviving educational ideal of the Caroline period; metaphysics, logic and dead languages were unnecessary or at any rate should be cut down. In a fascinating analysis of the conditions at Uppsala in 1783, Melanderhjelm, the astronomer, urged that this should be done as soon as possible. The old weeds had still not been cleared out and Melanderhjelm took a strong line: the Skyttean professor, with the help of an assistant, could take care of Latin single-handed; Hebrew should be combined with Greek, and formal logic and metaphysics, which were both useless, should be completely withdrawn or combined with the equally superfluous professorship of moral philosophy. "It is pitiful", wrote Melanderhjelm, "that such charlatanry should have been allowed to continue to exist for such a long time".

These were the opinions of a modern man. Gustav III, who was undoubtedly of the same opinion, reduced the number of old-fashioned professorships, as we have seen, by simply abolishing them. Also in other respects, Kellgren's fundamental contempt for the University lost some of its point in the course of developments. Towards the end of the 18th century, the philosophy of the Enlightenment and modern literature both gained recognition in Uppsala.

More detrimental to the University's reputation was the criticism of a different and almost diametrically opposite kind, which had been growing stronger since the 1760s. It amounted to saying that the old thoroughness had disappeared, so that the young graduates were rushing out onto the labour market after insufficient study. This view was not without justification; it will be remembered that the new civil-service degrees led to the curriculum being gone through more rapidly. Höpken took up the matter in the spring of 1764, when he visited the University as Chancellor; a superficial attitude had gained ground and the desire to study had diminished; the question was whether the blame lay with the professors or with the students. A few years later, Carl Gustaf Löwenhielm, the Chancery President, uttered a severe condemnation of the Swedish universities in his address to the Royal Academy of Sciences on the education of the young. The learning inculcated at the universities during a few short years was not worth much; a graduate who knew something of mathematics, history and geography, in addition to Latin and a little Greek, was regarded as a prodigy of learning. The complaints were rather intensified during the Gustavian period. The professors at Uppsala themselves mentioned the lowered standard of knowledge and that rapid courses of study for subsequent careers were the only attraction to students. We catch a glimpse of the general wretchedness of the time and the depravity of the young people. In his analysis, Melanderhjelm also attacked those who slandered the University; it had now reached such a pitch of disrepute that the nobility were no longer sending their sons to Uppsala. It is hardly possible to decide how pertinent this cogent but loosely expressed criticism was, nor the extent to which it contributed to the fall in the number of students.

Calm prevailed, on the whole, in the Senate and the university establishment during Gustav III's reign. The new constitution made political disputes between the professors impossible, and the monarch's direct supervision of the University subdued any excesses of passion, as during the autocracy of Charles XI. However, personal antagonisms flared up from time to time. Gustavian Uppsala harboured a notorious trouble-maker of long standing—Pehr Niclas Christiernin, the Professor of Theoretical Philosophy from 1771 onwards. He had a keen brain and was zealous and capable, but his constant quarrelsomeness was a source of continual irritation to both the Senate and the Chancellor. Time and again, Christiernin started pointless feuds; he accused Melanderhjelm (whom he detested) of teaching materialism to a criminal extent and in 1780, in his capacity as Rector, he started legal proceedings against Frondin, the Librarian, for alleged dereliction of duty. His last tragi-comic battle will be described in another connection.

The greater part of the professorial body had been renewed during the 1770s and 1780s. The prominent men of the Age of Freedom had gone; when Ihre died in 1780, both Anders Berch and Linnaeus were already dead. The newcomers included at least one leading light, namely, Torbern Bergman, but he died in 1784 while still in his prime. The natural scientist who came next to him in ability was Daniel Melanderhjelm, who was older than the others and who had been Professor of Astronomy since the 1760s. In mathematics, Fredrik Mallet administered the legacy of the great Klingenstierna, while Carl Peter Thunberg, the industrious botanist from Småland who occupied Linnaeus's chair in 1784, maintained Sweden's international reputation in botany (cf. below, p. 198).

The typical Gustavian academics—the standard-bearers of the new age—were to be found in the Faculty of Arts. They included Johan Floderus, a famous Professor of Greek in his time, who guided students of antiquity towards new goals, and Johan Adam Tingstadius, the Professor of Oriental Studies, who later became Bishop of Strängnäs. The learned Neikter has already been mentioned, but in 1787 he left his post as Professor of Literature for the Skyttean chair, in which he succeeded Jacob Lindblom, an ambitious and engaging young man who was restored to Uppsala in the fullness of time as Archbishop. Daniel Boëthius, a future disciple of Kant, was Professor of Philosophy, together with the troublesome Christiernin, from 1785 onwards. The professor who occupied the chair of history into the next century was Erik Michael Fant, an honourable man and a popular lecturer; he was an incredibly productive author but had hardly any sympathy with new ideas, either in his own field or in anyone else's.

Accordingly, when Gustav III left the stage in 1792, the University of Uppsala was not in a bad position, as regarded instruction and studies. It had a number of teachers of excellent quality and its voluble and contemptuous critics were, from this point of view, in the wrong. It is true that the University no longer held the same central position as it had in Linnaeus's time. Lund and Åbo had lately made good progress and Uppsala was hardly the national university in the same sense as before. But there was reason to face the future with confidence, though the signs were ominous—Duke Charles had been appointed Chancellor and the bigot Reuterholm was the real ruler of Sweden.

3

In the preceding pages, we have caught a glimpse of the basic features in the history of ideas at the University of Uppsala in the 18th century. This history began with the substantial theological and humanistic learning inherited from the period when Sweden was a great power. This was soon pushed aside by the natural sciences and economics, until finally, during the Gustavian period, new aesthetic and philosophical trends asserted themselves.

During these developments, theology and Latin, on the whole, retained their positions on paper. Even *c.* 1800, Lutheran doctrine and a solid knowledge of Latin formed the foundation of university education in Sweden. But, through being constantly nibbled away, they had in practice more and more declined in importance.

Towards the end of the century, academic theology appeared to be an empty shell. In Uppsala, some of the learned Caroline theologians were still at work at the beginning of the Age of Freedom, but afterwards the Faculty's reputation waned continuously. Its professors probably did their duty and dinned into their students' heads the Scriptures and the compulsory textbook in dogmatics, Jacob Benzelius's *Repetitio theologica,* which took two years to go through. But they were unable to give Lutheran orthodoxy a living content and their message became in time more and more attenuated. In the middle of the century, the Uppsala theologians were, as a rule, applying the new Wolffian philosophy (see below, p. 126) and were consequently pursuing a kind of dry scholasticism, an "enlightened" or natural theology, in which they thought rational thoughts about God. The Wolffians in the Faculty were led by Nils Wallerius, the Kalsenian professor and the only theologian who was productive as an author (*Praenotiones theologicae,* 1756–65). Wallerius was a man of inflexibly orthodox type and did not touch upon Biblical revelation, but the main task of Wolffian theology was to demonstrate the greatness of the Creator with the help of reason and thus to confute the atheists and the naturalists. The arguments used were often trivial and theology gradually lost its connection with the numinous and the incomprehensible. This process was hastened during the Gustavian period. What was left of Lutheran orthodoxy at the University of Uppsala was ridiculed by Kellgren and his brothers-in-arms; fashion favoured instead watered-down "neology", which saw the essence of Christianity in virtue and a tender heart. Leading Gustavian "neologians", such as Tingstadius and Magnus Lehnberg, had received their education at Uppsala. But there was little to be learned from the professors of theology. By the end of the 1780s, the Faculty had reached its nadir; two of its three professors were on leave on account of advanced age.

Nevertheless, the theologians tried, as far as possible, to predominate, as they had done in former times. The Faculty still had the right to censor objectionable theses and from time to time there were cases of persecution and trials for heresy. The new Moravian movement was very vulnerable; in 1757, the University Chancellor was instructed to investigate the extent to which it had penetrated into Uppsala and the Moravians' errors were revealed in a number of disputations. In 1763, Nils Wallerius, who was by virtue of his office the administrator of theological hatred in Uppsala, attacked a heretical theological compendium by J. D. Michaelis, the famous Göttingen professor, and succeeded in having it prohibited.

But greater dangers were looming up as a result of the general secularization of life in the name of the Enlightenment. The gospel of earthly happiness inherent in utilitarianism and the triumphal progress of the natural sciences were accompanied by new values and many people began to call into question what happens in the hereafter. This also applied to some natural scientists in Uppsala; both Anders Celsius and Klingenstierna should probably be described as religious sceptics; at any rate, the former spoke irreverently of sacred things. Linnaeus's orthodoxy was doubted by his theological colleagues. This had nothing to do with the advanced materialism of the French Enlightenment, but it gave the orthodox sufficient grounds for standing guard on the walls of Zion and striking a blow, when necessary. Wallerius was indispensable for these activities; he found his lawful prey in any unduly enlightened way of thinking. As a young assistant lecturer, he took part in the Knös–Ihre affair. In 1742, Anders Knös wished to defend a thesis, under the presidency of Johan Ihre, on the relationship between natural and revealed theology. However, the Faculty of Theology forbade the disputation. When, nevertheless, Ihre boldly allowed it to go ahead, this gave rise to a great wrangle. The proceedings lasted for nine hours and Knös was hard pressed, especially by Wallerius. The theologians, who were chiefly irritated by the fact that, contrary to the constitutions, a delicate theological subject was being discussed in a disputation in the Faculty of Arts, took the matter to the Chancellor and won him over to their side. The prohibition on the discussion of theology by members of the Faculty of Arts was re-enforced; on such subjects, people were not allowed to argue too freely. Anders Knös's promising academic career was cut short for ever and the Faculty of Theology adhered to its prohibition when he wished to defend a further thesis. But Ihre also got into difficulties. The controversy about orthodoxy flared up again in 1745–7; because of his encouragement of Knös, Ihre was accused of having supported a heretical theology of reason. The Cathedral Chapter at Strängnäs, the Uppsala theologians, Wallerius and the Estate of the Clergy in the Riksdag were ranged in opposition to

123

Ihre. He put up a manly and drastic defence: "I have neither sufficient genius nor stupidity to be a heretic, let alone sufficient ill will." He came off well, but the clergy triumphed on the question of principle. By a royal rescript, a fine of six months' salary was imposed on any professor who allowed opinions which conflicted with pure Lutheran doctrine to be expressed in a thesis defended under his presidency.

Solid, classical learning was undermined in the same way as theology; the spirit of the age was not favourable to it. Eighteenth-century Uppsala had no counterparts to Schefferus or Norrmannus. There was practically no scholarly research in Graeco-Roman antiquities and philology. Latin rhetoric still flourished but was nowhere near as important as formerly. There were no virtuosi of the Caroline class and the once fluent voice of Latin poetry began to fall silent. As we have seen, one of the Latin professorships was abolished in the 1770s, after sustaining a long series of attacks. But Latin and the culture of antiquity were, of course, never abandoned as a kind of permanent frame of reference for the intellect and the emotions. Now as formerly, the Professors of Rhetoric, Poetry and Greek and the holder of the Skyttean chair lectured on their Latin and Greek authors, giving explanations of and comments on the text; Cicero still held pride of place among the prose writers. Ekerman, who occupied the chair of Latin rhetoric for more than 40 years, attracted great crowds of students to his subject by his unashamed industry in connection with disputations. His successor, Pehr Svedelius, who also lectured on poetics, was accounted one of the best teachers in the University in the Gustavian period. The aim of education was still to acquire a fairly elegant Latin style, but the requirements had been lowered. The natural scientists looked askance at their silver-tongued Latinist colleagues, like Linnaeus, whose expressive "Svartbäck Latin" would have been unthinkable in the previous generation.

The advance of Swedish provides a measure of the decline of classical education. Swedish gradually came into use in lectures and academic publications during the 18th century. There was pressure from outside, prompted by the spirit of bourgeois public utility. The sciences should not be concealed, like some kind of esoteric trade secret, behind a language which was unintelligible to the man in the street. The decision of the Royal Academy of Sciences to publish its proceedings in Swedish was deemed to be exemplary. In Lund, a suggestion had been made as early as 1723 that lectures could be given in Swedish. At Uppsala, the first initiative was taken in 1738, when a thesis on the Norrland fisheries defended under the presidency of Anders Celsius was published with the Swedish text in parallel columns. The fruits of economic science should be available to the common people. When Berch's chair of general economic management was established in 1741, it was decided that he should speak his mother tongue at lectures and disputations. The Education Commission wished to go further and to allow its use in other subjects as well. This proposal met with opposition, for the humanists and the old-fashioned scholars rallied to the support of Latin as the basis of academic culture. If it was abandoned, Sweden would "sink into barbarism" and become a realm of ignorance. Johan Ihre gave voice to these feelings in a notable speech at the conferment of doctoral degrees in 1752. Latin was the medium of international scholarship and it would be foolish to abandon it in favour of a long series of modern languages. On this point, he could, in the main, count on the support of the natural scientists, who addressed themselves to readers in Europe; it would never have occurred to Linnaeus or Bergman to publish their scientific investigations in Swedish. However, Ihre seems earlier to have adopted a more liberal attitude; he arranged elocution classes in Swedish for his students and in 1745 presided over a disputation (P. N. Torger's thesis *An scientiae lingua vernacula tradi possint ac debeant*), in which Torger defended the use of the mother tongue in scientific works and academic instruction. Developments were inevitably moving in this direction. Theses on law were also published in Swedish in the Gustavian period and public lectures—not to mention private *collegia*—were often held in Swedish. But the death throes of academic Latin culture were to be long drawn out.

The oriental languages, which had been greatly cherished in Uppsala in the Caroline period, were not to the taste of the utilitarians of the Age of Freedom either. The main language here was Hebrew, for the benefit of prospective clergymen. However, in Carl Aurivillius (who became Professor of Oriental Languages in 1772), the University acquired a learned and productive philologist who had mastered all the Semitic languages, as well as Turkish, Georgian, etc., and who was hailed in Germany as a master of his science.

The scientific study of the Swedish language occupied an exceptional position. It had no professorial chair of its own. Runes and Icelandic literature had gone out of fashion after the Rudbeckian mists had been dispelled. To the ordinary extrovert patriots of the Age of Freedom, on the other hand, the care and cultivation of the mother tongue were a most important matter, which the universities should not shirk either. This demand gave birth to modern Scandinavian philology in Sweden. Its creator was Johan Ihre; oddly enough, in virtue of his position as Skyttean professor, he was bound to safeguard the supremacy of Latin, which he certainly did. But at the end of the 1730s, almost by chance, he had begun work on a much-needed Swedish dictionary. It progressed slowly, as he became absorbed in investigations concerning etymology and comparative philology. When

125

his famous Swedish–Gothic dictionary, *Glossarium sviogothicum,* was published in 1769 with the aid of a grant from government funds, it proved to be a work of the most penetrating learning. Ihre emerged as one of the shining lights of Germanic philology, on account of his keen perception of the sound changes in the Indo-European languages. The *Glossarium* called for thorough research in the Old Icelandic and Gothic languages, of which Ihre was accounted a master. He showed that Snorri Sturluson's *Edda* was a handbook for Icelandic poets and carried a good deal further the study of Bishop Ulfilas's Gothic translation of the Gospels.

Under its two professors, philosophy in 18th-century Uppsala slowly progressed from Descartes to Kant. At the beginning of the Age of Freedom, a vague eclecticism prevailed, in which Descartes was responsible for the natural philosophy but otherwise his principles were combined with remnants of scholasticism, the ethical teachings of antiquity and the tenets of natural law. Then, in the 1720s, a new interpretation of the world arrived from Germany and a decade later managed to acquire the status of the university philosophy at Uppsala. This was Wolffianism. It had been created by Christian von Wolff at Halle and was intended to summarize and develop the basic ideas in Leibniz's philosophy into a logical system. With its lofty faith in reason and its optimism about mankind and the world, Wolffianism represented a kind of cautious philosophy of the Enlightenment. Its rigid mathematical method of demonstration attracted the natural scientists. Uppsala became one of its main strongholds outside Germany. It was actually introduced by Anders Celsius, the astronomer, who recruited the first generation of Swedish Wolffians about 1730. The theologians were alarmed at first; Wolff postulated a natural knowledge of God (*theologia naturalis*) which appeared to threaten belief in revelation. In 1732, Cronhielm, the University Chancellor, was persuaded to issue a letter criticizing the dubious philosophical innovations at Uppsala.

However, the new ideas spread and in the 1740s Wolffianism reigned more or less supreme at the University. Its leading proponent was Petrus Ullén, the Professor of Philosophy, followed by the notorious Nils Wallerius, whose heavy *Compendium metaphysicum* (1750–2) was for long a plague to the students. As we have seen, Wolffianism had developed into a new kind of scholasticism in the service of Lutheran orthodoxy. As Wolffians, Ullén and Wallerius sought to show, by conclusive inferences, that God existed and that consequently atheism was unreasonable. After his transfer to the Faculty of Theology in the 1750s, Wallerius became increasingly fanatical in the pursuit of heretics; using reason uninhibitedly was as dangerous as not using it at all. One of the cardinal points in Wolffian natural theology was "physicotheology", the method of deducing the existence of an omniscient Creator from the order and beauty of a

126

J.Gillberg delin: et sculp. 1768

A. Littera inter Suiogothicas hodie prima, fed olim, ubi Runæ viguerunt, decima, ut videre licet ex Calendariis Runicis fcriptisque VERELII WORMIIque,palæographiam Borealem illuftrantibus. Et quum in hoc diffideant majores noftri non tantum a cognatis fuis, quibus ULPHILAS veritatem Euangelicam prædicavit, fed etiam a ceteris Europæ gentibus; indicio id forte fuerit, Runas a Scythicis gentibus inventas ufurpatasque, antequam cum ceteris Europæ incolis bellis commerciisque commifceri, eorumque inftitutis imbui cœperant. A, particula infeparabilis, apud Scriptores medii ævi non infrequenti ufu rei privationem denotans. *Awita* in LEGE BIRC. c. 14. §. 34. notat amentem, a *wit* ratio: *alag* iniquitatem, vel potius illegalitatem, a *lag*, lex. KON. STYR. Edit. SCHEFF. p. 144. *Sva óde ok forderwar girugr höfdinge fit land med allum alagum ok margfaldan orätt:* i. e. ita exhaurit corrumpitque terras fuas Princeps avarus per iniquitates & multiplices injurias. cfr. KNITL. SAGA p.54. His adde *amægtig*, impotens, a *magt* potentia. NEHEM. 4: 2. SAP. 15: 8. cfr. VERELII index p. 12. *amæli*, qui fine opprobrio eft, quum omnibus linguis vetuftioribus eam communem fuiffe, videamus. Ignorat nemo Græcorum α ςεϱητικὸν, ut ἄΦϱων, ἀνομία, quæ refpondent fuperius allatis *awit*, *alag*. Latini licet α illud per *in* fere

exprimant, remanet tamen in non paucis, notante HENRICO STEPHANO in Thefauro L. Gr. T. I. p. 2. e. g. *a-mens*, *avius*. Anglo-Saxones idem retinuiffe, docent varia compofita. Ita *agild* iis dicebatur, cujus ob necem pretium *Wirgildi (mansbot,)* non pendebatur. v. SPELMANNI Achæologus, p. 22. & DU FRESNE Gloff. Lat. B. in voce. Ex veterum ALEMANNORUM fcriptis haud pauca hujusmodi adfert FRANC. JUNIUS in *annot*. ad WILLERAMUM, p. 301. e. g. *amaktig* impotens(confr.nuper allatum *amægtig*) *aweig* devium, *awis* infipiens. Nos circa hanc particulam notamus 1.) Eandem non tantum præfixam nominibus, fed etiam adjunctam verbis, negationem defignaviffe apud veteres Gothos, tefte GUDMUNDO ANDREÆ in Annot. ad EDDÆ *Volufpa*, Str. 3. e. g. *vara fandur*, non erat arena; ubi *a* ultimum in *vara* negationis nota eft. 2.) Citeriori tempore *a* hoc negativum a nobis in *o* commutatum fuiffe, ut fuo loco amplius dicetur, a Danis in *u*; cui, nefcio an ad imitationem Latinorum, *n* adjunxerunt Germani. 3.) Particulam hanc feparabilem plenius olim fcriptam fuiffe *af*, id quod multa adhuc refidua veftigia indicant. Apud ULPHILAM *afgrunditha*, *Luc*. 8: 31. æquipollet Gr. ἄβυσσος, ortum a *grund* fundus, & *af*, quod τῷ α ςεϱητικῷ in Græca voce refpondet: nos hodieque *afgrund* dicimus. Sic habemus apud veteres *afkapad* pro informi, ἄμοϱΦῳ: KONUNG. STYRILSE. p.112. *Dtukinfkapr gör manzins ánlite lyt ok affkapat*. i. e. Ebrietas vultum hominis turpem creation governed by laws. Physicotheology also drew its inspiration from other sources and was often flat and trivial but was included as self-evident in the picture of the world that prevailed in the Age of Freedom and was elevated by Linnaeus into a touching religious devotion.

Wolffianism stubbornly held its own in Uppsala, though it sometimes came under attack. In theses published during his sojourn in Göttingen in 1756, the rebellious Forsskål denied the very foundations of Wolff's philosophy; this later gave rise to a violent dispute between him and Wallerius. Even towards the end of the century, Wolffian scholasticism was still a force to be reckoned with. Its dominating position long prevented fresh philosophical stimuli from being introduced into the University. Locke, above all, was kept at a distance. Locke's empirical philosophy—the self-evident basis of the view of mankind and society held in the French Enlightenment—did not begin to be generally accepted in Uppsala until about 1770. The Wolffians were opposed to the Lockeans, who were led by the polemical Christiernin, who in this respect made a decisive contribution by lecturing on Locke's *Essay concerning Human Understanding* and by expounding its doctrines in a series of disputations. Christiernin taught Locke's doctrines to Daniel Boëthius, Neikter, Leopold and other representatives of the younger generation. But Locke had come to Uppsala at the last minute, for *c*. 1790 Kant appeared over the horizon and opened up a new heaven to Swedish academic philosophy.

Research in natural science, which reached its climax in Uppsala at the middle of the century, borne on the intellectual currents of the age, was a surprising and unexpected phenomenon. To carry out independent scientific work was no more a part of the professors' duties than it had been before; in that sense, the Education Commission's hope of turning the University into a training school for civil servants was well grounded. But, as things were, scientific books and discoveries were coming out of Uppsala in a steady stream and it was impossible to prevent them; the very idea gave Linnaeus insomnia. The Estates had themselves encouraged this development, by supporting the establishment of institutes and laboratories for the needs of research.

The enthusiasm for economics, which was highly favourable to the natural sciences, found its most important Swedish representative in Anders Berch. Berch's classical work, *Inledning til almänna hushålningen* (Introduction to General Economics) (1747) develops in textbook form the fashionable contemporary doctrines on industry and *Kameralwissenschaft*. But Berch also pursued studies in individual branches of husbandry. In his "Theatrum oeconomico-mechanicum", he collected models of tools and samples of raw materials to illustrate manufacturing processes and agriculture. He was an expert on different designs of plough. The

JOHANNES IHRE
REG.CANC.CONS, PROFESSOR R.ET
SKYTT.EQV.AUR. DE STELLA POL.

*40. Johan Ihre, the
Skyttean Professor and
philologist. Copperplate
engraving.*

Borgströmian professor later lectured on what was in part the same subject.

The central figure in scientific research in Uppsala—Linnaeus—embraced the economic gospel of the times. The purpose of his journeys in the 1740s through the Swedish provinces, which were undertaken at the request of the Estates, was to make an inventory of all kinds of exploitable resources in the three realms of nature. But Linnaeus's deepest needs were satisfied only by purely scientific work. He had been born to bring order and method into the vast hosts of the plant and animal kingdoms. He had already published the pioneer works which had made him the

129

prince of botanists, primarily his *Systema naturae*, while he was a young man studying in Holland. After he had occupied the chair of medicine in 1741 and settled in Uppsala, he published new basic works—*Flora svecica* and *Fauna svecica* in the 1740s, the indispensable *Philosophia botanica*, in which he laid down the rules for the world's botanists, *Species plantarum* (1753) with its inventory of every known species of plant, the new and enlarged editions of *Systema naturae* and the long series of academic theses which often reveal fascinating and unexpected aspects of his personality. He did an enormous amount of work and wore himself out prematurely. He devoted the greatest care to his teaching. To attend Linnaeus's lectures became the fashionable thing to do; students from all faculties thronged to his lectures in the Gustavianum and many took private *collegia* at his house at great expense. During the spring and early summer, the botanical *herbationes* began—excursions on which the master, at the head of a small army of enthusiastic disciples, roamed the countryside round Uppsala, hunting for plants and butterflies.

Linnaeus had at once restored the dilapidated Botanical Garden in Svartbäcken. It was redesigned with rectangular flowerbeds in the French style and Hårleman's orangery for exotic plants, in which parrots, monkeys and other animals were also housed, was erected in the background. Seeds and bulbs were sent to Linnaeus from all over the world and soon the Uppsala Garden was competing with the finest in Europe. The prefect's house erected by Rudbeck in one corner of the Garden was Linnaeus's home for the rest of his life. It was there that he kept his enormous herbarium and his collections of shells, insects, fishes and minerals until 1768, when he moved them to a small museum near his summer cottage at Hammarby.

Linnaeus was unrivalled as a teacher. No one in Uppsala has ever had so many devoted pupils as he had, and no one has supervised them more firmly. Probably not all of them had such splendid talents as Linnaeus's benevolence led him to think, but his itinerant disciples who ventured life and limb in unknown continents left their marks on the history of science. Pehr Kalm travelled in North America, Osbeck went to China and Pehr Löfling to South America; Forsskål met his fate in Arabia, while Daniel Solander and Anders Sparrman sailed as naturalists with Captain Cook on his voyages round the world; Carl Peter Thunberg returned from his many years of travel, loaded with natural-history specimens, after Linnaeus's death. But Linnaeus's fame also attracted foreign students from many parts of the world to Uppsala, where they learned the elements of the new science of botany. In time, they formed a large body, mostly consisting of Norwegians, Danes and Germans but also including the occasional Dutchman, American and Russian. Linnaeus sought to exercise a

41. Linnaeus. Oil painting by Per Krafft the Elder (1774). Royal Academy of Sciences, Stockholm.

kind of international dictatorship in his science and, as long as he lived, European botanists turned their gazes towards his throne in Uppsala.

Nils Rosén von Rosenstein, Linnaeus's colleague in the Faculty of Medicine, brought new life to practical medicine; together, the two of them inaugurated a new epoch in medical studies at the University. Rosenstein,

131

who resigned his chair as early as 1756, was a skilful anatomist; he began to carry out dissections again and was soon assigned an assistant for this work. But he preferred to work at the bedside. The *nosocomium academicum*, the University Hospital in Riddartorget, was repaired and re-opened with 7–8 beds and regular instruction was given in the outpatient department. Rosenstein had a large private practice, which gave him the experience which underlay his classical work on paediatrics, *Underrättelser om barnsjukdomar* (Information about Children's Diseases) (1764), which was translated into several languages and acquired European fame.

Anders Celsius led astronomy in Uppsala into a new era. Today he is best known as the inventor of the centigrade thermometer scale ("degrees Celsius"), though his right to it is to some extent doubtful. This scale was derived from a paper by Celsius published in 1742, in which the fixed points were decided, but centigrade thermometers had long been in use and the "reversed" Celsius scale now in use did not come into existence until 1746, after Celsius's death, when it was introduced at the Uppsala Observatory. At any rate, this instrument had been developed there, as a stage in the making of meteorological measurements. Anders Celsius had been Professor of Astronomy for several years and had made his name as a participant in Maupertuis's expedition to Lapland to measure a degree of the meridian, when he began to work for the establishment of an observatory in Uppsala. The observatory building was designed by Hårleman and paid for by the University; it was completed in 1741 and is still standing in Svartbäcksgatan. Celsius procured quadrants, telescopes and other instruments from England. His own research in astronomy was chiefly devoted to methods of determining the stars' light intensities. He also made investigations of terrestrial magnetism, in which he had a skilful assistant in Olof Hiorter, who became the observatory officer in 1746. They made an important discovery at the beginning of the 1740s—that the magnetic needle was disturbed during the northern lights and therefore there must be some kind of connection between the northern lights and magnetism.

After Celsius's early death in 1744, which was soon followed by that of Hiorter, the study of astronomy declined in Uppsala. But the routine observations continued and in Daniel Melanderhjelm, who was Professor of Astronomy from 1761 to 1796, the University once more had an astronomer of European fame. Melanderhjelm was chiefly a theorist—he was a devoted Newtonian—and sought to discover the equilibrium conditions in the universe with the aid of mathematical calculation. Erik Prosperin, who was his observatory officer during the Gustavian period, acquired a reputation as an outstanding expert on comets.

In mathematics and physics, Samuel Klingenstierna was the great name

42. *The botanical garden in Svartbäcken restored by Linnaeus with Hårleman's assistance. In the foreground is Carl Eldh's statue of Linnaeus. Sture-Foto.*

in Uppsala and in the whole of Sweden. He was hailed as an equal, even in his youth, by the leading mathematicians in Europe and, as Professor of Mathematics in the 1730s and 1740s, he trained the younger generations of Uppsala students in advanced mathematical analysis. But

43. *Electricity-generating machine, probably acquired by Samuel Klingenstierna about 1740. Frictional electricity was generated by rotating the glass cylinder. Institute of Physics, University of Uppsala.*

he shunned printer's ink and published only a few of his mathematical discoveries. Few also were his papers on physics, in which he did his most important work. Even before he took over the new chair of experimental physics in 1750, he gave lectures on this subject and procured from England a collection of instruments, which was housed in the University Hospital in Riddartorget. He was particularly fascinated by the new discoveries in electricity, performed numerous experiments himself and put forward visionary ideas about electricity as a universal force of nature, possibly identical with magnetism. But Klingenstierna's mastery of his subject was displayed in geometrical optics. Quite unabashed by Newton's authority, he demonstrated theoretically in a paper in 1754 that the dispersion of light in astronomical lenses (the chromatic aberration) could be corrected; inspired by this paper, Dollond, the English optician, succeeded in making his famous achromatic telescope. Klingenstierna—"an intelligence of incomparable steadiness", according to Linnaeus—resigned his professorship prematurely. The abilities of his successor, Samuel Duraeus, were hardly equal to the post and physics in Uppsala stagnated for a long time to come.

The tradition of chemical research in Sweden had grown up from mineralogy and mining engineering and the same is true, in a way, of chemistry at the University of Uppsala. The first Professor of Chemistry, Johan Gottschalk Wallerius, had been trained in medicine but soon settled on mineralogy, in which he became one of the leading authorities of his time. His *Mineralogia* (1747), which was translated into several languages, contained the first properly arranged mineral system ever devised. He published an epoch-making handbook on chemical metallurgy and was

44. *Torbern Bergman.*
Copperplate engraving
by F. Akrel after an oil
painting by Lorens Pasch
the Younger.

also something of a pioneer in agricultural chemistry. Wallerius worked in the University's new chemical laboratory on Västra Ågatan, which was completed in 1754. The building, which was originally a long, low house containing two laboratories, is still standing, with the upper floor added by Bergman. An annual grant to cover the running costs was paid from University funds and in 1757 Wallerius was assigned an associate professor of chemistry to act as his assistant.

His successor, Torbern Bergman, led Uppsala chemistry into its most brilliant period. During the 1770s, when Bergman and the outstanding, self-taught, experimental chemist, Scheele, were working side by side in the town, Uppsala was a place of interest to chemists all over the world. Bergman did not take up chemistry until late in life. As a brilliant young man, who was more versatile than any other Swedish natural scientist, he made independent and to some extent remarkable contributions to entomology, astronomy, electrical theory and physical geography. His *Physisk beskrifning öfver jordklotet* (A Physical Description of the Earth) (1766) was published by the small Cosmographical Society which then flourished in Uppsala and became a standard work in many countries. When Wallerius resigned his professorship in the following year and Bergman took

135

his place, he mastered the subject of chemistry while learning its basic principles. He renovated the "Laboratorium chemicum", which had been badly damaged by the serious fire in Uppsala in 1766, fitted up and arranged the University's collection of mineral samples there, and had models made of equipment used at mines and foundries. Prospective mining engineers always constituted the majority of Bergman's students and his teaching was devoted to a large extent to applied chemistry. His increasing reputation attracted several foreign students, including the Elhuyar brothers from Spain, to Uppsala to learn advanced chemistry in his laboratory. It was like the palmy days of Linnaeus; Uppsala was not to begin to attract foreign scientists again for another 150 years.

Bergman, who collected the results of his experiments in the series of publications entitled *Opuscula physica et chemica* (1779–83), was an excellent analyst, who worked out new methods of investigating ores, minerals and metals. His work on carbonic acid was of fundamental importance, his famous tables of the chemical affinities were based on countless experiments and his proposals for a new chemical nomenclature represented a great step forward. Clarity and logical acuity characterized all his work and he stimulated his many pupils, led by J. G. Gahn and Hjelm, to make important discoveries in mineral analysis; the three new elements manganese, molybdenum and tungsten (wolfram) were all discovered under the guidance of Bergman and Scheele. Bergman kept the tradition of scientific research from the Age of Freedom alive into the 1780s but died, in poor health and worn out, at the age of 49 and chemistry fell into decay.

The scholars of Uppsala had had their own scientific association ever since the beginning of the Age of Freedom. This was the Royal Society of Science, which had developed from Benzelius's small group of learned men (see above, p. 75) and which was raised in 1728 to the rank of a royal academy, the oldest in Sweden (Societas regia literaria et scientiarum Upsaliensis). This Society, which was of an erudite Latin character, was active in the 1720s and 1730s, when Anders Celsius, as its secretary, edited its scientific transactions, but was later overshadowed by the more up-to-date Royal Academy of Sciences in Stockholm and became dormant during Linnaeus's long period as secretary. It was not until 1773 that the Society again started to publish papers, which continued to appear under the title of *Nova acta* down to our own times.

The new trends which manifested themselves in Gustavian Uppsala were not of a uniform stamp. In the first place, the modern philosophy of the Enlightenment, which had been shouldered aside by Wolffianism and the surviving remnants of Latin scholarship, had to be given its chance. The radical French philosophers were not unknown. Ihre, who

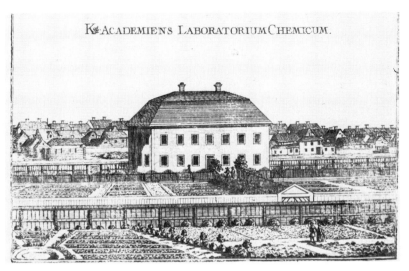

45. *The University chemical laboratory on Västra Ågatan, built at the beginning of the 1750s by Johan Gottschalk Wallerius and improved in the period 1768–70 by Torbern Bergman. Engraving by F. Akrel in Busser (1769).*

was head and shoulders above his colleagues, dealt familiarly in the 1760s with the writings of Montesquieu, Voltaire and Helvetius, and Rousseau's cultural criticism could be traced in the disputations at an even earlier date. But it was only in the cultural climate of the Gustavian period that the philosophy of the Enlightenment was able to permeate the academic world. Now, as we have seen, Locke was accepted at the University and Jacob Fredrik Neikter, who became Professor of Literature in 1785, had learned not only from him but also from Voltaire and Montesquieu; in a long series of disputations, he defended Montesquieu's celebrated climatic theory.

However, Neikter, who was a leading Uppsala figure towards the close of the 18th century, discussed primarily aesthetic problems. They had come to the fore among the younger generations. In 1767, Olof Bergklint formed the private society called "Apollini sacra", in which the contemporary lovers of literature in Uppsala came together. They were soon confronted with new and revolutionary ideas, which represented a radical break with the prevailing requirement in French classical thought for reason and good taste; a new epoch was looming. Rousseau's emotional gospel and Montesquieu's climatic theory had already broken the ground and now the exotic and the picturesque, the irregular and the naive, were taking on aesthetic value. The moribund academic humanism was renewed

137

by Winckelmann and the sentimental passion for antiquity, which cast longing eyes back to the elevated calm of the Greek monuments and saw in the half-barbaric Homer the greatest of poets. This neo-humanism had its stronghold in Göttingen, which was visited by many Swedes. At the same time, the humanists discovered the majestic Hebrew poetry of the Old Testament and thrilled with awe at the "wild and gigantic" elements in Shakespeare or Ossian, whose works were now conquering Europe. But Neikter was still hesitant. He was too firmly rooted in the French Enlightenment to swallow the new aesthetics whole; poetry, he thought, should not be written just anyhow. But there were no eternally valid rules and creative genius must have a free hand. Johan Floderus, the Professor of Greek, had already oriented his teaching towards the educational ideal of neo-humanism. He loved the great Greek poets with an insight previously unknown in Uppsala and lectured on Homer, whose timeless simplicity soon won the hearts of the students. Johan Adam Tingstadius, who became Professor of Oriental Languages in 1786, performed the same service for Hebrew literature. He found the oldest poetry in the world—fiery, full of imagery and magnificent—in the books of the Old Testament and sought to bring out these values in his own translations (he was a member of the Bible Commission). This yielded him, alone among the Uppsala professors, a seat in the Swedish Academy.

Times were changing in Uppsala too. Romanticism was just round the corner and when the philosophy of common sense was abandoned and Kant laid hands on the young people, the break-up was final.

4

The students' daily life as members of the University—marked out by lectures, disputations and examinations—changed little during the 18th century. The professors continued their fixed courses, as before, in public lectures and private *collegia* and the students made verbatim notes. The pace of study was still a jogtrot. It could take 4–5 years to go through one subject and the same classical authors were ploughed through term after term. As the Skyttean professor, Ihre lectured almost continuously on Livy. However, he and some other professors, such as Linnaeus with his drastic sense of humour and later Floderus, Neikter and Fant, were among the most popular lecturers and often packed the auditoria. Sometimes stimulating innovations were tried; thus, at the beginning of the Age of Freedom, politics and contemporary history were read from foreign newspapers. A good deal of trouble arose over the question of attendance checks and continuous questioning during the lectures, which were urged time and again by the authorities but were resisted by the professors, principally Linnaeus, who detested any suggestion of school routine. Sometimes attendance was checked and questions were asked, sometimes not. Neither teachers nor students would normally seem to have been weighed down by excessive instruction. The breaks during the terms were frequent and the vacations were long—from Midsummer to 1 October and from 21 December to 28 January in the Gustavian period.

The examination system too remained largely the same, despite the attempts at reform. The only substantial innovation was the above-mentioned examinations for entrance to the courts of justice and the civil service, introduced in 1749–50. All students who passed through the Faculty of Arts and wished to take a degree there had still to undergo final examinations in all the Faculty subjects by all the professors, which usually took four hours. As time went by, many candidates began to find this unreasonable. The ideal of encyclopaedic academic education, which was a legacy from scholasticism and humanism, was now felt to be antiquated in progressive circles, especially among modern natural scientists, who were unwilling to spend time on metaphysics and ancient languages. The conflict between general studies and specialization is a main topic in Swedish academic debates from the end of the 17th century to the beginning of the 20th. In Uppsala in the Age of Freedom, the professors sometimes modified tacitly the instructions in the constitutions; students who proved to be proficient in certain main subjects were let off lightly in the others. But when in the 1770s explicit demands were made that the examination system should be re-organized and that examinations should only be held in a selection of subjects, these demands encountered opposition and the old system was retained for a long time to come (cf. below, p. 168). However, the requirements were not high; even very scanty knowledge was rewarded with a simple *admittitur* ("he is admitted"). But then the grades *approbatur* or *laudatur* were required in other subjects if a pass was to be granted. The other examinations for the first degree in the Faculty of Arts were the traditional ones—an examination in theology, two Latin translation tests and a disputation *pro exercitio*. These, together with the oral examination, formed the ingredients of the examination for the bachelor's degree. For the master's degree, they were followed by a disputation *pro gradu* and two formal lectures.

The theses were written and publicly defended on the old pattern. Their volume did not increase appreciably during the 18th century, but it was taken for granted that they should in some sense make fresh contributions to scholarship. This was connected with the fact that it became increasingly common for both theses *pro gradu* and theses *pro exercitio* to be written by the professor who acted as president and not by the respondent.

139

Linnaeus himself was responsible for every word in the many theses which he wrote and the industry with which Ekerman, the Professor of Latin, produced theses was mentioned above. The authorship is, of course, obvious in those cases—like Thunberg, the botanist, and Fant—in which a continuous series of theses were publicly defended under the same president. There could still be lively scenes at the disputations. The shows which Gustav III ordered as Chancellor or as monarch, with or without Thorild at the lectern, occupied a place apart. Fierce battles were fought at some of the disputations for professorships held in accordance with the constitutions. Abuse came thick and fast when the hot-tempered Christiernin, who yearned for a chair of theology, came to loggerheads with his rival Palmberg in 1777; there was a long discussion as to whether Palmberg could be regarded as being intelligent or not (cf. the scandalous scenes at Johan Gottschalk Wallerius's disputation for a professorship, above, p. 96).

The conferment of masters' degrees—the most impressive of University ceremonies—still took place only every third year, in the Carolina since early in the Age of Freedom and after its demolition in the Cathedral. The question of the number of degrees to be conferred gave rise to much discussion. The authorities thought it important to keep the number down, in order to increase the honour and not to create superfluous masters. A royal ordinance limiting the number to no more than 50 was issued in 1731, but not much attention was paid to it at the time. The number of degrees conferred was often much greater; in 1743 it reached the record figure of 118. As Chancellor, Gustav III insisted that no more than 50 masters' degrees should be awarded and his will prevailed, despite complaints by the University. The actual conferment ceremony took place with the traditional pomp, including a procession, the ringing of bells and music. The auditorium where "Parnassus" stood was covered with red cushions. The recipients of degrees were clad in black silk gowns, which could be hired from the Faculty for a small charge, and received from the presenter their laurel wreaths, which had now finally replaced the hats used during the previous century.

Examinations and disputations in the higher faculties became more common in the 18th century than they had been before. However, the special final examinations in theology prescribed in the 17th-century constitutions were never really generally accepted. The first degree in theology (*teologie kandidat*) was not established until the 1750s; it was taken by a large number of students but was by no means essential for prospective candidates for holy orders. Only five persons obtained the licentiate of theology during the whole of the century. No candidates sought the distinguished degree of doctor of theology, for it remained a rarely awarded mark of

46. *Hats designed for everyday wear by Doctors of Divinity. On the left, the hat worn by Dean Anders Knös (1844) and on the right, that worn by Bishop Frithiof Grafström (1868). Nordic Museum, Stockholm.*

favour, conferred at ceremonies that were seldom held. Similar conditions obtained in the Faculty of Law, where formal examinations (for the *juris kandidat* and *juris licentiat* degrees) did not commence until the middle of the century. Two conferments of doctorates of law were held, the first in 1752, when there were five recipients.

The situation was more favourable for the doctors of medicine. The doctoral degree, which was essential to obtain the right to practise, was, as will be remembered, almost invariably obtained abroad. But now Rosén took the matter in hand. The Swedish universities should be encouraged to confer doctorates of medicine and in 1738 the first such conferment for a very long time took place in Uppsala. The prosperity of the Faculty of Medicine under Rosén and Linnaeus and the high standards which it maintained during the Gustavian period meant that conferments of doctorates took place frequently; a total of 172 doctorates of medicine were awarded at the University up to the middle of the 1790s. Medical studies were more thorough than those in any other faculty. There were preliminary examinations in theology and philosophy, which were by no means a matter of form, and a disputation *pro exercitio.* These were followed by an examination on the theoretical aspects of medicine (*medicine kandidat* degree) and another on its practical aspects (*medicine licentiat* degree), before the disputation for the doctorate could take place, followed by the conferment of the degree, with Hippocrates' works opened and a silk hat for the recipient. The whole process usually took about 10 years. But, in addition, from the 1750s onwards, all who wished to be-

141

come municipal or district medical officers had to do at least six months practical work in surgery at the new Serafimer Hospital in Stockholm.

Medical students did not cease to make study tours abroad under the new system. Such tours were no longer compulsory, but the more ambitious doctors found it necessary to perfect their skills at foreign hospitals under famous teachers. Halle and, above all, Leyden were their usual destinations until 1740, when Paris became more attractive, and several Gustavian doctors found their way to Edinburgh. But students from other faculties also continued during the 18th century the beneficial custom of travelling abroad, though in diminishing numbers. Their choices fell almost invariably on German universities, where theology and philology flourished. At first it was generally Halle and then Göttingen, the stronghold of the Muses and the principal point from which Swedish academic culture reached Europe. Young Uppsala students attended the University of Greifswald, which belonged to the Swedish Crown, for other reasons; the master's degree could be acquired there in no time, to the annoyance of many people. It was not until the turn of the century that study tours abroad by Swedish students ceased, after having gone on without interruption for over 500 years, and the Universities of Uppsala and Lund became entrenched in national self-sufficiency.

The students' way of life changed as the social behaviour of the period became more refined, but the process of change was slow. Even towards the end of the Age of Freedom, we read of fights and riots of the lively Caroline type and as late as 1772 the Senate sentenced a student to death. With academic arrogance, the students harassed the Uppsala citizens and the town watch; they particularly liked to don masks and gatecrash the weddings of the citizens and play all kinds of pranks. However, towards the end of the century, the old coarseness seems to have been refined away. Melanderhjelm says explicitly that disturbances hardly ever occurred and the students were noticeably more civilized. At any rate, the sons of both the nobility and the gentry became increasingly elegant as the century went on. Complaints were raised about young dandies with purses and whips in curls and cuffs and the Stockholm newspapers of the Gustavian period printed disparaging rumours about the University's gilded youth lounging about at assemblies and dancing clubs. But the large numbers of poor students lived frugally, as in the past, and sometimes attended lectures in dressing-gowns and slippers.

Thus, the 18th-century student's cost of living varied enormously. The conditions were completely different for the many who lived on supplies of food brought from home or shared an evening meal bought from the innkeeper and the count's son with his tutor and his servant. There were still the royal scholarships for poor and diligent students, but the fall in the value of money made them less important than before and, for this reason, they were reduced in 1780 from 145 to 56, distributed by faculties; at the same time, the amounts were increased. In addition, there were what were called the "magnate scholarships", which were supplemented by new donations. Thus, a considerable proportion of the student body was living on scholarships in one form or another and posts as tutors were available to the rest. These posts played an increasingly important part in the financing of studies. This was a form of teaching work which was permanently incorporated in University life and whose palmy days in Sweden were between about 1750 and 1850. It was an important part of the professors' duties to procure good tutorial posts ("conditions") for their pupils in wealthy homes or at the University. Exact figures are available from the latter half of the 18th century; periodically, well over 100 students, i.e. approximately one Uppsala student in five, were supporting themselves as tutors at the University or elsewhere. Tutorial work was often well paid and also offered a welcome opportunity to penetrate into influential circles and to get on in the world.

The students of noble birth retained their privileged position during the 18th century. They still took precedence in the University processions and were not, as a rule, enrolled in the usual student nations. Gustav III, who had a sympathetic feeling for noble splendour as long as it was politically harmless, gave orders as Chancellor in 1768 that a special nation for noble students was to be established. It actually started, with Ihre, the Skyttean professor, as its inspector, but was soon dissolved. The number of noble students at Uppsala, who were always mostly young boys in the charge of tutors, remained at about 10% of the total during the century. For some obscure reason, it declined in the 1770s and 1780s to about 6% (equivalent to between 20 and 30 students) but later increased again. The contemporary endeavours to secure social equality and to restrict the privileges of the nobility called forth responses in Gustavian Uppsala, but they did not change the social reality. In a sense, the noble students were more segregated from the University community at this time than ever before. While the young aristocrats of the previous century had endeavoured to acquire the Latin learning that was necessary for future high office, the complaint was now heard that their fellow nobles at the University were ignoring serious studies and were only taking up the frivolous noble exercises. Melanderhjelm did not mince his words: he said that these students were usually aiming at careers as Army officers and their only desire was to ride and fence; they strolled about the streets in riding clothes, with whips in their hands.

To these students, it was a *sine qua non* that Rudbeck's establishment for the noble exercises should continue to function undisturbed. The

143

young nobles for whom it had been created remained faithful to it. The riding, fencing and dancing masters taught their aristocratic skills well into the 19th century. The riding school had been discontinued for a long time and the stable wing at the "Exercise House" had fallen into disrepair, but about 1740 it was revived and, with the support of government funds, entered upon its heyday under Johan Lewin Eklund, the finest horseman in Sweden in his time. He used to begin his lectures by saying "Gentlemen, when God created man, he also created the horse". The post as fencing master was held from the 1730s in unbroken succession by four generations of the remarkable Porath family of fencers. To parry the Porath rapid passes required great skill.

Modern languages were still taught as part of the noble exercises. But the times had changed and during the 18th century they seem to have been learned by an increasing number of ordinary students. Instruction in Italian, German and the new language—English—was given more or less sporadically. Only the inevitable French language was permanently on the timetable. A well-known teacher of French was Jean François de la Bourdonnière, who became interested in Sweden through reading Voltaire's *Histoire de Charles XII* and for 40 years—well into the 19th century— taught the language of the Enlightenment and the *philosophes* in Uppsala. It was to be a long time before the modern languages were regarded as anything more than fashionable exercises and became regular academic subjects.

The importance of the student nations increased in time. All students, except the young nobles, had to be enrolled in one of them and their activities became increasingly versatile. The *studentexamen* (matriculation examination) which the freshmen (except the young boys in the charge of tutors) had to pass in the presence of the Dean of the Faculty of Arts on their arrival in Uppsala was only a formality and several nations therefore began to introduce, on their own initiative, a more rigorous entrance or "nation" examination. The intellectual exercises in the form of orations and discussions of Latin theses were carried on with great ardour, and there were numerous nation festivities—"conventions" and "provincial parties"—in beer cellars or on hired premises. Owing to subdivision, the nations as a whole had a much more varied appearance than they have today. They were, in all, 21 in number, but some of them, such as the Roslagen, Kalmar and Västerbotten nations, were very small and had only about 10 students. The inspectors who superintended them were now appointed at free elections. The office of inspector was increasingly coveted, since it gave the holder influence over the students and yielded handsome fees in the form of valuable inspector's silver. Several professors—particularly theologians, who were in a position to help their young fellow-

47. A couple of specimens of "inspector's silver" from different periods. In the middle, the gift presented by the Östgöta nation to Professor Jacob Fredrik Neikter in 1790; at the sides, the gift presented by the Södermanland-Nerike nation to Rutger Sernander, Professor of Botany, in 1931.

countrymen in their clerical careers—held inspectorates of two or three nations at the same time, while their less useful colleagues often, to their regret, had none. In fortunate cases, the relationship between the inspector and his young fellow-countrymen was marked by the sincerest affection. A legendary glow surrounds Linnaeus and his cherished Småland students, while several other inspectors are praised for their paternal care and it was customary for students to attend the inspector's *collegia* free of charge.

The social recruitment of the students underwent a slow change, as time went by. This was a result of the increasing secularization of society. The number of sons of the clergy at Uppsala (there was the same development at Lund) declined intermittently from about 40% at the beginning of the 18th century to about 25% at the end of the century. Instead, the sons of the gentry and citizens (for the nobility, cf. above, p. 143) were gaining ground cautiously and already exceeded the number of sons of the clergy during the Gustavian period with their 40% of all matriculated students. The number of sons of farmers seems to have remained fairly unchanged throughout the century, oscillating around 20%. In the international context, this was an exceptionally high figure and bears favourable witness to the solid popular basis of the old Swedish educational system. The sons of farmers still mostly sought careers as clergymen or

145

school-teachers, which were otherwise natural goals chiefly to the sons of the clergy. But the course of developments was characterized by a gradual decline in the attractions of the clerical career. While, at the end of Sweden's period as a great power, considerably more than half of the Uppsala students sought posts in the Church, the corresponding figure towards the end of the 18th century was about 35–40%. On the other hand, the number of prospective officials in the state and municipal administrations increased under the influence of the new civil-service examinations.

Thus, the tendency was clear: the students were no longer reading for ordination to the sacred ministry as self-evidently as before. As yet, there was no question of any radical structural change. It was not until well into the 19th century that the University of Uppsala became what might primarily be called a university for civil servants.

CHAPTER V

Uppsala in the Age of Romanticism

1

There is every reason to mark a new stage in the history of the University of Uppsala as beginning about 1800. The age of romanticism was at hand and was to leave its mark on the intellectual and emotional life and the forms of social intercourse in the little university town of Uppsala for generations to come. The change from the worldly utilitarianism of the Enlightenment was a radical one. Man no longer lived by bread alone but was a spiritual being, labouring to perfect himself. About 1800, academic Uppsala gave birth to the literary revolution which overthrew the dominion of French classical taste and spread German neo-romanticism over Sweden. As never before or since, Uppsala was the focal point of the aesthetic debate and Beauty, together with Truth in its most elevated sense, were the main objects of the endeavours of academic romanticism. Its period of glory lasted only for a few decades, but in a more general sense the romantic attitude to life retained its hold until long after the middle of the century. As harmless post-romanticism, it permeated poetry and emotional life, and as high-toned idealism in patriotic and moral connections, it gave professors and students the intellectual pabulum for their journey through life.

This romantic idealism had an educational kernel which led to its being deemed indispensable at the Swedish universities. From this point of view, the phrase "the age of Uppsala idealism" would be the aptest designation of the whole epoch. It expresses the belief in mankind's possibilities of self-realization and refinement which developed from the German academic philosophy of the early 19th century. In this philosophy, Kant's gospel of freedom, the soulfulness of romanticism and the neo-humanists' aesthetic and ethical view of mankind were combined. The concept of *Bildung* was endowed with a new meaning and this transformed the aims and methods of higher education. In Germany, Schleiermacher, the theologian, and Wilhelm von Humboldt, the man responsible for the newly founded University of Berlin, were the foremost advocates of the new idea of a university. Sordid utilitarianism and the empirical sciences, with their accumulation of dry facts, were held in contempt. Academic education should consider human knowledge as an organic whole and penetrate into the innermost nature of reality by taking a kind of intellectual view.

147

Philosophy became the science of sciences. Under its aegis, the student would realize his fundamental talents and become aware of his powers and his obligations. Classical antiquity, interpreted in a high-flown, romantic spirit, provided the pattern; its noble and harmonious figures taught us what human perfection really meant. This neo-humanism meant that the study of Greek and Roman literature was to predominate for generations to come.

Nevertheless, public utility and future careers as civil servants were still conceived to be the chief aim of university education. However, this aim could not be attained by submission to short-term, current demands. Independent of the State, the universities should train a civil élite, who would be aware of their responsibilities and could relate the problems of the day to eternal criteria from a higher, theoretical viewpoint. Plato's guardians and China's mandarins became examples or parallels to the teachers, judges and civil servants of the 19th century.

In this environment, the university students acquired a new status, at any rate, in Germany and the Scandinavian countries. There was a complete change of attitude. From having been an anonymous, industrious or clamorous and window-breaking mob, they became the hopes and the darlings of the nations. The academic romanticism of the 19th century was, to a large extent, student romanticism. It was the age of student songs, student meetings, patriotic speeches and punch-drinking. Borne on the wave of idealism, the students appeared as the knights of light, irradiated by the glow of innocent youth. They knew their worth. To be a student —in Uppsala or elsewhere—was not only an enviable way of life but also offered opportunities for effective expressions of opinion and political action.

The new attitude was not fully developed in Uppsala until well into the 19th century. But it had its basis in the rebellious currents of ideas in the student world of the 1790s, when political freedom and Kant's transcendental philosophy aroused the enthusiasm of the young. This section must therefore begin in that period.

However, the University did not, for the time being, undergo any fundamental change in structure or organization during the 19th century. New routines were introduced and things were patched and mended, but the old constitutions applied unchanged throughout the first half of the century and when they were finally replaced by new ones in 1852, scarcely any radical reforms were introduced. This may seem remarkable, because, from the 1820s onwards, discussions about the universities in Sweden were exceptionally lively. They were concerned with the fundamental questions of the aims of higher education and the status of the universities in civil society.

48. View over the Uppsala of the late romantic idyll from the north. In the background is the Carolina rediviva. Wood engraving after a drawing by A. Nay in Förr och nu *(1875).*

These discussions were to a large extent official, the fruit of royal committees and interventions. Two opposing camps faced each other. On one side, there was the majority of the academics, led by the Uppsala teachers and captivated by the reactionary educational standards of romanticism, and, on the other, the liberals, who usually hailed from Stockholm. They were faithful to the ideas of the Enlightenment and held fast to social utility as the lodestar of university education. In the age of incipient industrialism, the universities must serve the aims of economic progress and mankind's earthly happiness. The antagonism between these two programmes was the very nerve centre of university policy in 19th-century Sweden. The future existence of the two Swedish small-town universities—primarily Uppsala—depended on the outcome of the conflict.

149

The discussion was first concerned with two problems—the university jurisdiction and the organization of medical education. It then broadened out and in what was called the "Grand Education Committee" (appointed in 1825) was expanded into a comprehensive analysis of the entire university system.

Right from the start, the aggressive liberal demand that the University of Uppsala should be closed and transferred to Stockholm presented a deadly menace to the established order; a central university for the whole country might perhaps be established there. There were foreign precedents, chiefly in Germany, where one small-town university after another had lately been closed down. The idea was first voiced by the liberal pioneer Johan Gabriel Richert. The dividing line between the two contending parties was drawn in the encounter between Richert and Erik Gustaf Geijer, the leader of the conservative wing in Uppsala. The issue was the University's jurisdiction, which Richert, as a member of a royal committee appointed in 1817, wished to abolish in all except official and disciplinary cases. He expounded his point of view in a pamphlet published in 1822 and entitled *Ett och annat om corporationer* (Some Comments on Corporations). He found the jurisdiction which the University had exercised over its members since the Middle Ages to be unreasonable, a survival of the guild philosophy which had no place in modern society. In Richert's eyes, the University of Uppsala as a whole was a mouldering monument to a bygone age, remote from the life-giving influences of the present time. The only remedy was to move it to Stockholm, where professors and students could work amid everyday political and economic life and thus focus their disciplines on the improvement of society. Geijer—the University's spokesman and a romantic—was horrified. He put forward his arguments in a pamphlet against Richert entitled *Nytt ett och annat i anledning af frågan om academiska jurisdictionen* (Some More Comments on the Question of University Jurisdiction) in 1823. The separate jurisdiction was in fact the seal on the freedom and integrity of the universities and of scholarly thought. Protected from government supervision and the passions of party politics, as in a "protected sanctuary", the University of Uppsala would work out its profoundest purpose in an idyllic small-town environment. This purpose was purely theoretical, because, to Geijer, the whole object of the University was to promote speculative thought and personality training in the neo-humanistic sense; every practical aim should be alien to academic education.

At the Riksdag of 1823, the liberal reformers renewed their attack on the University's "guild spirit". Richert's views provided the guide-lines; the bourgeois Stockholm press had disseminated them. Some of the reformers went to great lengths; Carl Henric Anckarsvärd was almost inclined to abolish the Swedish universities altogether. Gustaf Hjerta thought that at least the practical faculties (medicine and law) should be located in the capital, with is hospitals and its courts of law. Like many others, he dreamed of a flourishing central university in Stockholm, permeated by the progressive social and political currents of the time.

The new liberal ideas included the demand for up-to-date medical training. This was put forward by the Karolinska Institute, the newly founded school of medicine in Stockholm, which had a brilliant spokesman in Berzelius, the great chemist. The problem was evident and has already been indicated: should the young medical students derive their knowledge from books or should they be trained in an experimental and empirical spirit at laboratories and clinics in Stockholm? The question had a formal aspect. The Karolinska Institute had been planned as a purely practical "school of applied medicine", intended for the training not of real doctors but of "barber-surgeons" in what was at that time their "craft". After the decision in 1812, that university-trained doctors who aspired to public medical posts must also obtain the degree of Master of Surgery at the Institute, there was increased tension between the Institute and the university faculties of medicine. The Institute, whose teaching staff, headed by Berzelius, could easily stand comparison with the faculties at Uppsala or Lund, soon gained further ground. The surgeons who graduated there were given the right to practise medicine as a whole and a regulation in 1822 enlarged the examination which all prospective medical officers had to take at the Institute, besides their probationary service at the Serafimer Hospital in Stockholm. Berzelius, who was responsible for the regulation, wished to go even further. In his view, the Institute should have the statutory right to give complete medical training, in all respects equal to that provided by the medical faculties. As a matter of fact, it should be of higher quality, on account of the opportunities offered by the big Stockholm hospitals.

There was great resentment at this in both Uppsala and Lund. It was bad enough that the Karolinska Institute—which was really an ordinary school for craftsmen—had monopolized an examination which should devolve only on the universities. It would be a sheer catastrophe if the ambitions of Berzelius and the Institute were to be satisfied *in toto;* the medical faculties would then become superfluous and perish. In Uppsala, attempts were made to sabotage the new regulations as far as possible. At length (1829), a thunderbolt was hurled at Berzelius, modern research in natural science and the re-organization of medical training. It took the form of a polemical pamphlet entitled *Om Carolinska Institutet* (On the Karolinska Institute) published under the impenetrable pseudonym of

E.R.U.F. (the initial letters of the Swedish phrase *En Röst Ur Fängelset* (A Voice from Prison)) by Israel Hwasser, who was at that time Professor of Medicine at Helsingfors (Helsinki) but who moved to Uppsala in the following year. This pamphlet is a masterpiece in the uninhibited neo-romantic genre. Fanatically loyal to its conception of philosophy and the sciences as an indivisible, divinely instituted whole, Hwasser asserted that the removal of the Uppsala faculty to Stockholm would involve a violation of the eternal order. Medicine in the higher sense (the only kind that was valid to Hwasser) was not an empirical science but a visionary knowledge of the innermost essence of life, which, as a fundamental idea, should permeate all other sciences, including statesmanship. Thus, as it was the noblest of the faculties, it could fulfil its destiny only in a privileged university environment, in which nothing would disturb the profound contemplation of its devotees.

The Grand Education Committee had already presented its report when Hwasser was writing. This report, it was thought, would decide the fate of the Swedish universities and the Swedish educational system. The effort was an impressive one. The leading intellectual and cultural personalities of the time sat on this Committee (it was referred to as "the geniuses")—Tegnér, Geijer, Johan Olof Wallin, Berzelius, Carl Adolf Agardh, of Lund, Hans Järta, Samuel Grubbe, the Uppsala philosopher, and August von Hartmansdorff, the politician. It was in the nature of things that so many brilliant cooks would be unable to make a strong broth. The work of the Committee was crippled by profound internal antagonisms. However, the conservative camp was the more numerous and succeeded in getting its own way on essential points, as regarded both the university policy and the schools. It was led by the three men from Uppsala—Geijer, Grubbe and Järta, who was an experienced, practical politician. They fought for pure and elevated scientific research, unblemished by current considerations, and therefore defended the traditional, provincial universities as indispensable; no good could be expected of Stockholm. They were opposed by an insignificant left wing, represented by Berzelius and Agardh, the botanist, who wanted a thorough reform of both the universities and the grammar schools. A centre party, including Tegnér and Hartmansdorff, mediated between the two others. To the minority, the question of the content of higher education was of fundamental importance. This question came to a head in their attitude to the classical languages. As eminent natural scientists, Berzelius and Agardh regarded their dominating position as harmful; Agardh, in particular, took a hard line and condemned high humanistic culture as a kind of "anaesthetic". Euclid was just as indispensable as Plato; the times demanded that Latin and Greek should give way to the modern natural sciences, in which

152

men inquired into the causes of objective phenomena. Neither he nor Berzelius gained the hearing they sought. Berzelius, who also continued to
struggle on behalf of the Karolinska Institute and again demanded that all
medical training should be concentrated there, soon gave up, disappointed
and embittered. There was nothing he could do about the "obscurantists"
and the "illiberals" (Geijer and Järta) and he refused to attend the Committee's discussions. Neo-humanism was firmly in the saddle. It was
promoted primarily by Järta; studies of the classics gave the student a
feeling for the Beautiful and the Noble, which raise mankind above the
beasts.

The main report of the Education Committee (1828) is an exemplary
summary of the conservative majority's view of the university. Grubbe,
the philosopher, was responsible for the wording. The background of
German romanticism, chiefly the influence of Schleiermacher, is obvious.
There was an "idea of the university" which must not give way to the

49. *Israel Hwasser, the
legendary Professor of
Medicine, in four silhou-
ettes by Bernard Hwas-
ser. At the top, Hwasser
is "walking along, look-
ing at the stars" and "taking his wife home on a
winter evening"; at the
bottom, he is "having a
little quarrel" and "walking in his garden with a
casquet on his head".
Nordic Museum, Stock-
holm.*

clamorous demands of the modern age. This meant that the function of the universities was to imbue the nation's youth with the true scientific spirit and to serve as the focal points of its intellectual life. Education must therefore be universal, must join together all the sciences to form a harmonious whole and must strive unceasingly towards "the higher and the ideal". It was precisely this that constituted its usefulness to the state and society. In undisturbed tranquillity, prospective civil servants at the universities would be pervaded by an attitude to life and a comprehensive theoretical knowledge without which they would relapse into contemptible "mechanical routine" in their future professions; only then could they become "living organs in the great system of society". The study of the classical languages and literatures occupied a key position in this training in intellectual and moral awareness, but the natural sciences were also of value, provided that they were pursued in a philosophical spirit. The Committee was of the opinion that all these purposes could be successfully realized only at the two universities that already existed in Uppsala and Lund. The idea of replacing them by a national university in Stockholm was rejected. It would prove costly, but that was not all. For moral reasons, the capital, with its temptations, would be a dangerous place for the students (this "noble association of youth", as Hwasser called them). The political discussions in the capital also seemed harmful, as they might prematurely confuse the students' immature minds and impede their true education. The matter could hardly be more lucidly stated—the universities were to inspire society by remaining outside it. The practical "schools of applied arts and crafts" (primarily the Karolinska Institute), whose sole aim was to prepare the student directly for an occupation, represented something entirely different; they could with advantage be located in Stockholm. But they could never replace the universities, and studies at them should be preceded by academic studies of the true scientific culture, which gave practical experience a higher value.

The Education Committee stood up for tradition; Uppsala and Lund were permitted to retain their universities and academic education its basic character of aloofness from the world. Even towards the mid 19th century, Sweden was still a backward agricultural country without a flourishing urban culture; from this point of view, it was natural that its intellectual life should still be concentrated in the two country towns that had universities.

But the question of siting universities in provincial towns or in big cities was still not yet settled. The discussion about the Karolinska Institute could still be used as a battering-ram. At the end of the 1830s, a fresh feud flared up between Berzelius and Hwasser. The former reiterated his claims that Stockholm was superior as a place for medical training, where it should also be possible to acquire the degree of Doctor of Medicine (1837). This proposal was naturally rejected in Uppsala and Lund. Three years later, Hwasser published the documents in the case, together with an important addition: Stockholm and the Karolinska Institute were the home of the most detestable materialism; only at a complete university could medical students and others learn to comprehend science as the doctrine of "the eternally true, the essential in the world of thought". At the Riksdag of 1840–41, Berzelius's claims on the Institute's behalf were received with sympathy by the liberal opposition, but no fundamental decision was made.

When the university question in its widest sense again came to the fore 10 years later, it had to some extent changed its character. The most grandiose romantic arguments in Uppsala's favour had lost their cogency. Financial reasons and considerations of practical suitability now played a greater part. But the problem itself was as acute as ever: should the University of Uppsala (and possibly Lund as well) be closed down and replaced by a university in Stockholm? This question was raised again and again at the Riksdagar in the 1850s; the liberals and the farmers, supported by the *Aftonbladet* newspaper, were eager supporters of the proposal. "These monstrosities, which continue from century to century" was how a member of the Estate of the Peasants in the 1850–51 Riksdag referred to Sweden's provincial universities. Two years later, a fellow-member of the same Estate demanded that they should be removed to the capital. As in the Gustavian period, an outcry was raised in progressive Stockholm circles against Uppsala's decay and obsolescence. This was at a time when the Uppsala students in the Scandinavian movement were coming forward as the heroes of the bourgeoisie. At the Scandinavian student assembly in 1856, Pehr Henrik Malmsten, a professor at the Karolinska Institute, made a speech in which he said that it was deplorable that the capital of Sweden had no university of its own; it must become the centre of the nation's intellectual life, like Copenhagen and Oslo. This theme was immediately taken up in *Aftonbladet*, oddly enough by an advocate of Uppsala humanism, Carl Edvard Zedritz, the Professor of Latin. He was of the opinion that Stockholm had many advantages as a university city. There was "a freer outlook on life and on society" there, theatres and concerts for aesthetic education and opportunities of earning additional income.

In the autumn of 1856, the question was again raised in the Riksdag after motions had been submitted from several quarters. The traditional strains were heard; it was time to abolish the small-town universities and at least the faculties of medicine and law should be moved to Stockholm. When the matter was discussed in committee, any radical change was

155

50. "Uppsala depicted in 12 views and on the topographic plane". Lithograph by Johan Way, the drawing master of the University (1842).

opposed; on the other hand, the central school of medicine in Stockholm for which Berzelius yearned was recommended. There was great disquiet in Uppsala. Gustaf Svanberg, the Professor of Astronomy, intervened in Uppsala's defence in a witty and pointed pamphlet entitled *Hufvudstad och universitet* (Capital and University, 1857); this was followed by a lively and at times violent debate in the press. The result of all the fuss was that the Riksdag requested an inquiry into the position of the medical faculties. This was held in 1858 and was, on paper, a success for the Stockholm interests; however, Mesterton, the surgeon who

156

was the Uppsala representative on the committee, dissented from the report of the inquiry and urged that the university faculties should remain in being. A new storm broke out in the Riksdag of that year, in pamphlets and in the press and extended to the university question as a whole. Hwasser, who was still alive, again laid his authority on the scales and Svanberg, Mesterton and Ribbing, the philosopher, also fought for Uppsala's cause, emphasizing, amongst other things, the cost of moving the university. The liberal *Aftonbladet*, which was always their main opponent, did not mince its words: it said that the bright students were dazzled by the atmosphere in Uppsala and the duller ones became "lunatic dreamers and conceited and intolerant pedants".

But such outbursts made no difference. When it came to the crunch, the Riksdag was no more willing than before to disturb the *status quo*. Uppsala and Lund were also permitted to retain their faculties of medicine. The only concession which the Karolinska Institute gained was that in future it might also award the Licentiate of Medicine degree (1861). The old passions flared up again for the last time at the Riksdag of 1862–63, but this was the last round. All the old arguments and a few new ones were aired. A new champion on behalf of Uppsala and against Stockholm now appeared, remarkably enough in the person of the young liberal fighting-cock, Adolf Hedin, who found it impossible to accept the idea that the transfer of the allegedly stagnating University of Uppsala to Stockholm would miraculously transform it. After that, things calmed down. No one wished any longer to overthrow the University of Uppsala, least of all after the new Stockholm *Högskola* opened in the 1870s and the Karolinska Institute received the right in 1873 to award the Bachelor of Medicine degree.

2

While the great university controversy was in progress, everything was going on as usual in Uppsala. Whether the attacks of the liberal progressives were justified or not, it is in any case arguable that between 1810 and 1850 the University went through a period of some distinction, of which both its contemporaries and posterity were well aware. It was not of the same kind as that which had occurred in the 18th century, when brilliant natural scientists brought Uppsala European fame. During the age of romanticism, the University was turned in upon itself (this was precisely what its enemies complained about); it was a purely national educational establishment, where a series of excellent teachers captivated the students and felt that they had done their duty if they raised Swedish humanistic culture to a higher intellectual level. It was these men—primarily Geijer, Grubbe, Atterbom and other romanticists, such as Törneros and Palmblad—who gave Uppsala its distinctive character. Hwasser soon appeared on the scene and the Boströmian philosophy took shape as the purest expression of academic idealism above the storms of time. All this could be regarded as reactionary and old-fashioned, even when compared with the University of Lund, where fresher breezes were blowing. But no one denied the intellectual influence which emanated from romantic Uppsala and this explained the intensity of the attacks.

The Education Committee had also been busy with minor matters and had scrutinized the universities' needs on point after point and called for improvements. These improvements were carried out only to a limited extent and new proposals for reform were issued in the following period. They concerned both universities, Uppsala and Lund, in an endeavour to bring them under common regulations. The many minor rules and ordinances which had come into existence over the years necessitated an overhaul of the old university constitutions. But it was not until the Riksdag of 1840–41 that it was actually decided that they should be revised. Committees at Uppsala and Lund set to work on the task—the Uppsala committee even produced complete draft constitutions—and in 1846 a royal committee was appointed to draw up a definitive proposal. On this committee, Uppsala was represented by Elias Fries, the botanist. But progress was slow and it was not until 2 April 1852 that the King-in-Council issued the new statutes governing the Universities of Uppsala and Lund. This meant that both the Swedish universities were now subject to uniform national legislation, in the interests of modern bureaucracy.

The 1852 constitutions were hardly a masterpiece (the members of the committee had proceeded cautiously) and the regulations on examinations in the Faculties of Arts, which were announced separately in 1853, were also short-lived. There was general dissatisfaction with them at the universities and in 1865 the King-in-Council requested that the two universities should produce proposals for something better. There was a lively discussion in the Faculty of Arts at Uppsala and the matter dragged on. The new regulations, issued finally in 1870, were based mainly on the Uppsala proposal. They were in part an expression of radically new ideas and lasted in important respects for nearly a century. However, minor defects were discovered immediately and the necessary amendments were made by letters patent issued in 1877 and 1879.

The main constitutions of 1852 did not prove to be adequate in the long run either. Just over 20 years later, it was again time for a revision, which was rapidly carried out by a committee under the chairmanship of Archbishop Anton Niklas Sundberg. This revision was, in the main, approved by the Government and formed the basis of the new university statutes issued in January 1876. These too were cautious but contained some innovations in the university organization which are still in existence.

Throughout the 19th century, the Chancellor, the Pro-Chancellor (the Archbishop), the Rector, the Senate and the Council were responsible for the administration of the University of Uppsala. After the lamentable death of Axel von Fersen, the last Gustavian Chancellor, in 1810, Prince Karl Johan, the new successor to the throne, was chosen to succeed him, and the revived royalist tradition was retained for the time being. First Prince Oskar and the Prince Karl acted as University Chancellors in both Uppsala and Lund, as a sign that the old particularism was fading away. But at the election of Chancellor in 1859, the royal family was again abandoned and Gustaf A. Sparre, the President of the Court of Appeal, was chosen as joint Chancellor of both universities. As regarded the Chancellor, the constitutions of 1852 merely said that the same man could hold the post at both universities but that this was not necessary. Besides, an attempt to co-ordinate the universities at the Chancellor level had been made as early as 1801, when a Chancellors' Guild was formed, consisting of the Chancellors of the three existing universities, their task being to be responsible for educational work in Sweden. This Guild took the initiative in some valuable projects but was dissolved in connection with the revolution in 1809.

In the course of time, the Rector (*rector magnificus*) gained greater influence on the University administration. Even under the statutes of 1852, each Rector-elect was to take office according to the date of his authorization, but the mandate period was extended to one academic year and the constitutions of 1876 went even further. As a result of the multiplicity of new teaching posts and institutes, it was found to be important to confer a degree of permanence on the local executive officers and it was therefore decided that the most suitable candidate should be chosen as Rector for a period of two years, irrespective of length of service. The same reasoning motivated the change in the Council elections which was made at this time. Its members, who had hitherto changed annually, were henceforth to be elected for a three-year period. The Senate still consisted of the assembled body of professors and was ultimately responsible for the University's scholarly and financial affairs, but, from 1826 onwards, it dealt only with questions of major importance. Minor administrative matters were dealt with by the Council, which now ceased to decide or prepare the financial business, which was instead entrusted to a financial committee (established in Uppsala in 1869) consisting of the Bursar and three members appointed for three years.

The Senate's work load was reduced in one important respect from 1852 onwards. The University jurisdiction was finally abolished. The stubborn resistance to this reform offered by Geijer and other members of the University had long prevented its implementation. Thus, after exhaustive deliberations, the Education Committee decided in its report of 1828 that the universities' jurisdiction should be retained. The report makes no mention of its significance as a safeguard of academic freedom. Its wording is practical and concrete: the special jurisdiction could not be separated from the "paternal authority" which the Senate exercised over the students and to which the teachers also might well be subjected. But the demands for its abolition were not silenced. The question was raised in the Riksdag of 1840–41, and in the two committees which afterwards worked in Uppsala and Lund on the new university statutes, the jurisdiction was one of the main issues. The Uppsala professors wished to retain it as long as possible but finally yielded and in the spring of 1852 the matter was settled by the promulgation of letters patent. The Senate and the Council were allowed to retain their disciplinary powers over the students and their right of inspection as regarded the teachers, but their jurisdiction was to cease immediately in all other cases, which were to be referred to a public court. The Swedish universities thereby lost their mediaeval corporative privilege and were finally fitted into civil society.

Their isolation was also broken in another important field—that of finance. The change was most striking at Uppsala, where the University had lived well for 200 years on the yield from the Gustavian hereditary estates. These estates proved to be insufficient as the University grew during the 19th century through the coming into existence of new professorships, institutes and buildings. The Education Committee produced a good survey of the situation in the 1820s. At that time (1826), the University's total income in corn and cash from Gustavus Adolphus's donation amounted to 75,419 riksdaler, including the yield from the estates given by Charles XI for the upkeep of the noble exercises. The total expenditure, as stated in the budget for the University in 1813, amounted to 74,137 riksdaler. Thus, there was a small surplus, but this was due to casual circumstances and the outlook was thought to be gloomy. The new Library building was swallowing up large sums, the professors' salaries must, according to the Committee, be raised until they reached at least the same level as those in Lund, and many of the current grants (to the Library, the Hospital, etc.) were not sufficient. If the University was to be able to carry out its tasks and keep abreast of the times, the State must finally intervene and order a fixed annual grant to be paid for its running costs. The Education Committee's demand yielded results. The Riksdag of 1830 decided that the Universities of Uppsala and Lund should receive annual government grants, primarily in order to raise the teachers' salaries. Uppsala was allocated 8,550 riksdaler, which were included in the ordinary budget from 1834 onwards. This was an insignificant amount but was later continuously increased, so that the total government contribution to the University's costs—now by no means intended for salaries alone—rose to over 300,000 crowns by the end of the 1870s.

For a long time, the teachers' salaries were calculated in the old way —in corn—and they consequently varied with the price of corn. In the 1820s, a professor on the permanent staff had to support himself and his family on 215 barrels (1,430 riksdaler), while an *adjunkt* (assistant) had to manage on 65 barrels. Only the theologians and a couple of others held prebends and prospered; the rest still had to eke out their salaries by giving private tuition (*collegia*) until far into the 19th century. However, with the newly acquired government grant, the professorial salary gradually increased and the amount was fixed; about 1860 it was 4,500 crowns (three-quarters in corn and one-quarter in government grant) and in the 1870s it was 6,000 crowns. The *adjunkter* now received half of a professor's salary and were obliged to give two public lectures per week. In 1852, six fellowship grants for the previously unpaid *docenter* were introduced; in the 1870s, the number was increased to 16, each of 1 000–1,500 crowns and payable for three years with a three-year extension. This created, for good and ill, the present institution of the temporary *docent*, which is peculiar to Sweden but is still maintained, although the subject of much discussion. The introduction at long last (1873) of the right of a jaded professor or *adjunkt* to retire at the age of 65 and enjoy his *otium* was a blessing both to the individual teacher and to the University. But the reform cost money in the form of additional *emeritus* salaries over and above the few which already existed.

The development indicated here, with the Swedish State as the increasingly open-handed contributor of funds for the universities' work, led to changes in the external conditions of both of them. Even in earlier centuries, the University of Uppsala had been subjected to control and often heavy-handed interference on the part of the State authorities. But as it was financially self-supporting, it was not dependent at every instant on the favour of the Government or the Estates but retained its status as a privileged corporation of teachers and students. The situation was different when the State began to assume responsibility for running the University. It now became one educational establishment among others in the bureaucratic society of the 19th century and had to defend its interests in accordance with the rules of the political game. This defence was conducted mainly in the Riksdag, where, especially about the middle of the century, university questions played an important part and where the decisions were made. It was therefore of importance that, from the 1828–30 Riksdag onwards and as long as the Riksdag of the four Estates lasted, the two Swedish universities had the right to send their own representatives to the Estate of the Clergy (two members of a secular faculty from each university). Geijer was chosen as the first representative of Uppsala and was later followed by Elias Fries, the botanist, who was a mild man but by no means unversed in worldly matters. The universities' interests could now be brought up directly in the course of the Riksdag's work. Moreover, the establishment of the Ministry of Education and Ecclesiastical Affairs in 1840 opened up an easier means of access to the government, the more so as several outstanding academics held the post of Minister, including, in the 1860s and 1870s, F. F. Carlson, the Uppsala historian, who was one of the re-organizers of the Swedish educational system and worked energetically to reform the universities. Under these circumstances, the office of Chancellor lost its old significance. The Chancellor was now shared by both the universities and became merely an intermediary between the academic authorities, on the one hand, and the Riksdag and the government, on the other, with no opportunity to exercise either paternal power over those below him or any real influence on those above him.

During the 19th century, the work of reform was concentrated to a large extent on the expansion of the University of Uppsala by the creation of new professorships and institutes. In a few decades around and after the middle of the century, the University changed more rapidly than at any time since Gustavus Adolphus's reign. The number of professors on the permanent staff was 21 (22) in the 1820s, i.e. scarcely more than during the 17th century; in addition, there were 22 (24) *adjunkter* and 21 unpaid *docenter*. Fifty years later, the professors numbered 34, the *adjunkter* (temporary professors) 18 and the *docenter* 54, together with 4 assistants (110 university teachers in all). The structure of the teaching body was also changed at this time. After prolonged discussions and complicated manoeuvres, the issue of letters patent in 1877 implemented the suggestion which had originally emanated from Uppsala—that the ancient institution of the *adjunkt* should be abolished at both the Swedish universities. The under-paid, dependent and over-worked university *adjunkter* were gradually replaced by non-established professors (18 in Uppsala). However, their salary was still less than that of an established professor and the holders of the new independent posts had to carry out the full teaching duties but were not members of the Senate. The creation of the new *docent* fellowships led to the *docenter* being incorporated on a firmer footing into the scholarly and educational activities of the University.

The new professorships and new subjects created during this period

162

reflected the progress and increasing specialization of the different disciplines. It is significant that the Faculty of Theology remained unchanged; no new top posts were created there. The Faculty of Arts acquired five new professorships from the 1830s onwards. The first of them—and the first new chair to be established in Uppsala for many a long year—was the professorship of aesthetics and modern literature (1835), which was now separated from the post of Librarian; its first holder was Atterbom. Two new professorships were established in 1858—one in Scandinavian languages (Carl Säve) and the other in modern European languages (Carl Wilhelm Böttiger). The natural sciences were reinforced by two chairs—one in mineralogy and geology (1852), which was detached from the old chair of chemistry and was long occupied by the Walmstedt family, father and son, and the other in zoology (Wilhelm Lilljeborg, 1854). Moreover, the professorship of botany was at this time transferred from the Faculty of Medicine, by converting the Borgström chair of economics (see above, p. 106), which was long occupied by Elias Fries, into a combined chair of botany and practical economics. Thus, natural science received its due share of the improvements, despite the prevalent atmosphere in Uppsala. The tendency is even more obvious if we consider the Faculty of Medicine, the number of whose permanent professorships was doubled during the same period. A chair of surgery and obstetrics, separate from that of anatomy, came into existence in 1837. In the 1850s, the Linnaean chair of natural history was converted into a professorship of pharmacology and medical chemistry and a new chair of pathology was established, with Per Hedenius as its first occupant. Somewhat later (1864), Uppsala and Sweden gained their first Professor of Physiology in Frithiof Holmgren, and a temporary professorship of psychiatry was established at the same time. In a short time—as a kind of retort to the challenge from the Karolinska Institute—the Faculty of Medicine was transformed and expanded in accordance with the requirements of modern research and teaching.

The lawyers did not go away empty-handed either. The two professorships which the Faculty possessed at the beginning of the century had become five by the 1860s. The new creations were a chair of criminal law and legal procedure, a chair of Swedish constitutional law with ecclesiastical and international law, and a chair of Roman law with general jurisprudence and the history of law.

The demands made on the professors were gradually made more stringent. It was no longer possible to take possession of a professorial chair without scholarly qualifications. The statutes of 1852 contained for the first time the classical wording that only "the degree of scholarly ability displayed" should be adduced in the appointment of a professor. At the

163

same time, it began to be regarded as a matter of course, almost as a duty, that the professors should be actively engaged in research. They could publish their results in the *Uppsala universitets årsskrift*, which was issued from 1861 onwards.

The expansion of the teaching staff in the mid 19th century had hardly any immediate connection with a corresponding increase in the number of students, which remained more or less constant at this time. But *in toto*, throughout the period 1790–1875, the number of students attending the University rose steeply, from about 500 at the turn of the century to approximately 1500 in the 1870s, i.e. a threefold increase. This represented a considerable educational expansion, but it occurred by fits and starts, with the first real increase between 1805 and 1825 and the second from about 1860 onwards. Between these dates, the number of students remained fairly constant at about 900. This figure was rather less than that which had obtained during the greater part of the 17th century.

One of the main objects of university reform in the 19th century was the academic instruction and examinations. As will be recalled, at the end of the previous century everything in this respect was still more or less as it had been in the old days. The students in the two largest faculties—the Faculty of Arts and the Faculty of Theology—were not purposefully prepared for their future careers. The attempt to make the Swedish universities serviceable at last in these respects was an important task.

The reforms began with the training of the clergy. At best, the ordinands might learn a little theology at the universities, but this was not essential for prospective ministers and there was no mention of the art of preaching and other pastoral skills. The training of the Swedish clergy, it was said in 1800, was beneath contempt. Reforms were introduced in 1806 in Uppsala (and in 1809 in Lund). The Chancellors' Guild took the initiative in instituting a special theological seminary, attendance at which was compulsory for all ordinands and where they could learn the elements of practical theology in a one-year course. The director of the seminary was Samuel Ödmann, the finest intelligence in the Faculty at this time; he was always bed-ridden on account of an imaginary illness but was otherwise, in spite of his continual tobacco-smoking, fitter than any of his colleagues. However, as the years passed, complaints were raised that the seminarists were being released with far too little knowledge of real theology and in 1831 the theological studies were re-organized in

51. The teachers in the Faculty of Medicine in 1863. In the left-hand row, from the top, Dr. Edvard Clason (anatomy), Professor August Almén (medical and physiological chemistry) and Dr. Fredrik Björnström (theoretical and practical medicine); in the middle row, Professors Carl Mesterton (surgery), Olof Glas (theoretical

and practical medicine), Fredrik Sundevall (anatomy) and Per Hedenius (patho-logy); in the right-hand row, Dr. Frithiof Holmgren (physiology), Professor Gustaf Kjellberg (psychiatry) and Dr. Robert Fristedt (pharmacology).

165

accordance with the proposals of the Education Committee. The seminary was closed and instead it was prescribed that the ordinand should have secured pass marks in all the Faculty subjects and have some training in preaching (what was called the "dimission degree"). This meant that the ordinands were actually compelled to read theology, but they did not as yet have to pass an examination for the degree of *teologie kandidat* (B.D.). In 1865—later than in the other faculties—a propaedeutic examination in the Faculty of Arts was introduced prior to entry on theological training.

What was called "clerical or pastoral medicine" (introduced by letters patent in 1813) was a peculiar element in this training. The idea went back to Linnaeus and the 18th century. On account of the poor or non-existent medical care available in the country districts, it was desirable that the clergy, after a period of medical training, should be able to help sick parishioners to recover their health. The question had been raised at the 1809 Riksdag by Carl Trafvenfelt, a well-known doctor. From the funds allotted, 50 scholarships in "clerical medicine", worth 100 riksdaler each, were arranged and 34 of them went to the University of Uppsala. The holders had to pledge themselves to undertake several terms of medical study. The arrangement seemed to work well. However, it soon fell into disuse; the ordinands found it a burden to have to struggle with medicine in addition to their ordinary training and in 1841 Uppsala and Lund ceased to hold courses and examinations in what was actually called the "Medico-theological Faculty".

Progress was slow in the Faculty of Arts. The traditional idea that the prospective masters should browse through all the Faculty subjects survived almost throughout the 19th century. It was explicitly defended by the Education Committee, which had no other idea than that the students should strive in the old way to acquire the broadest possible general education. At Uppsala, the public examination for the bachelor's or master's degree, which was held in the Senate Hall, called for a pass or *approbatur* in at least eight of the 13 subjects taught in the Faculty; an *admittitur* (he is admitted) sufficed in the remaining five. In his memoirs, Gustaf Svanberg, who later became Professor of Astronomy, gives a vivid picture of the procedure of taking degrees in this Faculty in the 1820s. Svanberg, who was a model student, started off on the way to Parnassus by passing the compulsory "great" theological examination (it was in fact a mere trifle); he then wrote his first Latin composition, defended a thesis *pro exercitio* and after that wrote his Latin composition *pro gradu*. He was bent on getting his master's degree at the 1824 conferment and, as the date of the ceremony approached, began to take *viva voce* examinations at a rapid rate in one subject after another. He sat these examinations at the homes of the professors, who made notes of the

52. *Samuel Ödmann, the perpetually bedridden Professor of Theology. Oil painting by J. G. Sandberg (1830). The Småland nation.*

grades awarded for their own use. It was only then that the public examination took place before the assembled Faculty, as prescribed in the constitutions. Everything depended on this and all 13 subjects were included. But the professors knew the ability of each candidate on account of the preceding private examinations; they were loth to change their assessments and the public examination therefore became mostly a matter of form. Svanberg succeeded brilliantly; he received altogether no less than 25 marks (on the average, approximately a *cum laude* in every subject) and, after he had defended his thesis *pro gradu*, could begin thinking about his graduation robes. That year, his record was surpassed only by Boström, the philosopher.

The conferment of masters' degrees was still held only every three years, in the Cathedral, with about 75 recipients. Svanberg—if I may dwell on him—donned under protest the regulation garb: a hired black jacket dating from the previous century, a red silk sash round the waist, a cloak, knee-breeches with red rosettes, white stockings and a low-crowned black hat under one arm—in short, what was called the "Swedish costume". The conferment ceremony was followed by a grand dinner in the Linnaeus Hall at the Botanical Gardens. Svanberg himself regarded the conferment ceremony almost as a joke and so, but to a greater extent, did his fellow-sufferer, Erik Sjöberg-Vitalis, a cynical poet, who gave vent to his feelings in his poem "Promotionen" (The Conferment of Degrees):

> In Solon's time, there were in Greece
> Counting all the islands
> And the whole of Asia Minor, seven wise men;
> But in eighteen hundred and twenty-four
> Upon the bare banks of the Fyris
> Seventy-six came out of nothing ...
>
> We had also already undergone
> The really difficult test of knowledge,
> The publication of a small printed work
> Which a professor had written on our behalf
> And we had also defended it from the lectern
> In high-sounding, empty phrases ...
>
> The thin legs shine in white stockings.
> Each graduate walks to the heights of honour
> As silver-footed as Homer's Thetis,
> And where the short breeches reach their limit
> Red roses grow upon our knees.

It soon became increasingly clear that the time-honoured system of education in the Faculty of Arts had outlived its usefulness. The criticisms bore especially on the scope of the bachelor's degree and the defence of the master's thesis. The old omnivorousness was out of place in modern times, especially as new subjects—chiefly the natural sciences—had been admitted to the Faculty and were clamouring for attention. But the first step was not taken until the new degree regulations were issued in 1853. These laid it down that candidates for degrees in arts and sciences need no longer pass examinations in all the subjects taught in the Faculty; it would be sufficient if they obtained 12 pass marks, which were to be gained in six compulsory subjects and certain other optional subjects. However, this reform was regarded as being half-hearted and in the 1860s a lively discussion began in university circles concerning the scope of the bachelor's degree. The Government referred the matter to the universities for their comments. The proposal drafted in Uppsala formed the basis of the new regulations on degrees in arts and sciences introduced in 1870. They inaugurated a new era and in some respects are still valid today. Studies in arts and sciences were divided into two stages, each with its own degree (the bachelor's degree and the licentiate). The bachelor's degree called for eight pass marks, but the candidate need take only five

53. Uniforms for beadles and cursors at the University. These uniforms, which came into existence in the reign of Karl XIII, were still in use in the middle of the last century. From Minnen från Nordiska museet *I (1879–85).*

compulsory subjects (theoretical philosophy, Latin, history, Scandinavian languages and mathematics or one of the natural sciences). Other subjects were added only if they were needed to reach the required total marks. However, the bachelor's degree still had a humanistic stamp. Only one of the five subjects was a science, a circumstance which was soon found to be unreasonable; the defect was rectified by a regulation in 1877, whereby prospective scientists were allowed to take degrees which included only two compulsory humanistic subjects. Latin was one of these. The question of its status in university education had become increasingly controversial. The idealistic guardians of tradition held stubbornly fast to the requirement of Latin, as a safeguard against barbarism, and when in 1879 only one compulsory subject was considered to be sufficient, it was Latin that was retained. But Greek and the Latin composition for the bachelor's degree were abolished.

The licentiate degree, which was introduced in 1870 and was to survive for a century, involved a further specialization in preparation for the doctorate. It comprised at least five marks in three subjects and a licentiate thesis in one of them. Studies in the Faculty of Arts were becoming vocationally orientated.

The old type of public disputation in defence of the master's thesis survived until 1852, though it became increasingly old-fashioned and the subject of controversy. It then ceased to be a proof of good Latinity and dialectic skill and became instead a specimen of scholarship, for which the respondent alone was responsible; at the same time, the old disputation *pro exercitio* was abolished. Under the new constitutions, the master's thesis was always to be written by the respondent and to be defended by him without interference from the president. In addition, Swedish was admitted for a wide range of subjects; the thesis could be written and defended in Latin or in Swedish and before long the modern European languages were also permitted in certain cases. The opponents (two at most) were chosen by the author. The conferment of masters' degrees could still be arranged only every three years, but the number of recipients was no longer limited; however, it was reduced by the new and stricter requirements. The titles created certain problems. Candidates from the Faculty of Arts were still made only masters, but the master's diploma of the 1850s used the double Latin title of "philosophiae doctor et artium liberalium magister" and the recipients unblushingly used the title of doctor. This practice was not officially confirmed until 1870, after which date the graduates of the Faculty of Arts were awarded the doctorate, thus introducing full equality between all the faculties.

Medical training in Uppsala, which had been severely attacked during the battle with the Karolinska Institute, underwent few changes. The question of how much basic general knowledge a medical student needed was elucidated by the 1852 statutes and a supplementary regulation providing for a preparatory "medico-philosophical" examination for eight marks, which every medical student had to pass in the Faculty of Arts. The medical studies proper were divided, as before, into a theoretical part (*medicine kandidat,* M.B.) and a practical part (*medicine licentiat,* L.M.), separated by a period of clinical training in Stockholm. When the Faculty of Medicine at Uppsala emerged from its conflicts with the Stockholm doctors in a stronger and hardier condition and its continued existence was no longer threatened, the organization of medical training in Sweden was laid down by law in 1861. The *medicine kandidat* degree could be taken only at Uppsala or Lund, while the *medicine licentiat* degree, with its clinical specialization, could now also be gained at the Karolinska Institute.

From 1852–53 onwards, candidates seeking basic training in law (the

54. *Master's diploma printed on silk in 1857 for Robert Fristedt, who later became Professor of Pharmacology. University Library.*

171

degree of *juris utriusque kandidat*) had also to undergo a preliminary examination in the Faculty of Arts (what was called the *juridikofilen*). The *kandidat* degree was followed by the degrees of *juris licentiat* and *juris doktor*, which, then as now, few candidates passed. The majority of students in the Faculty of Law had much more modest ambitions. The civil-service examinations introduced in the 18th century for rapid entry into the civil-service departments still flourished; they were primarily legal in character, demanded little knowledge and were therefore very attractive. They were now four in number—those for the Courts of Appeal, for the central Government Offices, for mine officials and for the public-revenue departments (introduced in 1799). These examinations did not enjoy any great esteem, least of all that for entry into the public-revenue departments, which only required two terms' study, and those who worked for them were disdained as a kind of second-class students. Complaints were voiced again and again; according to the Education Committee, the examination for entry to the public-revenue departments was a sheer travesty and in the 1830s it was generally considered at the universities that the civil-service examinations were an unnecessary burden on the professors of law. But they were not re-organized until 1863, when the examinations for the Courts of Appeal and the Government Offices were retained, while the examination for the public-revenue departments was abolished and that for mine officials was transferred to the Faculty of Arts.

In the mid 19th century, the Swedish universities were still male corporations, where the students performed male rites. But the question of women's rights to higher education could no longer be dismissed. At the 1865 Riksdag, it was explicitly urged that Swedish women should be able to take degrees and to defend doctoral theses in the Faculty of Arts and the Faculty of Medicine. A lively discussion ensued in the Riksdag and at the universities. Woman's quiet role as wife and mother was praised, but even the reactionary Uppsala philosopher Sigurd Ribbing regarded her as suitable for medical training, though not, on the other hand, for such studies as called for "the use of sheer, isolated intellect". When this delicate problem was discussed by the Uppsala Senate in 1867, the flora of male arguments blossomed; greater intellectual culture would involve the malformation of women's minds and its acquisition would lead to risks of indelicate liaisons arising with their male fellow-students. The King-in-Council was largely of the same opinion. Letters patent issued in 1870 gave Swedish women the right to take the university-entrance examination and to be trained in the Faculty of Medicine for the medical profession, which was so well suited to their motherly instincts. The other faculties remained closed to them. But the fence was torn down only three

55. *Ellen Fries, the first woman Doctor of Philosophy in Sweden, received her doctoral degree in Uppsala in 1883. She eventually became Director of Studies at the Åhlin School in Stockholm.*

years later; women received the right to take all university degrees, except the licentiates of theology and law. This had only a moderate effect, as young women hesitated to grasp the outstretched hand. The first woman student in Uppsala was enrolled in 1873 and, 10 years later, Ellen Fries became the first woman Doctor of Philosophy at Uppsala and in Sweden.

Throughout the greater part of the 19th century, the instruction was given in the old, soporific forms. Public lectures and private *collegia* were for a long time the only forms of instruction offered. Individual teachers of brilliant talents, such as Geijer, could attract large and enthusiastic audiences, but most of the professors still read aloud monotonously from prepared manuscripts. It is true that the factual level had been raised. Elementary knowledge was avoided; according to an explicit direction in the 1852 constitutions, the lectures were to be aimed at "the students' independent scholarly development". But this did not make them any more interesting to the majority of students, and towards the middle of the century the situation appears to have become critical; the lecture halls were deserted. This applied chiefly to the courses in the humanities, which

173

were not organized on modern lines until the 1870s. It was then that the first seminars on the German model were instituted, in which the students themselves, prompted by the professor, discussed texts, questions of method and scholarly problems. A classics seminar had been founded in Lund as early as the 1860s, but it was not until 1878 that Uppsala adopted the new form of instruction in a three-part philological seminar. This form of instruction was financially supported by special government grants and was widely practised from the following decade onwards.

The students had already formed their own associations for scientific discussions and lectures. A tentative beginning was made in the 1840s, but these associations, from which the professors were usually excluded, were not established in permanent forms until a somewhat later date. The Students' Science Society was founded in 1853; it was soon divided into three sections. The Historical Society came into existence in 1862, the Philosophical Society in 1870 and the Aesthetic Society, which was founded by Carl Rupert Nyblom, in 1872.

The death struggle of Latin as the official academic language took place during the 19th century in Uppsala and the rest of the world. In the middle of the century, it was abolished as the compulsory language for disputations, while Swedish seems to have been accepted almost completely in lectures as early as the beginning of the century. The language of the Romans held its ground for a little longer at university ceremonies, such as the installation of a new Rector and the like, but here also the battle was largely won by about 1850 and thus an era came to an end. In the spirit of progress, the University of Uppsala was opened to the bourgeois world around it.

Its development in the 19th century was marked by the erection of a series of new university and institute buildings, which not only provided more favourable conditions for research and instruction but also transformed the little town of Uppsala, which about 1840 still had no more than 5000 inhabitants. The transformation began with the Botanicum and the Carolina Rediviva. Then, in mid century, the renovation of the institutes of natural science and medicine began, which confirmed that the University's continued existence after the years of crisis was assured for the future.

The new Institute of Botany in Slottsträdgården, for which Gustav III had donated land and money, was not ready for inauguration until May 1807, on the centenary of Linnaeus's birth. The herbaria and other natural-history collections had by then long been accommodated there. This splendid building, with its large orangery and its memorial hall to Linnaeus designed by Desprez in strictly neo-classical style, stood in the middle of the garden; it was at once a temple and a lecture hall and was generally

56. Prince Charles (later Karl XV) and Prince Gustaf attending a lecture on law by Professor Johan Chr. Lindblad in the Theatrum oeconomicum. Lithograph dated 1846.

regarded as the most splendid sight the University could show. Carl Peter Thunberg, the Professor of Natural History, made a lofty speech in Linnaeus's honour, followed by dinner amid the palms and the cypresses in the orangery and on the following day the Pro-Chancellor, the popular Archbishop Lindblom, entertained a large number of guests. But the real object of the temple service—the larger-than-life statue of Linnaeus in marble—was not set up until 1829, to the accompaniment of much choral singing. This statue was carved by Niclas Byström and was paid for by a collection among the students.

The history of the building of Carolina Rediviva was equally prolonged. The overcrowding of the book-rooms at the Gustavianum had become increasingly troublesome since Gustav III's plans for building a new Library had come to nothing (cf. above, p. 118), but no agreement could be reached on the solution of the problem. Then Karl Johan, the heir-apparent, intervened when he visited Uppsala in 1811 for the first time as

57. The new Institute of Botany in the former Castle Garden (Slottsträdgården),
built in neo-classical style by Jean Desprez and opened in 1807.

the University Chancellor. On a stroll through the town, he pointed to the
brow of the hill along Drottninggatan and decreed that this greatly desired
building should be erected there ("Well, that's settled then"). The site was
a magnificent one and Carl Fredrik Sundvall, the Royal Architect, soon
prepared designs for an equally magnificent palace, but, when the building
work began about 1820, the plans had become somewhat less pretentious.
Carolina Rediviva ("the Carolina resurrected"), as the new building was to
be called, finally took the form of a tall structure three storeys high, with
book-halls on the two lower floors and a hall for University banquets on
the upper floor, which was reached by an over-large staircase at the rear
of the building. The work progressed at a snail's pace and cost large sums
of money—315,000 riksdaler in all, of which the University paid all but
30,000, which Karl Johan donated from his private purse. It was not until
1841 that all the Library's 100,000 volumes were transferred from the
Gustavianum, under the direction of Johan Henrik Schröder, the Chief
Librarian, who was known as "Tiny" Schröder and was a well-known
figure at the University in his time, notorious for his servile fawning on
royalty and persons who could flaunt many decorations. Unfortunately,
during the removal he made a real mess of the collections, which had been

176

58. Interior view of the new Library premises in Carolina rediviva. Lithograph by A. Nay in S. Nordström's Upsala i taflor (1870).

increased by splendid donations since the turn of the century, principally the Nordin collection of manuscripts and the large libraries of Claes Fleming and Carl Gustaf von Brinkman. There was no special reading-room for visitors in the new building, but the book-halls were spacious and freely accessible.

The ceremonial or "Carolina" hall on the third floor, which could accommodate 2000 people, was a complete success, despite its bare and unadorned state. At conferment balls and Scandinavian student festivities, blazing with the light of innumerable wax candles, it expressed the new corporative spirit of the University, which united professors and students in the pomp of public ceremonies. But it served this purpose for only a few decades. The growing masses of books at Carolina Rediviva laid claim to the entire building and after the completion of the new University building in the 1880s, a thorough reconstruction was begun and resulted in the great staircase being demolished, reading-rooms being fitted up and the banqueting hall, which constituted a serious fire hazard, being gradually converted into a book store.

The great period of new buildings was the 1850s and 1860s. One institute

177

59. *The new University Hospital opened in 1867 at the old Castle toll-gate (Slotts-tullen). Photograph by Henri Osti. University Library.*

after another, in rapid succession, was then erected in the periphery of the old University area. The new Observatory on Kyrkogårdsgatan was completed in 1853; it was entirely the work of Gustaf Svanberg, the practical and capable Professor of Astronomy, who, together with Johan Way, the University draughtsman, was himself responsible for the plans and, like a latter-day Rudbeck, supervised every detail of the building. In 1859, it was time to abandon Torbern Bergman's old chemistry laboratory by the river and to move into the new Chemicum in the Carolina Park, an impressive multi-storey building in the Gothic style characteristic of the period, which also housed the Institutes of Mineralogy and Physics with their associated collections and the official residences of four professors.

However, the Faculty of Medicine was in the greatest need of better working conditions. In addition, the current situation required that the Karolinska Institute should be given tit for tat, by emphasizing ostentatiously that first-class medical training could be provided in Uppsala. The work began with the anatomists, who had long endured wretched conditions on the ground floor of the Senate House. The University itself paid for the building of a new Anatomicum at Islandet; it was completed in 1850, enlarged by later extensions and in use up to quite recent times. It was even more important, both for the students and the wretched patients, to improve the clinical instruction, which was the sphere in which everybody acknowledged that Stockholm was superior. A surgical clinic

178

was established in 1858 in Aurivillius (Ekerman) House near the Gusta-vianum, and at the same time Olof Glas extended the medical clinic in the old University Hospital (Nosocomium) in Riddartorget. But these measures were not by any means sufficient and within a short time a new era began to dawn for medical studies in Uppsala. A completely new and spaciously designed University Hospital was completed in 1867 on the Bleket site near Slottstullen, from which the modern Hospital area was later to expand. This was a great step forward; most of the cost was defrayed by the University, with contributions from the county and the town. In the same year, a building to house the newly established Institutes of Physiology and Pathology was erected in Trädgårdsgatan. The cost had been defrayed by a donation from a benefactor of the University, Anders Fredrik Regnell, a remarkable Swede long resident in Brazil, who was both doctor and botanist. Twenty years later, the physiologists split off and opened their own institute in 1892 in a more imposing building almost opposite. This too was paid for by the indefatigable Regnell ("Donavit Regnell" is inscribed over the main entrance) and, like the first "Regnellianum", is still in existence.

The University of Uppsala, the centre of idealistic academic philosophy and student song, was, after all, moving with the times. The 1870s had seen the creation of facilities for scientific and medical research and instruction which again brought the University up to a decent European standard.

3

The process of becoming a student in Uppsala in the age of romanticism was a simple matter until 1831, when a new form of university-entrance examination was introduced. Previously, everything had gone on in the old way; each new arrival merely produced his leaving certificate from the *gymnasium* (if he had one) and was then orally examined by the Dean of the Faculty of Arts. In 1802, at the suggestion of the Faculty, specific requirements were laid down regarding the standard of knowledge to be displayed in this examination, but it remained a pure formality which did not scare anyone. The requirements were made more stringent by letters patent in 1831; the Dean was now to be assisted in the examination by five *adjunkter,* each of whom examined the candidate in his own subject. As a result, many candidates were rejected or spent a long time preparing for the university-entrance examination, and these "provisionals"—mostly young boys taking private lessons—constituted a noisy group who were a problem to the University authorities, until they faded away in the

1850s. The old form of entrance examination at the universities was then on the verge of abolition. After lively discussions, which went on for decades, it was determined by a royal decree of 1862 that the university-entrance examination should be held in the *gymnasia*; it became a school-leaving examination which did not in itself necessarily lead on to university studies.

The social composition of the Uppsala student body slowly changed during the 19th century. The rise of the middle classes and the increasing secularization of society led to a decline in the number of clergymen's sons from about 30% around 1800 to just over 15% in the 1870s. The corresponding increase was primarily in the number of the sons of commoners and other middle-class persons, who accounted for considerably more than half of all the students towards the end of the period. The number of farmer's sons scarcely increased (it rather declined somewhat), while the sons of the nobility—who were increasingly sending their sons to ordinary schools—increased in number at the University; towards the middle of the century, they constituted about 10% of the students. At the same time, the average age of the students at enrolment increased, i.e. the young boys under the supervision of tutors, who had previously been a normal feature of university life, gradually disappeared; in 1800, 9% of all the students were under 15 years of age, but in the 1830s this category no longer existed.

The students' choices of careers followed the same pattern. The more the theological studies were vocationally orientated, the less attractive the Church became as a career. The number of prospective clergymen at Uppsala steadily declined, until about 1860 it was less than 20%; the Faculty of Law was now the larger. A contributory cause of this was that the secondary-school teachers were now ordained only in exceptional cases. In the bourgeois and bureaucratic society which was now replacing the old class society, Church and school had been separated and this separation also left its mark on student life and the atmosphere at the universities. In the mid 19th century, a spirit of social fellowship generally prevailed there and was accepted even by the aristocracy; in this fellowship, the qualification of being a free student and a member of the fraternity of the white cap was all that mattered.

There is ample evidence as to the Uppsala student's way of life in the era of romanticism and idealism. Memoirs abound, as do published and unpublished correspondence. The student now also became the hero or anti-hero of novels and stories, such as Rudolf Hjärne's *Alexis* or, towards the end of the period, Strindberg's *Från Fjerdingen och Svartbäcken*. The quiet labour of study, the lectures and the *viva voce* examinations have their share of attention in these sources, not to mention the vivid portraits

180

60. A student being examined in Uppsala in the 1840s. Aquarelle by Theodor Beskow. In private possession.

of the eccentric professors who walked the streets of Uppsala. But the picture of the Uppsala student in the 19th century is dominated by his amusements, his companionship with like-minded young men at the nations or in the students' digs, and the great political campaigns.

The majority of the students still lived simply, many of them in poverty. This was partly due to the fact that fewer of them took posts as tutors (only 2% had "university conditions" about 1870) and so almost all of them had to manage on their own resources. All too often, this meant incurring debts with tailors and innkeepers or taking up rash loans in the Mälar Bank; it also meant keeping a close watch for registered letters on the Post Office's notice-board. It was now that the bohemian student appeared, getting along on borrowed money with an apparently cheerful air. However, the cost of living in Uppsala was low. Meals were still often fetched from some nearby "cook-shop". In the student's shabby room, which he often shared with a fellow-student, the charwoman and the wood-seller were responsible for what comfort there was—as they were right up to the 1930s. But naturally there were also the sons of wealthy parents, who were trying a different style of life, eating at the taverns and following the fashion. In the 1820s, this category included the *Zierbengel,* a coterie of self-indulgent, upper-class students, who walked the streets carrying riding-whips and generally showing off. Around 1840, a dandified student had to wear a blue tailcoat, a straw-coloured waistcoat and white gloves. At this period, the moustache be-

181

came all the rage among the students, accompanied by the cigar. The contempt for bourgeois philistines and artisans still survived and was to survive for some time to come, but manners had softened and the last great fight between students and journeymen took place in 1840.

The students' amusements became increasingly abundant and more varied in the course of the 19th century. At the middle of the century, Uppsala was amply endowed with cafés and taverns, which have gone down in history in the aura of student romanticism. At Åkersten's in Stora Torget, arrack punch, wine and liqueurs were sold. Out-of-town restaurants like Stora Fördärvet, Flustret (which still shows faint signs of life) and Eklundshof were the destinations of longer excursions. Students full of *joie de vivre*, like the members of the Juvenal Order, could run up impressive bills at taverns. But the festivities were mostly held in the nations. The heyday of the nations began in the 1830s or 1840s and lasted a good hundred years. Several of the old, small nations had disappeared on account of amalgamations (this was how the present Norrland nation originated in 1827 and the Uppland nation in 1830), and one nation after another began to build its own house. The first nation-house was that of Göteborg on St. Larsgatan (1822), soon followed by those of Uppland and Västgöta. In their new homes, the members of the nations could devote their attention to each other undisturbed, safe from the malevolent looks of outsiders. There were many "wet" nation suppers, animated "by the sacred fire of innocent joy and friendship". The individual nations' calendars of festivities, with their special events (Martinmas, St Lucy, etc.), were fully developed by the 1840s at the latest, but even before then the students gathered, without regard to which nation they belonged to, to celebrate Walpurgis Night on Castle Hill and to spend May Day in noisy enjoyment. But festivities also flourished in separate private circles, to which it was counted an honour to gain entry. In the 1830s, there was a coterie which played blaring janissary music and was therefore called "the Turkish Music Club". Ten years later, the Juvenals were formed —the cheerful student circle in which Gunnar Wennerberg was the *spiritus rector* and his *Gluntarne* (published in 1849–50) were written.

Many students, at least those of good family, were also admitted to the professors' homes. In the age of romanticism, social intercourse between academic families flourished at Uppsala as never before. Several professors kept open house and students were usually welcome there too. They could go every Sunday evening to the home of the romanticist Palmblad, the Professor of Greek. and have an open sandwich and a glass of beer. Other professors offered the company of girls, dancing and games. Geijer and his circle were to be found in the salon of Mrs. Malla Silfverstolpe. It was here that the poets and musicians of Uppsala gathered, especially

61. *A company of student volunteers in the 1850s resting after drilling in the Botanical Garden.*

the handsome and romantic students, who all too easily roused tender emotions in their hostess. By this time (in the 1820s), many noble families had settled in Uppsala and were anxious to form connections in University circles. Professors and presentable students mingled at their receptions, tea parties and balls. This development to some extent bears witness to the improvement in the Uppsala student's social standing in the new age.

Curiously enough, military drill was also counted as one of the student's pleasures. Ever since the 1810s, the students had been obliged to carry out suitable military training for one or two weeks each year. They were paraded by nations under officers and corporals in the Botanical Garden and learned to handle their blunderbusses, with frequent breaks for refreshment, when schnapps and punch flowed freely. In addition, many students took part voluntarily in the old-established noble exercises. The fencing master and the riding master drilled their pupils, but there was also an innovation in the form of Ling gymnastics, which were introduced at the University in 1812 by Gustaf Daniel von Heidenstam, the fencing master. He set up his apparatus in the cupola of the Gustavianum and arranged gymnastic displays before large audiences. Towards the end of the century, Uppsala student gymnastics—which were better suited to a democratic society than the traditional noble exercises—underwent a new period of glory in the spirit of national romanticism.

However, it was particularly student singing that gave 19th-century Uppsala its distinctive character. This was a creation of the Romantic Age and of the eccentric, German-born J. C. F. Hæffner, who became the University *director musices* in 1808. He was an impulsive enthusiast, who inaugurated a brilliant period for music in the University. He also reorganized the languishing University Orchestra and composed a long series of lofty pieces for four-part male-voice choirs to lyrics by Atterbom and others—mostly cantatas and anthems for performance at the commemorations and official ceremonies which now followed each other in regular succession. Soon, at least in the 1820s, the first student serenades sounded on spring nights. At the suggestion of Dr. Otto Fredrik Tullberg, the orientalist, the Allmänna Sången male-voice choir was formed in 1830; it was the stronghold of choral music in Uppsala for a long time to come. The Orphei Drängar (OD) choral society, which was founded in 1853 and was conducted by J. A. Josephson, the Director of Music, originally had a different and more classical repertoire. By the middle of the century, choral music sung by male voices in four parts had reached its peak; no University event took place without it. Songs such as "Vikingasäten, åldriga lundar", "O hur härligt majsol ler", Wennerberg's "Hör oss Svea" and other patriotic pieces, the singing of which has accompanied the events of the passing year in Uppsala down to the present day, roared forth from dais and platform. In the autumn of 1845, Allmänna Sången gave their first public concert in the Carolina hall and in 1867 the choir made its first visit to Paris, by which the singing of Swedish students under the baton of the legendary Oscar Arpi acquired a European reputation.

Student singing, as an expression of lofty feeling, conferred lustre and inspiration on Scandinavian student gatherings. With these gatherings, Scandinavian students made contributions of international political importance, which to a great extent helped to direct public attention to the university towns. However, spontaneous demonstrations that were of significance in forming the politically conscious type of 19th-century student had already occurred in Uppsala. They were intentionally subversive and took place in the 1790s in the wake of the French Revolution. For the first time, the Uppsala students, who were sensitive to the intellectual currents of the time, led the way in the development of new ideas in Sweden.

The demonstrations began in the late autumn of 1792 during the dark period when the freedom of the Swedish press was restricted by a new ordinance. Some resentful students in Uppsala decided to arrange a "funeral for the freedom of the press". They gathered at Östmark's tavern and then, dressed in crepe and wearing cockades, walked in procession into the town, singing songs specially composed for the occasion. In the New Year, the political ferment found further expression in what were called "conventions"—private debating societies, whose members met once or twice a week to praise the virtues of the French revolutionaries.

62. *The staircase march, a ritual performed after the concerts given by the students in the Carolina hall. The Allmänna Sången male-voice choir are marching down the staircase and out onto the crest of the Carolina hill, singing "Vikingasäten, åldriga lundar . . ." Wood engraving from* Ny illustrerad tidning *(1877).*

The students seemed to be abandoning Bacchus and Venus in favour of Freedom, Equality and Enlightenment. Duke Karl and the omnipotent Reuterholm, both timorous and despotic men, had the "conventions" forbidden and when the speeches made at the meetings were published in the spring of 1793, they were confiscated. But the spirit of freedom which had developed in the student world could not be stifled. The Christiernin affair was an inoffensive and grotesque interlude. P. N. Christiernin (cf. above, p. 120), a choleric and conservative philosopher who had a horror of revolutionary conspiracies, had several students, most of them completely innocent, arrested in the autumn of 1795, after hearing nocturnal cries of "Pereat!" outside his windows. He acted in his capacity as Rector but was compelled by the Senate to resign his post.

A few years later, the political unrest among the students reached its climax. Since Gustav IV Adolf had acceded to the throne, autocratic obscurantism had been further strengthened and there was great fear of "Jacobinism". The praises of Bonaparte and the French Republic were being sung in Uppsala. Towards the turn of the century, the radical opposition had its stronghold in the circle called the Junta, an association of

185

mostly older students in which Docent Gustaf Abraham Silfverstolpe, the *littérateur*, was the driving force and Benjamin Höijer, the philosopher, the leading intellectual authority; it also included the young Hans Järta, who now launched his assault on despotism. When a Crown Prince was born in the autumn of 1799, a scandalous ballad was sung, which led to a wigging from the Rector and a visit by Gustav IV Adolf, who resigned his office as the University Chancellor. The King's wrath was directed particularly against Höijer, who was the champion of freedom and the chief advocate of the Kantian philosophy and therefore stood out as the hero of the younger generation. He was excluded from the chair of philosophy, for which he was the obvious candidate, and afterwards left the country during stormy demonstrations of sympathy on the part of the revolutionarily minded section of the student body.

A last flare-up of political passions occurred in the spring of 1800, when the University was to celebrate the King's coronation with loyal speeches and music. This occurrence, which led to what was called the "Music Trial", was stage-managed principally by members of the Junta and created an enormous sensation. Silfverstolpe, who was himself a member of the University Orchestra, smuggled into the repertoire a piece containing an excerpt from the Marseillaise, but the fact was discovered at the last minute. The unfortunate Director of Music had then to present a Haydn symphony instead—with three musicians, because Silfverstolpe and his cronies refused to take part. A long trial followed before the Senate, which sentenced Silfverstolpe to lose his *docent* post and to be banished from Uppsala. The other accessories received minor punishments.

Then peace reigned. A new epoch dawned with romanticism, which was politically conservative. Royalism—preferably in Old Norse or Gothic garb—was enthusiastically embraced by professors and students alike. Royal births, weddings and name-days gave occasion to violent manifestations of joy on the part of the University. On Oscar's name-day in 1819, a magnificent feast with a Gothic temple, an illuminated letter O, anthems and souvenirs was arranged in the courtyard of the Gustavianum; Prince Oscar, who was then a student at Uppsala, received the tributes seated upon a throne. In 1826, when the news of the birth of Prince Karl reached Uppsala, the students collected money for a gold watch to be presented to the courier who had delivered the glad tidings. On his visit to Uppsala in 1834, Karl XIV Johan was given an ovation on the burial mounds at Old Uppsala by the assembled students, who, in the person of the Curator of the Stockholm nation, toasted the monarch in a drinking horn containing mead. These patriotic manifestations later prompted the commemorations of Sweden's great kings—Gustavus Vasa, Gustavus

Adolphus and Charles XII—which now began to be arranged by the students in forms which became traditional as the years went by.

Politically reactionary ways of thinking were still good form in Uppsala during the 1830s. But at that time—just when the most ethereal form of romanticism was going out of fashion—the students again began to adopt more progressive ideas. The middle-class and liberal opposition gained a foothold and *Aftonbladet* had many readers. J. V. Sprengtporten, the Governor of Stockholm dismissed for his courage, was hailed with singing and cheers when he passed through Uppsala in 1838. The same year, tremendous excitement was aroused by the defection of the high priest of conservatism, Geijer, to the liberal faith; it was announced in his own journal *Litteraturbladet* and was regarded by most of the students as a fanfare for liberty.

The political passions of the student body culminated in the Scandinavist movement of the following decade. This did not only mean that the students were united by a political programme which became of national importance. It also gave them a prominent position in the public consciousness and thus a corporative self-esteem which coloured their way of life and led to the formation of a joint student body for all the students at the University.

Scandinavism was a fruit of Danish propaganda. The young liberal nationalists in Denmark, faced with the German military threat to the duchies of Schleswig and Holstein, were seeking support from their Scandinavian neighbours. It began gradually with contacts between the students of Copenhagen and Lund. The first large demonstration followed in the summer of 1843. Nearly 200 students travelled from Copenhagen and Lund to Uppsala, where they received a splendid ovation. The Uppsala students now wore for the first time the white cap which later became a symbol of Swedish academic citizenship. A feast of welcome was held in the Carolina hall, at which oratory, song and punch flowed freely amid scenes of great jubilation, and toasts were drunk to Scandinavian unity on the burial mounds at Old Uppsala. This enthusiasm was somewhat hazardous in the reign of Karl Johan. Scandinavism was supported chiefly by the liberals and on account of its involvement in Denmark's affairs ran directly contrary to the King's foreign policy; he therefore tried to counteract it. A visit to Copenhagen planned by the Uppsala students in 1844, when even Geijer was playing the government's game, was cancelled. But it took place in the summer of 1845, when the liberally minded Oscar I had ascended the throne. One thousand four hundred Scandinavian students assembled in Copenhagen, 150 of them from Uppsala; the feasting and the toasting knew no bounds. The tone of the speakers became openly aggressive and attacks were now also made on Russia.

The Scandinavist movement reached a new climax in 1848, the year of revolution in Europe. Uppsala was in a ferment of political unrest. The revolution in France in February was celebrated at "revolutionary suppers" and the students marched through the streets under the red flag, singing the Marseillaise. Toasts to Poland, a united Italy and the Swedish royal family followed one another. But Denmark remained the chief issue. War had broken out between Denmark and Germany. At an impressive ceremony held in the hall of the Uppsala Gille, the students declared their loyalty to their Danish brothers and to all efforts to secure freedom in Europe. An address was sent to the Danish students. Young August Sohlman, who later became the editor of *Aftonbladet,* took a leading part in these activities. In order to collect funds to help the Danes, Allmänna Sången gave two concerts in Stockholm, which were attended by the royal family and were huge successes. It was as elements in this general Scandinavist delight that student singing and student oratory got a chance to develop. Orators and poets mounted rostra and rose at banqueting tables amid storms of applause. The unrivalled virtuoso in this genre in Uppsala was the bohemian poet, Johan Nybom, who was always prepared to gild the occasion with bombastic toasts in verse and prose. "What is a student?" he asked in 1848. "He is the living expression of a nation's noblest youth. He carries his country's future germinating in his breast." He was prepared to offer his life and his blood for "all that is great and noble in humanity". The Scandinavistic 1840s saw the beginning of the Uppsala student's real period of glory. Before the nation and before himself, he appeared in a transfiguring light as the guarantor of hope and brightness.

The Scandinavist student meetings continued during the 1850s and 1860s. The attendances were magnificent, but some of the old ardour had gone. In the summer of 1856, it was Uppsala's turn again. A dinner for 1,400 persons was served in the Botanical Garden, followed by a Gothic *allherjarting* (popular assembly) at Old Uppsala and a ball in the Carolina hall for no less than 2,200 persons. When the renewed war between Denmark and Germany in 1863–64 resulted in a catastrophic defeat for Denmark, the Scandinavist movement ended in a fiasco. What remained was the sense of Scandinavian cultural solidarity, which was reinforced in the generations to come.

The Uppsala Students' Union developed out of the Scandinavist movement. The time was ripe. In Lund, an organization (Akademiska Föreningen) which included all students had been formed on the Copenhagen pattern as early as 1830. But in Uppsala, the conditions were less favourable, by reason of the strong position of the student nations, manifested in the fact that they had their own buildings. After the student meeting in 1843, a tentative beginning was made with the formation of a Scandi-

63. In February 1869, at the Archbishop's House, the Students' Union paid their respects to Karl XV and the Danish Crown Prince Frederik, who were visiting Uppsala at that time. Wood engraving in Ny illustrerad tidning *(1869).*

navian Society in Uppsala, but this was soon dissolved. Instead, the Uppsala students began to consider the possibility of establishing an internal association, over and above the nations, which could look after their common interests. The question was discussed in pamphlets and in the short-lived *Studentbladet* (1845–6). A number of the student nations were opposed to the plans, but in the spring term of 1846, an Uppsala Students' Association was formed on the initiative of some leading Scandinavists. Its programme was an ambitious one. Premises were procured at the Gillet Hotel, a library was established, and magazines and newspapers were displayed. But the enthusiasm soon waned and after a year the Students' Association was also breathing its last. However, within a short time, the problem was finally solved. In connection with manifestations of Scandinavist opinion, it was felt to be important that the Uppsala students should be able to present a united front, as an official body. In the autumn of 1848, that year of unrest, the nations themselves, represented by the Curators' Convention, put forward a proposal for an official body and in March 1849, regulations were adopted for the Uppsala Students' Union, which began work at once. Accommodation was found at the Stockholm nation.

The Students' Union was (and still is) an association of the 13 student nations, which continued to exist unaffected by the new system. Under the direction of a board consisting of the representatives of the nations, its task was for a long time largely representative and ornamental; at the splendid banquets so beloved of the age, its chairman had to give lofty expression to the idealistic temperament of the Uppsala student.

4

Scholarly and intellectual culture in Uppsala during and after the age of romanticism was dominated by the philosophers and the aesthetes. Sweden was a cultural province of Germany; the romantic speculation imported from the south could take root and grow undisturbed by the din of the outside world in the sheltered, small-town universities of Lund and especially Uppsala.

The professors who gave backbone and stability to the new ways of thinking were the occupants of the chairs of philosophy. The pioneer was Benjamin Höijer, who was finally, after many trials and tribulations, appointed Professor of Theoretical Philosophy in 1809. Höijer, who had gone on from Kant's transcendental philosophy to Fichte as early as the 1790s and finally took up a position close to that of Hegel, played a decisive role as the inspirer of the first generation of Uppsala romanticists, in-

64. *Christopher Jacob*
Boström, the philo-
sopher. Photograph
taken in 1861.

cluding Geijer and Atterbom, to whom he also acted as cicerone in
aesthetic matters. After him, the torch was carried on by Biberg and
Grubbe. Nils Fredrik Biberg was an ultra-conservative and eccentric professor who independently developed ideas which he had borrowed from
Schelling and Schleiermacher and put forward his own views on the Absolute. His colleague, Samuel Grubbe, who succeeded Höijer in 1813, presented a less clear-cut philosophical profile. In long-winded lectures, he
expounded the mysteries of the True, the Good and the Beautiful, and his
concept of sensual beings as ideas in God's self-consciousness. All this
was Platonic idealism of the purest brand and was soon developed to an
unequalled pitch on a Swedish basis by Grubbe's pupil and successor,
Christopher Jacob Boström. No Swedish philosopher, and very few
Swedish university lecturers, on the whole, have exercised so great an
influence as Boström. The nucleus of his system, which he developed
by means of prodigious logical deductions, was the doctrine of the cha-
racteristics of God or the Absolute Being and of the finite personalities
as independent entities in God's infinite being. This "idea of personality",
which guaranteed the inalienable value of the individual, had already been
developed by Biberg, Grubbe and Geijer, but it was Boström who made
it an indispensable ingredient of Uppsala idealism. Boström's reactionary

191

65. *Erik Gustaf Geijer in an unconventional pencil drawing by Brynolf Wennerberg.*

philosophy of the State was also important; he regarded the State, too, as an idea or personality and found that the Riksdag of the four Estates was based on the eternal order of things. After Boström's death in 1866, his intellectual legacy was passed on by Sigurd Ribbing and Carl Yngve Sahlin, the two Professors of Philosophy. Ribbing, who was eccentric and the subject of many anecdotes, was an indomitable opponent of materialism, political radicalism and other modern heresies, while Sahlin, who was a younger man and a faithful advocate of his master's system, enabled Boströmianism to live on into the 20th century and thereby made Uppsala one of the last havens of refuge for philosophers who gave an idealistic explanation of the world.

Erik Gustaf Geijer was also numbered among the philosophers. During the age of romanticism proper, he was the most brilliant of the University's teachers and had an influence which extended far beyond the academic world. Geijer was at the centre of the educational life of his time and many paths led to and from him. He was Professor of History and at his famous lectures on this subject the crowds consisted not only of students but also of members of fashionable Uppsala society. In his unfinished book *Svea rikes häfder* (The Annals of Sweden) and in his *Svenska folkets historia* (The History of the Swedish People) (1832–36), he put into practice his theories as a historian. Geijer had come to history from romantic philosophy and in that spirit regarded the Swedish people as a living being, whose development he sketched in superb, sweeping strokes. The life of the State, with the royal power and the people as its two poles, was the real subject of historical research. Like his German teachers, Geijer embraced a conservative philosophy of the State, permeated by corporative and religious lines of thought, which formed the unshakeable basis of his actions in questions of social and University policy. However, he was no out-and-out neo-romanticist, least of all from the aesthetic point of view, and his austere realism gradually inclined him towards liberalism. Today, it is somewhat difficult for us to understand the tremendous commotion caused by Geijer's "defection" from the conservative view of society. It alienated him from his romantic friends and gave him in his last years a greater degree of self-awareness, which he expressed in his lyrical poems.

Side by side with the philosophers and under their inspiration, the aesthetes and the poets carried on their battle for the regeneration of Swedish literature. The central figure here was the young Atterbom. In his circle, the bodyguard consisted of his fellow countrymen at the Östgöta nation, of whom Vilhelm Fredrik Palmblad was the most prominent. The Aurora Society was formed in 1808 as the focus of the new aesthetic ideals, and in the summer of 1810 appeared the first, flame-coloured issue of *Phosphoros*, in which these ideals were made known to their astonished contemporaries. The breakthrough of romanticism—in what was called "Phosphorism"—was one of the most revolutionary contributions made by academic Uppsala to the history of ideas. Emotional and flowery poetry filled the romantic journals and almanacks, and the secrets of nature and religion were interpreted with the aid of Schelling's obscure philosophy. As the chief advocate of Phosphorism, the aloof and hypersensitive Atterbom was as much a philosophical thinker as a practising poet and aesthetic revolutionary. When at long last he was given a professorship, it was in theoretical philosophy and he did not take over the newly established chair of aesthetics, for which he was the obvious candidate, until 1835. He grew more temperate as the years went by and now set about writing the great work entitled *Svenska siare och skalder* (Swedish Prophets and Poets), in which he appeared as a pioneer of Swedish research into literary history.

Even in its heyday in the 1810s and 1820s, Phosphorism was pursued by only a limited clique of students and young lecturers. Most people in the academic world were quite indifferent or openly unsympathetic. If a man was a Phosphorist, he was consequently "melancholy and affected", says Gustaf Svanberg, who, as a natural scientist, had the firmly rooted belief in reason of an earlier age. Nevertheless, neo-romanticism brought about a lasting change in the academic atmosphere. Literature and aesthetics were given priority long after the middle of the century. A world view in which Beauty and Truth were harmoniously combined became the goal of the average talented student. There were many student poets in Uppsala in the post-romantic period, with Nybom and Wennerberg as the admired leaders in the 1840s. Böttiger and Malmström, the two Professors of Aesthetics who followed Atterbom, both won fame as lyrical poets. Otherwise, the handsome and emotional Carl Wilhelm Böttiger (who became the first Professor of Modern European Linguistics in 1858) made his principal contribution as the founder of the study of the Romance languages at Uppsala. Bernhard Elis Malmström, who gained his master's degree with a thesis entitled *Om konstens väsende* (On the Essence of Art) and made his name as a poet with his romantic elegy *Angelika,* turned towards the liberal camp and, as critic and literary historian, took up arms against the vulgarities of Phosphorism. The young Uppsala aesthetes explained their inoffensive literary programme in a series of poetic almanacks and magazines. Carl Lénström, a prolific author who edited the short-lived magazine *Eos* about 1840, played an important role in this connection.

New poetical flags were hoisted in the 1860s by the group of student poets known as the "Signatures", who gathered together in the Anonymous Society and the most promising of whom were Snoilsky and Carl David af Wirsén. But their attempts to get nearer to reality stopped half way. Pretty little pictures of everyday life and an increasingly insipid idealism, spiced with a few drops of Boström, constituted good aesthetic culture in Uppsala. It was still faithfully cherished by the influential Carl Rupert Nyblom, who was Professor of Aesthetics from 1867 onwards and was important on account of his work on the theory of the fine arts. But after his day, speculative aesthetics of German origin went into decline. Nyblom's pupil, Henrik Schück, remarked, "I would rather have back my kidney stones than read German aesthetics".

The gospel of neo-humanism (cf. above, p. 137f.) was preached in close association with romanticism. It taught the students to react to the departed glory of Rome and Greece in a sentimental and romantic manner; the aesthetic contemplation of the art and literature of antiquity was always in the focus of attention. However, it can scarcely be said that neo-humanism flowered abundantly in 19th-century Uppsala. It was a natural constituent of the academic atmosphere but was never advocated by any influential or inspiring teachers. The pious and modest Christopher Dahl, who administered what he had inherited from Göttingen and his teacher Floderus and who was arousing enthusiasm in his students for the beauty of Greek poetry about 1800, was perhaps an exception. But the subsequent holders of the two key professorships—of Greek and the now undivided subject of Latin (rhetoric and poetics)—do not seem to have given their instruction the same inspiring quality. Adolf Törneros, the wellknown Professor of Latin in the 1830s, was otherwise a highly cultivated aesthete and his letters written on his travels through Sweden in the summer gave convincing proof of his wit and romantic feeling for nature. Vilhelm Fredrik Palmblad, a romantic who was a glutton for work and became Professor of Greek towards the end of his life, made a significant contribution with his translations of the works of the Greek tragedians. But neither he nor his now-forgotten colleagues in the professorship of Latin in the middle of the century were able to give classical studies the leading position which they still occupied at other universities. The same applied to Palmblad's successor as Professor of Greek, Johan Spongberg, an aristocrat famous for his biting sarcasms but an aesthete and a neo-humanist to his finger-tips. After the post-mortem examination a Greek lexicon was placed in his empty cranium.

Historical studies in Uppsala had been given new life by Geijer in the spirit of romanticism and this tradition remained alive throughout the century. It was carried on chiefly by Geijer's successors in the chair, Fredrik F. Carlson and Carl Gustaf Malmström, both of whom were also politically active as cabinet ministers and were the authors of monumental works on Swedish history. Carlson wrote several volumes (published from 1855 onwards) on the history of the Caroline period, while Malmström produced an equally fundamental account of the Age of Freedom. Faithful to the legacy they had received from Geijer, they were heartily nationalistic and concentrated their attention on the life of the State; at the same time, they were austere and matter-of-fact and based their work on research in the archives on a hitherto unprecedented scale. The third in the series, Clas Theodor Odhner, had been educated in Uppsala and was appointed *docent* there in the 1860s; he later became a professor at Lund and Keeper of the Public Records. He took care of the history of the Gustavian period. Another by no means insignificant historian was Wilhelm Erik Svedelius, who emerged, in works written while he was still a young man in the 1840s, as a pioneer of the more vigilant criticism of the historical sources. As the Skyttean Professor from 1862 onwards, Svedelius laid the foundations of modern Swedish research in political science. But he was, above all, an enthusiast and an academic orator (not merely in virtue of his professorship) and his students loved him; as one of the many eccentric professors of that idyllic age he was notorious for his slovenly appearance and incredible absent-mindedness.

A few other Uppsala humanists acquired reputations for scholarly work in the mid 19th century. Otto Fredrik Tullberg, who put new life into oriental studies, was skilled in Sanskrit and Syriac. Anders Uppström, the temporary Professor of "Moeso-Gothic", carried on an illustrious tradition of Uppsala scholarship with his complete critical edition of Bishop Ulfilas's Gothic translation of the Bible (1854).

With a few isolated exceptions, research did not prosper in the three higher faculties in 19th-century Uppsala. At the beginning of the century, the Faculty of Theology had had an inspiring figure in the versatile Samuel Ödmann, but after his time it for long presented a rather shabby appearance. It had no outstanding or leading personalities in the sphere of scholarship or in the Church of Sweden; it bore no comparison whatever with the Faculty of Theology at Lund, which possessed some brilliant theologians, such as Reuterdahl and Thomander. The lawyers were in a somewhat similar case. The professors and *adjunkter* in the Faculty of Law were snowed under by the daily round of pedagogic drudgery, their days being filled with lectures, examinations and the compiling of handbooks. However, the long-lived Pehr Erik Bergfalk, who was an expert on constitutional and financial law, and Knut Olivecrona, Professor of Law in the 1850s and 1860s and an advocate of reform in Swedish penal law, enjoyed considerable reputations.

Little need be added about the Faculty of Medicine. It had manfully stood the test in the battle with the Karolinska Institute and the teaching, stimulated by the provision of the new professorships and institutes, steadily improved. But no vigorous medical research was carried on, for the time being, in Uppsala. The Faculty's leading personality at the beginning of the century, Pehr von Afzelius, a physician-in-ordinary to the King, was primarily a practical administrator, and Hwasser, the reactionary romanticist, despised modern medical science. His admiring pupils—the "Hwasserians"—abandoned their master's abstruse doctrines but themselves contributed little to the improvement of medicine. However, about 1870, fresh air began to blow through the Uppsala faculty. Frithiof Holmgren, who had been trained at German and Austrian laboratories and became Sweden's first professor of physiology in 1864, was a pioneer in experimental medicine. His discovery of the impulse current in the retina and his investigations of colour blindness won him international fame. The discovery by Ivar Sandström, while he was still a young medical student, of the hitherto unknown parathyroid glands created a sensation when it was published in 1880. From the 1830s onwards, medical

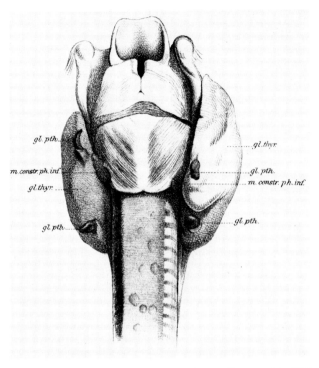

66. *While still a young man, Ivar Sandström discovered in 1880 the hitherto unknown parathyroid glands, which are depicted here from his own account in* Upsala Läkareförenings Förhandlingar *(1880). Gl. thyr.=glandula thyreoidea, gl. pth.=glandula parathyreoidea.*

men of all ages had had a meeting-place in the Uppsala Medical Society, which was founded by Hwasser, who remained its chairman until his death; current findings from the clinics and laboratories were published in its *Proceedings*.

On the whole, it was evident that the spirit of the age did not favour the natural sciences. In the eyes of the romantic or idealistic philosophers who reigned in Uppsala, they seemed unimportant or even vulgar. Thinkers such as Hwasser, Boström and Ribbing were quite definite on this point. The phenomena of the material world were not real in the same sense as the pure ideas in God's consciousness and were therefore of no real interest. Moreover, too intense a pre-occupation with them could lead to the most odious of all philosophies—a materialistic view of the world. Under these circumstances, it was inevitable that 19th-century aca-

197

demic research in the natural sciences in Sweden should be under the weather and far from experiencing a period of glory. The Stockholm medical men, gathered at the Karolinska Institute or the Royal Academy of Sciences, were more active; a more pungent spirit prevailed there, Berzelius in his laboratory providing the example and the inspiration.

The starting-point was not particularly favourable either. The natural sciences in Sweden, on the whole, went through a period of decline at the beginning of the 19th century. The only representative of the exact sciences in Uppsala who was at all distinguished was the physicist, Zacharias Nordmarck, who specialized in optics and theoretical hydrodynamics and who was an excellent lecturer. Jöns Svanberg, who became Professor of Mathematics in 1811, had already done his most important work (the expedition to measure the degree of latitude in Lappmarken); nevertheless, being witty, cheerful and talented, he enjoyed popular esteem. Chemistry and astronomy were in a bad way. The only science which continued to flourish was Linnaean botany. It was represented in Uppsala (still in the Faculty of Medicine) by Carl Peter Thunberg, who was now an old man but who went on working until his death at a great age in 1828. In his time, he was the University's most renowned professor, famous throughout Europe; in comparison with him, Geijer was only a local celebrity. The enormous collections of animals, plants and ethnographica which he made as a young man on his great journey to South Africa, Java and Japan and which he donated to the University were one of the sights of Uppsala, as was the old man himself. He kindly displayed his treasures at the Botanicum to visiting strangers; he was naive and brisk, sometimes slightly comical, filling his days with work and playing cards. His classical work on the Japanese flora had appeared long before, but it was not until 1820 that he finished his great work on the plants of Cape Province entitled *Flora capensis*. Thunberg's successor, the rugged recluse Göran Wahlenberg, also won European fame. He was an authority on the flora of Sweden and especially of Lapland (*Flora lapponica*, 1812) and also knew the flora of the Carpathians. Wahlenberg broke new ground in the field of plant geography—he investigated the dependence of vegetation on climate and soil and distinguished the plant regions in the mountains.

The botanists—and the biologists in general—were concerned with living, incessantly active nature. This meant that, when the time came, they were attracted to the romantic view of nature. German 19th-century romanticism was by no means a matter only for philosophers and aesthetes. Schelling had elaborated a very profound philosophy of nature, which was enthusiastically received by many natural scientists and medical students. This not only tempted them to indulge in singular extravagances; the romanticist's intuitive feeling for hidden connections in nature could also show the way to fascinating and fruitful lines of thought. In Sweden, there was as a starting-point in the Linnaean botanist's pious rapture at the wonders that God had wrought in nature; this, combined with Schellingian mysticism or a general Platonic idealism, made botany the most popular of the natural sciences, especially in Uppsala. Elias Fries, who had been trained in Lund (he was the Borgströmian Professor from 1834 onwards), was a brilliant representative of romantic biology and was second only to Linnaeus among Swedish botanists. He published a fundamental and internationally famous work on the systematics of the fungi (*Systema mycologicum*, 1821–33) and endeavoured to draw up a natural system for the entire vegetable kingdom. In this connection, he was inspired by the ideas of German *Naturphilosophie*, just as all his research was imbued by the conviction that nature is a manifestation of the Holy Spirit. Atterbom used a quotation from Fries as a motto for his cycle of poems entitled *Blommorna* (The Flowers). As a romanticist, Fries could not compare with his medical colleague Hwasser for uninhibited imaginative power, but he belonged to the same school, despite his humble respect for empirical facts.

On the other hand, Wilhelm Lilljeborg, the first Professor of Zoology at Uppsala (appointed in 1854), was a Linnaean systematizer of the driest kind. He also was trained at Lund, which was the real domicile of Swedish academic zoology. Lilljeborg concentrated his research on the lower crustaceans and the Scandinavian vertebrates. He worked in the Gustavianum, which was now and for a long time to come at the disposal of the Zoological Museum, which filled the old book-rooms and fairly soon the Rudbeckian cupola as well.

The more or less exact sciences, which could not be legitimated in the refulgence of Linnaeus's name, were still worse off. The chemists and the physicists did not feel the same need of romantic explanations of the world. They described nature in inexorably quantitative terms; in this sense, they were "materialists" and the chief objects of the dread and contempt of the idealistic academic philosophers, the more so as their results contributed to technological and economic progress, which was regarded with distrust by the guardians of the eternal verities. The scientists, chiefly Berzelius, counter-attacked and defended their positions. In the 1810s, Jöns Svanberg, the mathematician, who was faithful to the legacy of Newton, directed a tremendous salvo at romantic natural philosophy, which he described as sheer folly and a chaos of confusion and disorder. But such attacks did not help the exact and experimental sciences to secure esteem and well-being at the 19th-century, small-town universities in Sweden. They had only a few important representatives in

67. *Anders Jonas Ång-
ström, the physicist, who
was professor from 1858
onwards and a pioneer of
spectrum analysis.*

Uppsala. Despite the new observatory, astronomy attracted little attention, while chemistry, which at the beginning of the century had had a
capable representative in Anders Gustaf Ekeberg, had long been uncultivated. At long last, new life was put into it by Lars Fredrik Svanberg, the son of the Jöns Svanberg mentioned above, who was a pupil
of Berzelius and the driving force behind the building of the new Institute
of Chemistry, which gave the Uppsala chemists completely new external
conditions from the 1860s onwards. Otherwise, physics showed more
vigour. Fredrik Rudberg, who was Professor of Physics in the 1830s but
died prematurely, bought a collection of modern physical instruments in
Paris and made important investigations in thermodynamics which led,
inter alia, to improvements in the design of thermometers. But the great
name in physics—together with Fries, the University's only celebrity of
European fame around the middle of the century—was that of Anders
Jonas Ångström, who was Professor of Physics from 1858 onwards. This
rugged and sarcastic man made successful investigations in terrestrial
magnetism and the temperature of the earth, but his pioneering work was
done in spectroscopy, in which he and the German Kirchhoff were the
leading experts of the time. Ångström's celebrated work on the solar spectrum (*Recherches sur le spectre solaire*) was published in 1868; his name

is still recalled by the designation of the standard unit for measuring wavelengths of light (the Ångström (Å)=one ten-millionth part of a millimetre). His work in spectral analysis was continued by his colleague and successor, Robert Thalén, who determined the spectra of the rare earth metals, which were simultaneously investigated by Per Cleve, the Professor of Chemistry, who discovered the new elements holmium and thulium in 1880.

A new age was now at hand, which was to give natural scientists a stronger position in Swedish society and in the course of time also at the University of Uppsala.

CHAPTER VI

From the 1880s to the Second World War

1

About 1880, the outlines of a new age in the history of the University could be glimpsed. At the same time, two great events took place, both of which were significant milestones in the University's development. One of them—the quatercentenary celebrations in 1877—was devoted to the remembrance of times past and to the University as a centre of intellectual power in Swedish society. The other—the inauguration of the new University building ten years later—brought about better external conditions for the administration and the instruction.

The University's celebration of its quatercentenary in 1877 was in preparation for a long time; a committee was at work on the programme for several years. Including the preliminaries and the follow-up parties, the festivities extended over a period of four days, from the 4th to the 7th of September. Uppsala was decked with flags, a triumphal arch made of fir twigs was erected at the crossing of Drottninggatan and Trädgårdsgatan, fireworks were let off and there was general enthusiasm. The leading figures were King Oscar, Crown Prince Gustav, Carl Yngve Sahlin, the Rector, who was now presented by the king with the gold chain of his office, and Archbishop Anton Niklas Sundberg, the Pro-Chancellor. There were hundreds of invited guests from Sweden, the neighbouring Scandinavian countries and the rest of the world. On Wednesday, 5 September, a splendid procession walked from the Carolina Hall to the Cathedral, where the speech of welcome and the festival cantata, to the words of Carl David af Wirsén, were followed by a long series of harangues, congratulations and addresses. The ceremony was concluded by the Rector, who expounded the main theme of academic philosophy—the spiritual and the immortal part of man—in an oration entitled "On the power of knowledge". Then it was time for the material element. A temporary, roofed, banqueting hall with a canopy for the king had been set up between the two wings of the Institute of Botany. A magnificent dinner was eaten there, accompanied by toasts and the distribution of verses printed in Swedish and Latin—a kind of death throe of academic Latin humanism. At the same time, the student body and their guests partook of a separate banquet at the Uppsala Gille.

68. *The 400th anniversary in 1877 of the foundation of the University. The audience is assembled in the Cathedral on 5 September, the first day of the celebrations.* Carl Yngve Sahlin, the rector magnificus, *is on the rostrum. Wood engraving in* Ny illustrerad tidning *(1877)*.

On the following day, doctoral degrees in the four faculties were conferred in the Cathedral. There was an impressive row of Swedish, Norwegian, Danish and Finnish honorary doctors, accompanied by the "jubilee" doctors and the doctors who had passed examinations. But the conferment ceremony was made especially memorable by the performance of Viktor Rydberg's cantata, set to music by J. A. Josephson, the *director musices,* and made available to the foreign guests in a French translation:

> Des temps voilés par la nuit
> vers un but caché à tes regards . . .

Here, an inspired poet articulated the same creed as Sahlin, the disciple of Boström, had expressed in philosophical prose the day before.

No less than 1,500 guests sat down to dinner in the Botanical Garden after the conferment of degrees. A well-organized, popular festival broke out after the meal; over 2,000 people in evening dress gathered outside the open doors of the Linnaeus Hall, student songs mingled with military music, foreign notabilities offered congratulations, and Oscar II was carried through the throng by the students. The day's events, and the most brilliant festival in the University's history, concluded with a torchlight procession to the Castle, to which the king had retired.

The idea of a new University building was originally started by the quatercentenary committee, which hoped that at least the foundation stone could be laid in 1877. The old premises—the Gustavianum and the Senate House (known as "Kuggis")—began to seem cramped and old-fashioned, and the banqueting hall on the top floor of the Carolina Rediviva was both difficult of access and a fire risk; moreover, as we have already seen, it was required for the needs of the growing Library. By the mid 1870s, the plans of the new building were ready and a government grant of 740,000 crowns had been allotted, but after that progress was slow. The plans were changed and an architectural competition was announced, after which the more or less unknown architect H. T. Holmgren was commissioned to design the building. In the spring of 1879, Oscar II laid the foundation stone on the former site of the old building which Rudbeck had erected for the "noble exercises". But eight years were to pass before the building was completed and inaugurated in the presence of the king, in May 1887. A cantata by Wirsén and Ivar Hedenblad was performed in the Aula, and Sahlin, who was still Rector, made a high-toned speech about the Greeks, Kant and the importance of thinking not only freely but also rightly.

The new University building was, and still is, a palace in Renaissance style, monumental at least in the interior. The great entrance hall, with its side staircases and its three roof domes, has been adjudged to be one of the finest spatial creations of the last century in Sweden. Unfortunately, the sequence of frescoes representing the work of the four faculties, which was originally planned, was never executed. The richly decorated, semi-circular Aula—which is a centre of University festivities even today—was designed to hold 2000 people. While the Senate Hall with its royal portraits was located on the ground floor, the Chancellor's room and the faculty rooms were designed as a magnificent suite upstairs on the main floor; in the long gallery outside this suite, plaster casts of antique sculptures bore witness to the still unbroken power of neo-humanist aesthetics. The lecture rooms were much simpler. Georg Brandes, the Danish writer, who visited Uppsala in 1889, was struck by the contrast:

The vestibule is as rich as a Civil List, the assembly hall is as stately as a Court, the Chancellor's room is as costly as the Civil Service and the teaching rooms are on the plain side ... The whole building is well suited to instil into the young the desire to rise in the world, a useful ambition. Everything here calls to the young student: "Grow and climb and become a professor!"

204

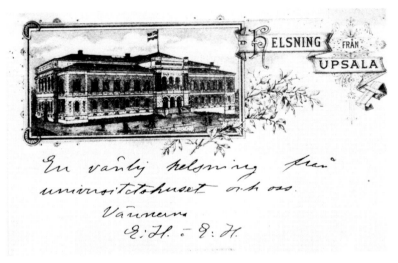

69. *This picture postcard, printed for the inauguration of the new University building in 1887, was sent to Miss Emma Svensson at Tierp and was post-marked on the day of the inauguration (17 May). In private possession.*

The new academic milieu was soon completed by John Börjeson's statue of Erik Gustaf Geijer in the University Park, which was unveiled in the autumn of 1888. It was significant that neither Rudbeck nor Linnaeus was considered for this statue—the *genius loci* selected was a humanist who personified man's endeavour to attain to the ideal world.

It was a long time before this endeavour ceased to be of current interest in Uppsala. Academic oratory poured forth from the University lecterns until far into the 20th century; high-minded ways of thinking were still good form and the celebrations commemorating the anniversaries of great men and events showed no tendency to decrease for the present. The tercentenary of the Uppsala Synod was celebrated in 1893 with great pomp and the conferment of doctoral degrees in the presence of the royal family, the Grand Duke of Saxe-Weimer-Eisenach, and a representative of the German Emperor. Linnaeus offered welcome pretexts. In January 1878, the centenary of his death was commemorated with speeches, lectures and verses by Frithiof Holmgren, the physiologist, who always had verses ready for such occasions. But the bicentenary of the birth of the "Prince of Flowers" was celebrated in the spring of 1907 with much more splendid ceremonies. Uppsala was decked with flags and triumphal arches, choruses were sung and concerts given, and a large number of foreign celebrities in the domain of natural science were made doctors *honoris causa* in the Cathedral. The royal family could always be counted upon to be present on these occasions. Oscar II stood out as a cordial patron of the sciences, and official Uppsala responded to this patronage with a heartily expressed loyalty. It meant a great deal that the King's sons were sent in turn to study at Uppsala; Crown Prince Gustav studied there in 1877–8 and his marriage to Victoria was celebrated with a banquet in the Carolina Hall. On the 25th anniversary of Oscar II's accession to the throne in 1897, the University presented him with a voluminous *Festschrift*.

As the 20th century advanced, the intellectual climate became increasingly harsh, as regarded the most inflated manifestations of academic joy. But the 450th anniversary of the University's foundation in 1927 was still celebrated in the traditional style. There were royal guests, illuminations and fireworks, mead-drinking at Old Uppsala "in old Swedish fashion", a commemoration in the Aula with cantatas by Hugo Alfvén and Gunnar Mascoll Silfverstolpe, and conferments of doctoral degrees in the Cathedral; the Oscarian era was breathing its last. Some monuments of the 1927 celebrations still remain: Christian Eriksson's statue of Archbishop Jakob Ulvsson on its porphyry column on the south side of the Cathedral, Eldh's statue of Prince Gustav, the "Prince of Singers", by the Carolina Rediviva, and the facsimile edition of the Silver Bible, the Codex Argenteus, made with almost incredible toil.

All the same, the last few decades of the 19th century saw the beginning of a new stage in the University's development. High-flown, increasingly stylized idealism now faced competition from other philosophies of life. In his book *Från Fjerdingen och Svartbäcken*, which was published in the quatercentenary year of 1877, August Strindberg from his own experience described the situation at the beginning of the 1870s. As critic and debunker, he was aiming at several targets; he scourged in disgust the students' predilection for convivial toping and the narrowness of the academic outlook. An attitude of disillusioned cynicism had begun to be adopted, to which the good, the noble and the beautiful seemed almost absurd; the word "idealist" had "become a nickname there". During the following decade, the radical zeal for reforming society penetrated into the student world and the window was thrown open to admit the contemporary winds created by the European movements for reform. The Verdandi Society gathered together the young political combatants, who made their way along with a great hullabaloo; from now on, the current problems of society and domestic policy were to keep both students and professors fully occupied. At the same time, the conditions and methods of research and instruction were gradually changed. The time-honoured humanistic educational ideal lost its hold. In the name of progress and optimism, the sciences, chiefly the natural sciences, acquired the power in society and the reputation which they still possess. With their increasing specialization, new subjects and new chairs came into existence, which called for new institutes, laboratories, museums and lecture rooms. The students became increasingly single-minded in their studies, which were arranged in more fixed forms, with precisely stated requirements and modern educational approaches.

The University was to largely remain in the state into which it had developed towards the end of the 19th century right up to the Second World War. It expanded slowly, but no far-reaching reforms were carried out. The new statutes which were promulgated in 1908 and which actually only intensified certain modern features in the 1876 statutes were to apply in all essentials right up to the mid 1950s; the new statutes which came into force in 1916 changed nothing in principle. The Swedish universities appeared to have taken their shape for an indefinite period to come.

The administration was still more centralized by the 1908 statutes. The Chancellor and the Rector were elected (the latter for three years) by the "University Congregation" (an innovation at this time), which consisted of the whole body of professors. Some Rectors were elected over and over again and consequently came—especially in representative contexts—to brilliantly personify the University for long periods. This applied to Carl Yngve Sahlin, the philosopher, during the Oscarian period, to Henrik Schück, the imposing literary historian, between 1905 and 1918, and to his successor, Ludvig Stavenow, the historian. A melancholy change was introduced towards the end of the period, when the office of Pro-Chancellor, held by the Archbishop, was abolished (1934). The ancient link between the Church and the University administration was thereby broken for ever. The Chancellor, who was now, in accordance with the statutes, common to Uppsala, Lund and the Karolinska Institute, was still the elected representative of these establishments of higher learning and safeguarded their interests in relation to the government in rather idyllic forms even in the 1930s.

From 1908 onwards, the University's real administrative and decision-making body—the Senate—no longer consisted of the assembled body of professors but of a limited number of representatives of the different faculties, which made it far more manageable. The Council and the Finance Committee continued in existence. The offices of Dean in the faculties and sections still changed holders in turn, according to seniority, which sometimes had unfortunate consequences. The financial administration, under the direction of the Bursar, was still run on the old lines. The University's ordinary running costs, which were regulated in revenue and expenditure estimates approved by the Government, were now defrayed predominantly by government grants. Of the good 1,000,000 crowns which constituted the University's income in the mid 1910s, the government provided 846,000 crowns, while the Gustavian donation yielded a total of 189,000 crowns in grain, rents from the freehold farms and income from the forests. The University Bailiff and the Forest Administrator were responsible for these lands. From the University's forests, there also came what was called "University firewood", which was assigned to certain officials as an extra perquisite. When the State took over responsibility for the running of the University, the yield from the Gustavian hereditary estates had become available for other purposes; it was substantially transferred to the reserve fund and was used, on request to the Chancellor, to pay for expensive scientific equipment or to cover other current needs.

The number of permanent professors, who since 1876 had been appointed after consultations with three experts, was drastically increased by a decision of the 1908 Riksdag. The transformation of the old *adjunkt* posts into non-established professorships (see above, p. 162) had meant an improvement but was soon found to be only a step on the way. Although the non-established professors had the same obligations as their permanent colleagues and carried the sole responsibility for often extensive subject fields, they drew much lower salaries and were not members of the Senate. The matter was being investigated at the universities as early as the mid 1890s and full equality was demanded. When the proposed reform was at length submitted to the interested parties for their comments, the Senate at Uppsala oddly enough objected to it (1903), but it could not be rejected in the long run and was carried out in connection with the promulgation of the new statutes. As from January 1909, all temporary professorships were given permanent status. After this date, there were only two main kinds of teacher at the Swedish universities —professors and *docenter*. The latter, who were appointed by the Chancellor, continued to work, and still do so today, under the old, insecure conditions; only a few held *docent* fellowships for limited periods. These fellowships amounted (1916) to 2,500 crowns *per annum*, while a professor's salary at that time was 7,500 crowns. However, the theologians still enjoyed special conditions. By tradition, they possessed prebends in parishes round Uppsala and received only any necessary increases from the salaries fund. This traditional link between the Faculty of Theology and the Church ceased only in 1937, when the Dean (the senior Professor of Theology) resigned the Vaksala prebend.

Certain important changes in the examination system were introduced during this period. They were chiefly aimed at finally abolishing the ideal of general education handed down from previous ages and at further increasing the vocational orientation of the studies instead. The preliminary examination for admission to the Faculty of Law was abolished in 1904 and that for admission to the Faculty of Medicine in 1907; only the preliminary examination for admission to the Faculty of Theology (in Greek, Hebrew and theoretical philosophy) remained and this was not abolished until 1955. The most extensive changes were made in the Faculty of Arts. The predominance of Latin in the humanities was broken for ever in the new regulations for degrees in arts and sciences in 1891, by which Latin ceased to be a compulsory subject. At the same time, syllabuses laid down by the Chancellor were introduced, with carefully specified requirements in each subject; the student's vague wanderings on the ocean of knowledge were brought to an end. The next regulations for degrees in the arts came in the autumn of 1907 and remained in force for a long time to come. They introduced a startling innovation—the modern Master of Arts degree, which was intended as a professional qualification for future secondary-school teachers. It was to include seven points in three subjects belonging to one of a number of fixed groups of subjects adapted to the needs of the schools, together with a teacher-training course. The Bachelor of Arts degree now required a total of six points in only three optional subjects. The requirements for the licentiate degree were also reduced; it was to be gained in only one subject. Printed university handbooks, giving the syllabuses, were introduced at this time—not only in the Faculty of Arts—and each student was given an examination record (*tentamensbok*) on enrolment in the faculty. The university handbooks had in fact been promoted by a resolute initiative on the part of the radical student association Verdandi, which published the first edition (for the Faculty of Arts) in 1887. It was rapidly followed by others, until the University took them over *ex officio*. At the beginning of the present century, which may be described as having been an eventful period in the history of the Swedish universities, the other faculties were also given long-term degree regulations—the Faculty of Theology in 1903, the Faculty of Law in 1904 and the Faculty of Medicine in 1907.

It was not until 1935 that all university degrees became valid throughout the kingdom. Moreover, their number was now increased by the establishment of a degree in political science and law and a corresponding degree in political science and philosophy, with economics, statistics and political science as compulsory subjects; in their way, they were modern replacements for the socially oriented civil-service examinations introduced in the 18th century but finally abolished at this time.

The reforms at the beginning of this century also involved a minor revolution in the Faculty of Theology. It will be recalled that, ever since the 17th century, doctors of theology had been appointed and conferments of doctoral degrees in theology had been arranged only on the orders of the King. It was only in the university statutes of 1908 and the special regulations in the same year that the Faculty was given the right to arrange conferments of doctoral degrees itself and to promote licentiates to the doctorate after the customary defence of a thesis. The Faculty held the first conferment of doctoral degrees under its own auspices in May 1911, when Nathan Söderblom officiated. Conferments of doctoral degrees in the higher faculties were by no means annual events. The first regular conferment of such degrees for all the faculties jointly was held in the University Aula in the 1930s; before this time, the ceremonies were usually arranged separately, in the Aula, in the faculty room or in the Cathedral.

The development of the University up to the Second World War can most easily be measured by the growth in the number of students and the increase of the teaching body. In neither case were there any drastic changes. The course of events had the character of a peaceful expansion, and barely that as far as the teachers were concerned.

The number of students at Uppsala between 1880 and 1945 will be given below. It is somewhat problematic. The figures, which are to be found in the student catalogues and refer to the autumn terms, give the total number of students enrolled in the nations. But this means that they are too high; as previously, the number of active students actually attending the University was much lower. During the 20th century, this tendency was reinforced, because former students who had gone out into the world but wished to keep in touch with Uppsala remained on the rolls of their old nations at reduced fees. It is not possible to decide for certain how numerous these nominal nation members were in various decades; it has been estimated that in the 1930s they amounted to 12–25% of the total number enrolled and accordingly the gross figures should be reduced by corresponding amounts, in order to arrive at the number of students who were actually attending the University. In Lund, where the nations were not of the same importance, the catalogue was drawn up on somewhat different lines; it included only active students and therefore exact comparisons of the numbers of students at the two universities are hazardous. Nevertheless, the higher and more certain gross figures are fully serviceable for a clear description of the growth of the student body in Uppsala. They give the following picture, on the whole. From a good 1,500 students in 1880, the number enrolled rose to about 4,500 in the autumn of 1945, i.e. it trebled in 65 years. The development was uneven at first. After a rise in the 1880s (with a maximum of 1,928 students in 1886), the number fell back to about 1,500 in the 1890s for reasons that are uncertain. Only after a few years of the new century did the fairly steady increase begin which characterized the picture to the end of the period and beyond:

210

STUDIEHANDBOK

FÖR DEM SOM VID

UPSALA UNIVERSITET

ÄMNA AFLÄGGA

FILOSOFIE KANDIDAT-EXAMEN

ELLER NÅGON AF DE

FÖRBEREDANDE EXAMINA

TILL TJÄNST

FÖR DE STUDERANDE VID

UPSALA UNIVERSITET och STOCKHOLMS HÖGSKOLA

UTGIFVEN AF

FÖRENINGEN VERDANDI.

— ✕ —

UPSALA
FÖRENINGEN VERDANDIS FÖRLAG.

70. Title-page of the first University handbook, published in 1887 by the Verdandi student association.

211

a good 2,000 students about 1910, barely 3,000 in the mid 1920s, a certain standstill around 3,200 during the first half of the 1930s, and thereafter a steady rise, which was accentuated in the war years, to 4,500.

No detailed comments on these figures will be given here. The expansion was an effect of the rise in the population of Sweden and of an increasing interest in education, chiefly among the middle class, whose members filled most of the higher posts and official appointments. In addition, the invasion of women students was an important new factor. After the first tentative efforts (see above, p. 172), there was a breakthrough in this respect about 1910, when the number of women students jumped to about 8% of the total, then slowly increased to 15% in the mid 1930s and subsequently escalated to 28% during the war years. However, the number of Uppsala students must also be seen in a wider national perspective. Towards the end of the 19th century, new private educational establishments were founded—Stockholm *Högskola* (1878) and Gothenburg *Högskola* (1891)—which offered academic instruction at the highest level. These colleges, which were supported by the generosity of donors and local enthusiasm, were at first incomplete; Stockholm *Högskola* originally concentrated almost exclusively on the natural sciences and Gothenburg *Högskola* on the humanities. But they were gradually expanded, especially Stockholm *Högskola*, which from the beginning of the 1920s had the right to confer degrees in the Faculty of Arts and Sciences and the Faculty of Law. Consequently, the two national universities were faced with competition, which reduced the influx of students to them. This was most clearly noticeable in Uppsala, whose proximity to the capital led to a considerable decline in the student nation which had long been the largest —Stockholm, in which law students predominated. As a result of the increased prestige of the Karolinska Institute, the Faculty of Medicine at Uppsala also lost some ground; moreover, even in the 1930s, Uppsala did not offer a complete medical training and some subjects had to be studied in Stockholm. As the provincial university of southern Sweden, the University of Lund maintained its position better and in fact shows a far greater increase than Uppsala; if only the number of active students is counted, the two seats of learning were of roughly the same size in the 1930s. By this time, developments had reached the point at which Uppsala no longer appeared to be the national university in the old sense. It now received only 24% of all the Swedish students attending seats of higher learning. As a result, its large catchment area in Norrland became increasingly important for its recruitment, a fact which is reflected in the vigorous growth of the Norrland nation, which has been the biggest of the nations since the 1910s.

The history of the development of the teaching body during the period

1880–1945 is not very edifying. This applies to the professors, alongside whom there were only a few scattered permanent teachers, such as *laboratorer* (associate professors in the Faculty of Sciences), a couple of foreign lecturers in modern languages (since 1888) and the throng of *docenter*. The domination of the professors was still absolute; everything depended on the professor, who was alone responsible for his subject field and at lectures and seminars also took charge of the elementary instruction. At the beginning of the period (1880), there were in Uppsala 52 professors in all, including the new non-established professors who later gained established status. By the end of the Second World War (1945), there were no more than 75, i.e. an increase of not quite 50% during a long period when the sciences, chiefly the natural sciences and medicine, were expanding continuously in the rest of the world and were being divided into specialist disciplines requiring their own professorial chairs. Thus, the government was not pursuing a liberal and far-sighted university policy in this respect, but the low rate of growth can probably also be explained by a certain lack of initiative on the part of the faculties and the Senate in Uppsala. When, at the same time, the number of students was trebled, this meant that each professor received an unreasonable increase in his work load. The 23 new professorships instituted during the period were rather unevenly distributed in time. During the first half of the period, there was a modest but steady expansion, until the number of professors increased to about 70 in the mid 1910s. Then, during the 1920s, there was a period of standstill or even decline; no new chairs were established until the 1930s (seven in all), but then nothing happened during the war years.

A glance at the different faculties will reveal some variety in the picture. The Faculties of Theology and Law did not expand at all after the turn of the century. There were invariably eight professors of law and also eight professors of theology (or, in the 1910s and 1920s, only seven). The stagnation in the Faculty of Medicine is the more remarkable. The number of professors there had increased in the last few decades of the 19th century from 11 to 14 but then did not increase until the 1910s, when another two were appointed, and remained at 16 or less to the end of the period. The nearly 100-year-old rivalry with the Karolinska Institute probably played a part in this; to the government authorities, it was more natural to invest money in the Institute, which now had the prestige of awarding the Nobel Prize, than to expand the faculty at Uppsala.

It is the Faculty of Arts and Sciences which attracts the greatest attention, with its two sections—one for the humanities and the other for mathematics and the natural sciences. It claimed the greater part of the increase in the professorial body (17 new chairs, 10 of which were in the humanities

213

section). Almost all of them were imperatively necessary, i.e. extorted by the needs of teaching and research. This applied especially to the modern languages, which towards the end of the 1880s were still being taken care of by a single Professor of Modern European Linguistics but were now (1887) divided between two chairs—a permanent chair of Romance languages and a non-established chair of Germanic languages, i.e. German and English. The latter was soon divided again, after a petition by students in Uppsala and Lund, which led to the establishment of two professorships in Germanic languages (1903–4), one in German and the other in English. Yet another group of living languages, the Slav, had been assigned a chair in 1890; this was long held by the eccentric J. A. Lundell, who is otherwise best known as the creator of the Swedish dialect alphabet. Fifteen years later (1905), a personal professorship of Finno-Ugrian linguistics was created for K. B. Wiklund, an expert on the Lapp language. The temperamental Karl Piehl, who died prematurely, was also primarily a linguistic scholar; he held the chair of Egyptology for a few years around 1900 and created the Victoria Museum of Egyptian Antiquities. Moreover, the other archaeological sciences in Uppsala were also expanded in the early years of the present century. They had become rather fashionable and could no longer be excluded from the academic curriculum. Schliemann's excavations at Troy had astonished the world and in Sweden Hans Hildebrand and Oscar Montelius had guided Scandinavian archaeology into new paths. The pioneer of modern classical archaeology in Uppsala, and in Sweden, was Sam Wide, who was the first to occupy the chair of archaeology (1909), after having produced an ample series of scholarly works on vase painting and the religions of antiquity. By this time, regular courses on Scandinavian archaeology had been given for some years, for the first time since Verelius had lectured on Swedish antiquities in the heyday of Gothic romanticism in the 17th century. But the chair of Scandinavian and comparative archaeology did not come into existence until 1913.

At the turn of the century, geography, which had long formed part of other subjects, at last acquired its own professorship in Uppsala; this also was extorted by student pressure (1901). During the years around 1910, when the government authorities proved to be remarkably favourable, a further two chairs in the humanities were created. One of them was a chair of education, which was regarded as essential for teacher-training. Teacher-training courses had been given in Lund and Uppsala as early as the beginning of the 19th century, primarily for the needs of private tutors, and a course in educational theory for prospective teachers was introduced at both universities in 1875. In 1908, after various travails, the University finally succeeded in obtaining the first chair of education in

71. *Henrik Schück wearing the rectorial chain. Oil painting by Anders Zorn (1915).*
University of Uppsala.

Sweden. The chair of statistics, which was established in 1910 and was
awarded to Gustav Sundbärg, the celebrated student of emigration, patriot
and popular psychologist, was characteristic of the period—a consequence
of the practical needs of society.

But then came the world war, and a period of wretchedness followed.

In the 30 years between 1915 and 1945, the University acquired only three new chairs in the humanities—one of them as a result of a private donation—and three in the natural sciences. The professorship of art history (1917) was the fruit of long preparation. It was split off from the old professorship of aesthetics, which included the history of both literature and art. Henrik Schück, who was responsible for this vast subject, lectured only on literature and was therefore desirous of having the subject divided. In 1907, art history was taken over by an assistant lecturer and became a degree subject in its own right. Ten years later, the professorial chair was established and was occupied by August Hahr. The other two chairs in humanistic subjects were instituted as personal professorships for two eminent scholars who had marked out the boundaries of new disciplines. Jöran Sahlgren was appointed in 1930 to the chair of Scandinavian place-name research and Johan Nordström in 1932 to the chair of the history of learning established by a private bequest. The straitened circumstances of the time, with its economic depression and unemployment, made further progress impossible. The lean years were at hand. The Universities Commission which was appointed in 1933 was instructed to propose measures of rationalization and joint planning by the universities, in order to save money for the government. The professorships of philosophy at Uppsala were among the posts which suffered; one of them was withdrawn until further notice in 1933 and the lack of talent of the remaining professor, who was responsible single-handed for the subject of philosophy over its entire range, meant that for a few years it went, generally speaking, uncultivated.

The chairs in the natural sciences were still far fewer in number than those in the humanities. Most of the seven which were newly established during the period were personal chairs or created through private generosity. In 1897, Frans Kempe, the Norrland timber magnate, donated funds for a professorship of plant biology. The University staff and students had long tried to urge on the creation of personal professorships for particularly deserving scholars by lobbying government departments and the Riksdag, usually with little success; however, the situation improved in the early years of the present century. In 1910, after persistent efforts, they succeeded in securing a personal chair of palaeontology for Carl Wiman, and two years later a chair of physical chemistry for The Svedberg, the brilliant young chemist. In 1919, Hugo von Zeipel was awarded a personal professorship of astronomy (with the right to examine students in geodesy). At the beginning of the 1930s, thanks to a private donation by John Andersson, the electrical engineer, a chair of electricity with special reference to atmospheric discharges (commonly known as "the thunder chair") was founded and the related institute (the Institute of High-voltage

216

Research) was erected outside Uppsala. The professorship of bio-chemistry created in 1938 for Arne Tiselius was also paid for by a private donation.

The slow rate of expansion did not prevent the erection of new institutes of medicine and natural science. As always, the humanists, theologians and lawyers made more modest demands and were accommodated wherever it was convenient in older buildings. The chief problem was to house the seminar libraries; thus, in 1898, Ekerman House on St. Larsgatan was assigned to the humanistic seminars. In the 1910s, the Institutes of Art History and Archaeology, which had their own collections, moved into the Gustavianum, which had been vacated by the zoologists. By that time, not only zoology but three other natural sciences had moved into new buildings. This took place during the short period after the turn of the century when the favour of the government authorities was unusually generous towards the University. The new chemistry building (Chemicum) was the first to be completed. The progress of chemistry and the rise in the number of students had made inadequate the institute building which Svanberg had erected in the English Park and which was not yet 50 years old. The Riksdag voted funds and the new institute was opened in 1904—a spacious building adjacent to the old Chemicum, still in use, with its laboratories and lecture rooms and the busts of Berg-man, Scheele and Berzelius over the entrance. The physicists obtained their own institute in 1908, having up to then been crowded into the old Chemicum. Their building was essentially the work of Knut Ångström, Professor of Physics, and was erected behind the new Chemicum, with a tower for the investigation of solar radiation and an iron-free room for magnetic research. The plant biologists moved in 1914 into the agreeable villa in Kåbo which they still occupy. In its vicinity rose the new Institute of Zoology in a monumental design inspired by national romanticism; it was completed in 1916 and has three large museum halls and a zootomic laboratory. A few years earlier, a station for instruction in marine zoology had been set up at Klubban near Fiskebäckskil (Bohuslän) with funds provided by a private donor. These developments meant that something which was beginning to resemble a quarter for natural-science research was taking shape beyond the Carolina Rediviva and the English Park. But then no further expansion took place until the 1930s. The mineralogists and geologists, who occupied the old Senate House on St. Erik's Square, were overcrowded, especially after the subject was divided and Carl Wiman became Professor of Palaeontology. Wiman was an enthusiast who gathered large collections of fossils from China, South America and Spitsbergen; he at length brought off the feat of extorting 791,000 crowns from the Riksdag to build an imposing Institute of Palaeontology, includ-

217

ing a museum, in the field behind the Zoologicum (1931). There remained the botanists, who lived in snug, old-fashioned quarters in Thunberg's old Botanicum until a new Institute of Physiological Botany was completed in the garden next door.

Progress was slower for the medical sciences. The main, theoretical, pre-clinical subjects were long housed in the old buildings on Trädgårds-gatan and Västra Ågatan. Histology (which had been a special examina-tion subject since 1886) shared the same accommodation as anatomy; when bacteriology finally acquired its own professorship in 1914, the In-stitute was housed for the time being in the first Regnellianum, i.e. the Institute of Pathology. From the beginning of the present century, the pharmacologists and the medical chemists occupied the old Chemicum, which they shared with the geographers. Thus, at the beginning of the 1930s, all the pre-clinical subjects were still housed in old premises dating from the previous century. But now a new building for the histologists was opened next to the Anatomicum by the river, and a few years later a spacious building for the Institute of Pathology and the Institute of Hygiene and Bacteriology was inaugurated on Stockholmsvägen.

The University Hospital, where clinical research and instruction were carried on at the patients' bedsides, was in a poor and antiquated condi-tion at the turn of the century. The main building, dating from the 1860s, with the medical clinic on the ground floor and the surgical clinic on the first floor, was overcrowded and no longer adequate. No detailed account will be given here of the way in which the Hospital, of which the Uni-versity and the county councils were the joint principals, extended over the old Bleket site with its new buildings and pavilions in the following decades. The periods of intensive new construction were the years 1901–4, when separate clinics were built for ophthalmiatrics and obstetrics and gynaecology, which had been independent subjects since 1891, and the mid 1920s, when the building work culminated in the new Department of Surgery. Radiology and paediatrics now acquired their own buildings. The mental-health services had long been housed in the—for its time—ultra-modern hospital at Ulleråker, completed in 1882. But the outpatient de-partments were accommodated to the very last outside the growing hospital complex; right up to the mid 1920s, ailing people made their way to Ekerman House by the Gustavianum, which the surgical and medical outpatient departments had occupied since the 1880s.

The University Library, Carolina Rediviva, underwent several drastic changes. The Chief Librarian in the decades around the turn of the century was Claes Annerstedt, the most outstanding holder of the post after Ben-zelius and Aurivillius and the author of a monumental history of the Uni-versity. He initiated the rebuilding work which became necessary after the

218

72. The new Institute of Chemistry, inaugurated in 1904, in the Carolina park.

Carolina Hall on the top floor had been released for the use of the Library. But it was not actually fitted up as a book store until the 1910s, while a new building containing reading-rooms was erected behind the main building. A third period of renovation began in the 1930s, when Anders Grape was Chief Librarian and the book stock (about 30,000 shelf metres) threatened to overflow all bounds. At this time, the general reading-room was enlarged with new reading-rooms at each end, and six rooms for research workers, together with a periodical room, were fitted up.

The Library was constantly enriched by new donations of books. The largest one came at the beginning of the period (1880–1), when the Library was given the enormous collection of books and manuscripts on Swedish history belonging to Jacob Westin, the great Stockholm collector. Westin also donated a considerable sum of money for the foundation of a scholarly society in Uppsala—the Royal Society of the Humanities—which started in 1889. The natural scientists in the University still gathered in the venerable Royal Society of Sciences, which had long had its own building on St. Erik's Square. These local academies played, and still play, an important part as intermediaries of the advances of science and as social clubs for overburdened professors.

2

Scholarship in Uppsala during the reigns of Oscar III and Gustav V was maintained primarily by a limited number of outstanding—in some cases brilliant—professors. Up to the 1920s, they were mainly humanists. The decades before and after 1900 were a period of unprecedented glory for the humanities at the University.

Three names shone with special lustre—those of Harald Hjärne, Adolf Noreen and Henrik Schück. They were followed, in a younger generation, by the two philosophers Hägerström and Phalén. Of Harald Hjärne, who became Professor of History in 1885, it may be said that his influence extended far beyond the boundaries of historical research. He was a monumental figure, exerting overwhelming authority. As a historian, he loved bold, sweeping lines; he was unusually free of prejudice and at the same time an austere realist, who saw the core of history in the concepts of the law and the State. In this, Hjärne carried on an earlier, idealistic tradition but gave Swedish historical research a new dimension by his alert source criticism and superb analyses of, *inter alia*, Sweden's European policy during its period as a great power. As the years went by, current politics came to fascinate him more and more; though very independent in these matters as well, he finally made common cause with the Conservatives, found the question of defence to be of prime importance and saw the will of God as the driving force behind world events. Harald Hjärne's greatness is perhaps difficult to understand today. He never concentrated on producing comprehensive scholarly works; his influence was exerted chiefly by his personal presence. According to the testimony of many witnesses, he was magnificent at the famous post-seminars or *Nachspiele* after the meetings of the Historical Association, when he spent hours analysing for his admiring pupils in his ponderous and powerful style the labyrinth of world politics and the play of historical forces. In the 1920s and 1930s, after Hjärne's death, history was again taught in more ordinary forms; Swedish historical research was then renewed in Lund and not in Uppsala.

Adolf Noreen was in all respects the complete opposite of Hjärne —quick, alert and informal, with an enthusiasm which attracted generations of students to his subject, Scandinavian philology. Noreen's post-seminars at Gästis were as famous as his colleague's, but they were more cheerful. Noreen became Professor of Scandinavian Languages in 1887 and had in his youth introduced from Germany—which was still Sweden's mother country, scientifically speaking—the new linguistic ideas of the *Junggrammatiker* or neogrammarians. This means that he was principally a linguist. In his copious works, Noreen dealt with Swedish dialects, etymological problems and basic grammatical questions. In his huge but

73. Harald Hjärne, the
historian, one of the
dominating figures in
Uppsala at the turn of
the century.

uncompleted work entitled *Vårt Språk* (Our Language) (1903–24), he intended to give a broad account of modern Swedish grammar but only
managed to finish the phonetical part. Scandinavian philology in Uppsala
continued to flourish under two of Noreen's pupils. Otto von Friesen
(*d*. 1942) had a historical and archaeological bent and was one of the foremost runic scholars of his time; his thesis on the origin of the runes among
the Goths on the Black Sea aroused lively discussion. His somewhat
younger colleague, Bengt Hesselman, emerges from his versatile and per-
ceptive writings as a dialect scholar, historian of language, publisher of
texts and *Realphilolog*.

The third of these great men, Henrik Schück, the literary historian,
was a glutton for labour and produced a greater number of scholarly works
than any other Swedish humanist. After a brief interlude in Lund, which
he did not like, he was restored to Uppsala in 1898 as Professor of
Aesthetics. But Schück was no aesthetician in the fastidious sense. He
turned away with distaste from the German idealistic aesthetics which
prevailed in the Uppsala of his youth and rejoiced when he was relieved
from the task of teaching art history (see above, p. 216). Schück regarded
the literary texts in a positivist spirit as historical documents which should
be treated by the normal historical method. He was a cultural as much

221

as a literary historian and had a wide-ranging and graphic style. Single-handed, he worked through the whole of Swedish literature from the Middle Ages onwards. He issued his great summary of it in *Illustrerad svensk litteraturhistoria* (An Illustrated History of Swedish Literature) (the 3rd edition, 1926–30, was entirely written by Schück), which was originally published under the names of Schück and Warburg and which devotes as much space to the history of learning and the material conditions of literature as to the poets and novelists. But Schück, who was as universal as Hjärne, also wrote an excellent book on Shakespeare and published an account of the history of world literature in six volumes (1919–25). As a teacher, he was exacting and a sworn enemy of all *beaux esprits;* his seminars, which were held between 8 and 10 in the morning, took the form of pedantic tests. Schück's work was of methodological importance owing to his endeavouring to place literature in the broad context of society and the history of ideas. This endeavour was continued in Uppsala by his pupil Anton Blanck, who succeeded him as Professor in 1922, and perhaps even more by Johan Nordström, who in 1932 became professor of the new subject of the history of learning and who was a pioneer of modern research in the history of science in Sweden. It has been spread by his pupils to other Swedish universities.

Nathan Söderblom may also be mentioned here. It is true that he was a theologian and a historian of religion, that in 1901 he was made professor of the amorphous subject known as "theological prenotions" and that finally he became Archbishop and Pro-Chancellor of the University. But, with his universalism, the enormous breadth of his interests and his complete freedom from dogmatism, he was likewise a great humanist. He came to Uppsala from Paris like an unpredictable breath of fresh air and right up to his death in 1931 he was regarded as an omnipresent spiritual force, admired by almost everybody. As a historian of religion, he was an authority on the religion of Iran; in his later works he gave his profoundly personal view of Luther and the Christian experience of God. From first to last, Söderblom influenced people by his personal charm, with increasing virtuosity as the years went by; he had the true artistic temperament and was a seducer whose public speeches and daily intercourse with people were characterized by dazzling improvisations and surprising approaches.

Other humanistic subjects also flourished at this time under eminent teachers. This applied especially to the classical languages. They had for centuries been the nuclei of Swedish and European academic culture, but now they were transformed into modern philological disciplines, in which the scholars kept within the bounds of the subject. O. A. Danielsson, who became Professor of Greek in 1891, was an imposing figure, a pioneer

222

of comparative linguistics in Sweden and immensely learned. He moved with the same ease in Greek, Latin, ancient Italian dialects and Sanskrit, and in later years devoted his acumen to studying the mysterious Etruscan inscriptions. His younger colleague, Per Persson, stands out as a pioneer of modern methods in Latin philology in Uppsala. But he too was primarily interested in comparative linguistics in the spirit of the age and was famous for his works on Indo-Germanic stem formation and word research. How classical archaeology acquired its own professorial chair (occupied by Sam Wide) has already been mentioned (see above, p. 214). In Axel W. Persson, from Lund, this chair had an occupant who brought Swedish field archaeology on classical sites up to the highest international level, at which his pupils maintained it for a long time to come. His own excavations at Asine and Dendra, where a royal grave full of treasure was discovered, shed new light on Mycenaean culture.

In H. S. Nyberg, the oriental languages at last found a representative of unusual versatility and breadth. Nyberg, who became Professor of Semitic Languages in 1931, was both a philologist and a historian of religion; he dealt with Arabic and Old Testament texts but made his principal contribution as a Persian scholar with a famous study of the ancient Iranian religions and with handbooks of Pahlavi.

The old Skyttean professorship was still full of life but on new terms. Oratory silently disappeared; from Svedelius's time onwards (see above, p. 195), the chair was devoted to political science in the modern sense. This did not prevent it from becoming a platform for current political propaganda. Oscar Alin, who was the Skyttean Professor from 1882 to 1900 and an implacable Conservative, was an expert on constitutional law who advised on the question of the Union between Sweden and Norway, which he expounded in the spirit of Swedish nationalism. The external conditions of European politics were investigated by Alin's pupil, Rudolf Kjellén (d. 1922), who was the Skyttean Professor in the last few years of his life. In private life an amiable and liberal man, he was inspired by German examples and became an ideologist of unscrupulous power politics; what he called "geopolitics" was one of the ideological properties of National Socialism. Political science at Uppsala was liberated from reactionary tendencies only by his successor, Axel Brusewitz. By his works on the structure and development of modern Swedish parliamentarism, Brusewitz stimulated a large number of his pupils, some of whom became journalists and were politically active.

Features of the national romanticism at the turn of the century are often conspicuous in the humanistic research which has been outlined here. Swedish culture and the distinctive Swedish character were favourite subjects; this is true of both Schück and Noreen, of Hjärne perhaps to a smaller extent. This romantic nationalist feeling reached its academic climax in the birth of modern Swedish art history. Here the leading figure was the young Johnny Roosval, who was still only an assistant lecturer in art history but about 1910 was arousing the enthusiasm of a whole crowd of students for the forgotten art treasures of the Middle Ages. They rode in caravans of bicycles through the countryside round Lake Mälaren to make inventories of the pictures, vestments and sacred vessels in the old churches; a very serious atmosphere prevailed at Roosval's seminars. The art and not the literary historians were the Uppsala aesthetes in the 1910s. A whole generation of leading Swedish art historians went out from Roosval's school. August Hahr, who finally became Professor of Art History, was equally typical of his time; his actual field of research was the national Renaissance architecture of the Vasa period. Hahr's successor, Gregor Paulsson, orientated Uppsala art history in the 1930s towards modern theoretical and sociological problems.

Philosophy in Uppsala took an interesting turn after 1900. The prevailing Boströmian idealism was disintegrated. The signs had been seen at an early date. When Pontus Wikner, who was beloved by the students, applied for the vacant chair of theoretical philosophy in 1885, the Boströmian experts would not accept him. Wikner, who was much more profound philosophically than his rivals for the chair, had differed from Boström in important respects and was therefore regarded as a heretic. But the new era of Swedish philosophy did not begin until Hägerström and Phalén appeared on the scene. The traditional idealism, and with it metaphysics, were thrown out, and philosophy became a specialist science, like the others, with limited aims. This "Uppsala philosophy" was developed by its two creators by a process of mutual give-and-take. Axel Hägerström, who became Professor of Practical Philosophy in 1911, took up chiefly law and ethics. He was a value nihilist and denied all objectively valid standards or rules of law; belief in such things was superstition —morality and law reflected only arbitrary and subjective feelings, accepted by convention. Hägerström developed his revolutionary value theory with a quiet fanaticism which made a great impression and even influenced Swedish jurists, including Vilhelm Lundstedt, the temperamental Professor of Civil Law in Uppsala. Hägerström's younger colleague, Adolf Phalén, who was Professor of Theoretical Philosophy until his untimely death in 1931, devoted his attention to the theory of knowledge. In opposition to the accepted idealistic doctrine, he asserted that there is an objective reality which is independent of the human subject. To Phalén, the main task of philosophy was the logical analysis of concepts, i.e. the critical scrutiny of the linguistic statements of philosophy, science and common sense. Both Hägerström and Phalén led philosophy

224

74. *Axel Hägerström,*
who induced the Uppsala
philosophers to abandon
Boström and take up
modern philosophy.

towards approximately the same goal as the modern currents of ideas on the Continent and in England, but there was no direct connection. The new Uppsala philosophy had its period of glory in the 1920s and 1930s, when it became part of the intellectual climate at the University and left its mark on many thinkers outside the circle of the professional philosophers. The situation was completely different in Lund, where Hans Larsson's gentle wisdom reigned and had little in common with the frosty search for truth in Uppsala.

Academic humanism in Sweden was still deriving its main stimuli from Germany, which was the leading scientific nation in the world up to the Hitler period. This applied even more to the theologians, who were bound by the Lutheran creed.

Uppsala theology was in a rather poor way towards the end of the 19th century. The only outstanding name was that of the mild and pious Waldemar Rudin, who was an exegetist and an authority on Kierkegaard. The situation became brighter after the turn of the century, when two rising

225

stars put new life into theological studies. One of them was, of course, Nathan Söderblom and the other Einar Billing, who later became Bishop of Västerås and was perhaps the more profound thinker in his struggle with the fundamental problems of faith. Otherwise, the overshadowing problem now was the new historico-critical method of Bible research, which appeared to threaten the foundations of Lutheran dogma. It gained ground in Uppsala, where Erik Stave, the exegetist, announced its results and the flexible and fearless Söderblom worked in the same candid spirit. To him, fellowship with Christ rather than dogma was the essence of Christianity. However, the Uppsala theologians were still so narrow-minded at this time that, when Torgny Segerstedt, Sr, in 1903 defended a thesis on the origins of polytheism, he was accused of lack of orthodoxy and excluded from his *docent* post in a scandalous manner. But in the long run, modern liberal theology was to win the day. Gillis Wetter, who died prematurely, created a stir in the 1920s by his association with the German New Testament scholars who consistently placed the Gospels against their historical and cultural background. Emanuel Linderholm, the eminent Church historian, was an implacable opponent of the established Church of Sweden and its dogmas; he himself was rooted in Pietism and the founder of the Swedish Association for Liberal Christianity and Religious Freedom. Such tendencies resulted in the Uppsala faculty being regarded in the 1920s and 1930s as not altogether orthodox or safe. This benefited the Faculty of Theology at Lund, which concentrated on the particular conditions of the Christian faith and thus attracted young ordinands of an orthodox turn of mind, especially from the west coast of Sweden. Tor Andræ, the historian of religion, who was a famous Islamic scholar and a religious psychologist with a subtle understanding of the essence of mysticism, was a pupil of Söderblom and, like him, as much a humanist as a theologian.

The work of the institutes of natural science went on just as usual, but there were few brilliant achievements for the time being. The appearance on the scene of a young genius at the very beginning of this period passed unnoticed. The man concerned was Svante Arrhenius, who in the most famous doctoral thesis ever defended in Uppsala (*Recherches sur la conductibilité galvanique des électrolytes*, 1884) laid the preliminary foundations of the electrolytic-dissociation theory, for which he was later awarded the Nobel Prize. Arrhenius was given only a *non sine laude approbatur* for his thesis and gained the status of *docent* only with difficulty.

The natural scientists with the widest international fame in Uppsala at the close of the 19th century would seem to have been Hugo Hildebrandsson, the meteorologist, and Nils Dunér, the astronomer. Hilde-

75. *Nathan Söderblom,*
Professor of Theology,
Archbishop from 1914 to
1931, and Pro-Chancel-
lor.

brandsson, who became the first Professor of Meteorology in 1878, investigated cloud formations and the circulation of the air in the upper atmosphere, while Dunér, who had been trained in Lund, drew up enormous catalogues of the stars and used spectroscopy to study the sun's speed of rotation. After the turn of the century, chemistry, physics and the biological sciences began to make progress on account of the new institute buildings, within whose walls special research traditions were developed. Here, if anywhere, the predominant stimuli and inspiration came from German universities and laboratories; the textbooks in use were German and the Swedish natural scientists published their results in German. It was chiefly through German intermediaries that the Darwinian theory of evolution made its mark on biological research and instruction in Uppsala from the 1880s onwards. This applied chiefly to zoology, in which Tycho Tullberg, who became Professor in 1882, introduced comparative anatomy with its evolutionary perspective; applied to small marine creatures, it subsequently became a speciality of Uppsala zoology. Other modern developments, such as zoophysiology and Mendelian genetics, were slower to gain a footing in the Uppsala of the early 20th century.

The Linnaean spirit long prevailed in botany, where it was reinforced by the emergence of national romanticism and the Linnaean centenaries. Consequently, systematics and floristic research at herbaria and in the field retained their prestige. It is true that Oscar Juel (who became Professor in 1902) introduced from Germany the new kind of botanical cell research based on microscopy (cytology). But Rutger Sernander, the most celebrated of the Uppsala botanists of the time, was essentially loyal to the Linnaean heritage. As Professor of Plant Biology from 1908 onwards, he became almost a legend in his lifetime; he was full of fire and flame, an eternal student who was loved far beyond the circle of his pupils. He made pioneering contributions to the investigation of the history of Scandinavian vegetation after the Ice Age, created the flourishing school of plant sociology in Uppsala and made great efforts on behalf of nature conservation in Sweden. Sven Ekman, the zoologist, whose great book on marine zoogeography (1935) became a standard work internationally, worked in similar spheres.

The more exact natural sciences entered on a very active period in the 1920s. The pioneer was Theodor (The) Svedberg, the most brilliant name in modern Swedish natural science, who became Professor of Physical Chemistry in 1912 and won the Nobel Prize in 1926. Svedberg, who began working on colloidal solutions as a young man, devised a method of determining their particle sizes by sedimentation under the influence of gravitation. From 1922 onwards, he was engaged in designing his ultracentrifuge, with which he finally achieved speeds of rotation which produced a power a million times that of gravity. At his laboratory—which led the world in research on solutions with large molecules—Svedberg and his assistants investigated proteins, enzymes, viruses and cellulose. In later years, he went over to atomic research at the Gustaf Werner Institute of Nuclear Chemistry, which was founded by a private donation and was inaugurated in 1949 (its cyclotron was completed in 1951). A large number of Swedish and foreign chemists were trained by Svedberg; for the first time since the days of Linnaeus and Torbern Bergman, Uppsala attracted research students from abroad. His most eminent Swedish pupil was Arne Tiselius, who gained the Nobel Prize in 1948 and occupied the chair of biochemistry. The extremely exact methods worked out by Tiselius (electrophoresis, adsorption analysis) opened up new possibilities of studying the chemistry of the proteins that are important in biology and medicine. Scientists from many countries were trained at his laboratory.

In physics, the light came from Lund, whence Uppsala succeeded in enticing two first-rate scientists—Oseen and Siegbahn. Carl Wilhelm Oseen, who was Professor of Mechanics and Mathematical Physics in the 1910s and 1920s, was a prominent international figure in hydrodynamics.

76. Five Nobel Prize-winners, two of them from Uppsala. From the left, The Svedberg, Alexander Fleming, Arne Tiselius, E. B. Chain and Hugo Theorell.

Manne Siegbahn, who became Professor of Physics in 1922 and gained the Nobel Prize three years later, was a pioneer in X-ray spectroscopy, in which, by using highly refined experimental methods, he achieved a previously unknown precision and extended the range of measurement.

Medical science did not show the same originality. The number of medical men in Uppsala from the end of the 19th century onwards who made scientific contributions of international importance is not large. The daily round of the professors was filled with clinical work, teaching and administrative duties. But a few names must be mentioned. Olof Hammersten was an imposing figure both physically and mentally. He was a pure theorist and a medical chemist who became professor of this subject in 1877. His achievements in the fields of enzyme and protein chemistry were of fundamental significance, his textbook on physiological chemistry being used in several countries. Salomon Henschen was a completely different kind of person—impulsive, polemical and the subject of polemics. He was Professor of Practical Medicine until he moved to Stockholm in 1900 and was famous for his enormous work on the pathology of the brain. His younger colleague, Karl Lennander, was the star surgeon of his day; he excelled in abdominal surgery and regenerated the Department of Surgery at the University Hospital. As early as 1896, he operated on a patient who had a bullet in the brain, which he located with the aid of Röntgen's new X-rays. Alvar Gullstrand, the greatest name in the Uppsala faculty, was scarcely a medical man in the true sense. His field was physical optics, in which he worked out a definitive theory for the image formation in the eye, for which he was awarded a Nobel Prize in 1911. The Austrian otologist Robert Bárány, who laid a new foundation for our knowledge of the labyrinth of the ear, was already a Nobel Prize-winner when in 1917 he was summoned from the horrors of the world war to Uppsala. Robin Fåhræus had also made his great achievement, the discovery of the sedimentation rate of the blood—an epoch-making advance in medical diagnosis—before he came to Uppsala, where he became Professor of Pathological Anatomy in 1928. He was a colourful personality and made no small impression on the academic environment.

Generally speaking, it was the natural sciences, in an increasingly close alliance with medicine, which were to give Uppsala science its strength from the Second World War onwards. Research in the humanities did not show the same vitality as in times past.

3

At the beginning of the Oscarian period, the University of Uppsala was firmly rooted in conservative, bureaucratic Sweden. The Scandinavist movement had ended in failure. The celebration of the quatercentenary of the University's foundation in 1877 was a brilliant spectacle but could not in itself instil new life into the academic community. Uppsala in the 1870s was not an encouraging sight, least of all in the student world. The majority lived listlessly with their conformist ways of thinking, which were becoming increasingly meaningless, and repeated academic rituals which marked Uppsala's character as that of a secluded idyll.

Then, in the early 1880s, a drastic change in the intellectual climate took place. The gateway to society and to the great world outside was thrown wide open. The stale air of high-toned idealism was let out and in advanced student circles demands for social and political reform were raised in the name of progress. The breakthrough of modern ideas and the storms of the new age left deep marks on Uppsala in the 1880s. Backward Sweden was becoming an industrialized country with a growing working class, and the serious social problems could no longer be waved aside by young people who were being trained for the intellectual professions. They derived inspiration from the radical pioneers at home and abroad—the young Strindberg, Ibsen, Georg Brandes and John Stuart Mill.

The student society known as Verdandi spearheaded the radical breakthrough. The commotion that its activities provoked can be compared to the two previous great conflicts of ideas in Uppsala—the Cartesian turmoil in the 17th century and the Junta's struggle for liberty in the 1790s. The situation was already tense at the beginning of the 1880s, when the young

Föreningen Verdandi hade i lördags å stora Gillesalen anordnat en offentlig diskussion öfver ämnet "Hvilka äro de viktigaste önskningsmålen i sedlighetsfrågan?" "Verdandisternas" kända rykte att äfven vara ytterst frisinnade i afseende på diskussionens form hade utöfvat sin verkan. Man väntade tydligen något pikant, ty salen var till trängsel fyld med folk. Efter en kort, ytterst ofullständig inledning, hvilken dock af inledaren afslöts med de om en viss själftillit vitnande orden: "sedan jag nu framstält sedlighetens utvecklingshistoria (sic!), vill jag" etc., vidtog diskussionen. Den var intressant därföre, att *allmänheten* här fick ett tillfälle att lära känna arten af det meningsutbyte, som äger rum vid den liberala studentföreningens sammankomster. Man såg här ett varnande exempel på, hvilken ensidighet och brist på objektivitet i uppfattningen, hvilken oförmåga att taga skäl, som ett under åratal fortsatt meningsutbyte emellan liktänkande, synnerligen under uppväxtåren, kan medföra. Förgäfves yrkade och sökte professor Rudin, som af intresse för sedligheten och för den studerande ungdomen föranledts att besöka mötet, bidraga till att åtminstone *något* objektivt angående sedlighetens begrepp lades till

Och *detta* meningsutbyte afhördes från början och till slut af *flere damer tillhörande stadens mest ansedda familjer*, hvilka naturligtvis genom sin närvaro, utan att ens protestera genom en så enkel åtgärd som att aflägsna sig, i viss mån gåfvo *sitt* bifall till diskussionens så form som innehåll. Man skulle verkligen tro sig förflyttad till det gamla Rom under Claudii eller Caligulas dagar, i stället för att vistas i det 19:de århundradets sedliga Sverge.

Någon anhållan till föreningen Verdandi att för framtiden förskona vår stads allmänhet från dylika "tillställningar" våga vi väl knappast framställa; en anspråkslös begäran synes man dock, utan att ens från det hållet anses kräfva för mycket, böra kunna få beviljad, och det är, att föreningen för sina "offentliga diskussioner" ville för framtiden upphöra med att importera osedlighetstalare från hufvudstaden eller andra orter. Föreningen synes verkligen själf ha frambragt nog af den varan för att kunna med framgång idka t. o. m. exportrörelse, och vi tro, att härvarande samhälle gärna skulle vilja uppmuntra en dylik "nationel" affär med några små bidrag i form af exportpremier. *Vällgren Vesig.*

77. An extract from the report in the Fyris newspaper of the notorious "morality debate" organized by the Verdandi student association in the spring of 1887.

Knut Wicksell began his work as a social reformer by giving lectures on the necessity for birth control. He was admonished by the academic Council. Two years later, when the question of freedom of religion was raised in the Riksdag, the Verdandi society was formed (1882). Its formation was promoted by Karl Staaff, a student from Stockholm like most of the original members (he later became a Liberal Prime Minister). In relation to the Conservative establishment, the Verdandi society intended to work for the introduction of the "principles of freedom of thought and speech" in Sweden. For the first few years, it led a quiet life, occupied in internal discussions, but in the spring of 1887 the storm broke. Verdandi arranged a public discussion in the Stora Gille Hall on what was called "the question of morality", in which the sanctity of marriage, prostitution and free love were dealt with and Hinke Bergegren, a visiting Stockholm anarchist, expressed himself in the crudest terms. *Fyris*, the

Conservative Uppsala newspaper, was horrified and soon other newspapers were as well. Demands were made for steps to be taken to discipline the subversive members of Verdandi (the "Wiksell clique"), and in a short time the Rector and the Council intervened. After an inquiry, all the members of the Verdandi board were sentenced to be reprimanded and warned, and two of them were also deprived of their scholarships. Individual members of Verdandi were subsequently persecuted, but they always had the support of Frithiof Holmgren, the broad-minded Professor of Physiology. A new storm blew up the following year, when Hjalmar Branting, the editor of the *Socialdemokraten* newspaper, was fined for publishing an abusive article and Verdandi helped him to pay the fine. The whole society was summoned into the presence of the Rector, Sahlin, who read them a lecture, and the chairman was also interrogated by Archbishop Sundberg. In the spring of 1889, there was trouble again. Georg Brandes was in Uppsala, and at the banquet which Verdandi arranged in his honour, outspoken toasts were exchanged. The chairman of the society said that he wanted to see some real leaders of youth among the professors, while Brandes (cf. above, p. 204) re-interpreted the famous inscription in the University building ("It is great to think freely, but it is greater to think rightly") and chose to read it as "Abandon hope all ye who enter here". New outcries were raised in the Conservative press, loyal students signed protest lists, and the Students' Union officially declared its respect for the teaching body. The persecution of objectionable members of Verdandi continued; thus, the Faculty of Medicine tried in vain to exclude one of the leading members of the society, Hjalmar Öhrvall, from a post as associate professor.

In time, the radical phalanx consolidated its positions. The basic questions of political democracy, primarily the question of the franchise, had become the concern of all citizens. In 1892, Verdandi was able to celebrate its 10th anniversary with a banquet for 500 liberal students from all the Scandinavian countries, a big public discussion and the singing of the Marseillaise. Popular education had now become perhaps the society's most important task. In this respect, its pioneering achievement in Sweden was its series of popular pamphlets on scientific and social subjects, which began to appear in 1888. As far as was tactically possible, they served the society's ideals but were strictly matter-of-fact in tone.

Verdandi's scandalous successes induced the Conservative students to organize themselves as well. *Fosterländska studentförbundet* (The Patriotic Students' Association) was formed in 1889; it was chiefly concerned about the country's defence and its patron was Oscar Alin, the political scientist, who was a keen persecutor of Verdandi members. Two years later (1891), the Heimdal society was founded as a national student association with wider aims. At first, it proceeded cautiously; officially, it sought to work only for "the calm and moderate development of society". It concentrated chiefly, in competition with Verdandi, on an intensive campaign of popular education with its own pamphlets (on Engelbrekt, on the Union between Norway and Sweden, etc.), the lending-library movement and lectures. At the beginning of the present century, the political antagonisms in the student world were not as intense as formerly; Verdandi and Heimdal could even arrange, in good agreement, a joint Scandinavian conference on popular education in Uppsala. At this time, the growing Labour movement acquired its own student forum in the Laboremus society (1902); it was formed by some members of Verdandi and soon became markedly Social Democratic in outlook. The student's choice of his general philosophy in Uppsala in the closing years of the 19th century and at the beginning of the 20th century was obviously connected with the orientation of his political beliefs. To many natural scientists and medical men, a positivistic belief in progress and reason seemed self-evident, a view which was nurtured by John Stuart Mill's writings and the Darwinian theory of evolution and was combined with political radicalism of the type prevalent in the 1880s. Its direct opposite, in a sense, was the romanticism of the 1890s, which attracted students to nationalism or to a refined aestheticism that bore no relation to reality. During the early years of the present century, Sven Lidman, Sigurd Agrell and John Landquist formed a literary coterie in which the first two, as juvenile poets, indulged in exotic preciosities.

Heimdal gradually gathered strength in the atmosphere of national romanticism and political development. An important part was played by Harald Hjärne, in whose impressive shadow several generations of students developed their patriotic temperament. The struggle over the Union with Norway yielded fresh support for the patriots and about 1910—by which time it was entirely dominated by Hjärne's pupils—Heimdal emerged as a Conservative campaign organization for students of nationalist views. At the same time, Karl Staaff, the founder member of Verdandi, formed his Liberal Government and the antagonisms in the student world were accentuated, the question of defence being the crucial issue. Heimdal received visits from generals and Conservative politicians, and the farmers' march and the "Borggård" crisis in February 1914 caused nationalist and anti-democratic enthusiasm to flare up again. Leading members of Heimdal hastily improvised a student march to Stockholm, in which 3,250 people from the four Swedish university towns took part and declared their loyalty to Gustav V. The women students contributed a Swedish flag which they had made themselves. Passions continued to run high during the first years of the war and the election of the President of the

233

78. *Women students gathered at the Central Station in Uppsala to present a Swedish flag to the participants in the march organized by the Uppsala students in February 1914.*

Students' Union in the autumn of 1915 was the stormiest in its history. The sitting President, who had sent a telegram of congratulation to the students of Berlin on his own authority, stood for re-election, but the members of Verdandi set to work and, after considerable commotion, succeeded in getting their own candidate elected.

The current of nationalism was also manifested in Christian student life. The young theologians, who had been combined in the Uppsala Student Christian Association since 1901, did not have a good market for their wares. Radical attacks on Christianity from Left-wing quarters and advanced Biblical criticism from their own ranks made their situation difficult. But things soon changed; in Söderblom and Billing they found leaders whom they could look up to and in 1908–9 what was called the "Young Church Movement" was born; it was led by Manfred Björkquist. In much the same way as the art historians gathered round Roosval at the same period, it wished to rally the people round the Church of their fathers; in "crusades" during the summer, its members preached the idea of a living Church, which would convert the people of Sweden into a people of God.

The discussion of political ideas slackened off after the end of the war. A fairly idyllic period followed, as far as the Uppsala student was concerned, in the 1920s; no major problems intruded. The intellectual at-

79. A gathering of literary students at the house of Erik Hemlin in May 1925. In front, from the left, Elsa Skantze, Erik Hemlin and Karin Boye; in the row above, Elof Ehnmark, Brita Benedicks, Clara Westman and Erland Ehnmark; at the top, Einar Malm, Barbro Linder, Allan Sjöding and Karl Larm.

mosphere had, of course, its own distinctive character and at any rate differed from that in Lund, where the great student generation was now blossoming which supported the *Lundagård* magazine and with Hjalmar Gullberg, Ivar Harrie,Tristan Lindström, Frans G. Bengtsson and others created a tradition of irreverent wit and literary playfulness which survived for decades. There was nothing like it in Uppsala, which presented a less uniform appearance, owing to the predominant part played by the student nations. In so far as it is possible to speak of a definite academic climate in Uppsala in the 1920s and 1930s, it was of a harsher type. The frosty dome of Hägerström's intellectual heaven arched over the more precocious students, irrespective of their faculty. The important poets who appeared among the Uppsala students of the 1920s—Karin Boye, Edfelt and others—were ardent persons or at least profoundly serious. When Karl Gustaf Hildebrand, the young lyric poet, made his debut in 1933, it was his peom on Uppsala nihilism and the jackdaws round the Cathedral tower which made him famous.

Otherwise, against the background of Hitler's Germany, the situation had changed at this time. Political fronts again began to take shape in the student world. Among the professors and students in Uppsala in the 1930s, open or half-concealed Nazism never attained the same proportions or influence as at the University of Lund. But it did exist, especially among extremely Right-wing students, and anti-Semitism was far from unusual. Verdandi, with the support of Laboremus and the Student Christian Association, revived its vigilance against the imminent barbarism. However, the great Students' Union meeting held in the Union's indoor tennis-court in February 1939 ended in defeat for the opponents of Nazism. The question was whether a handful of German Jewish doctors should be given entry and labour permits to enable them to take refuge in Sweden. In the discussion, views about competition alternated with racist slogans about protection for "our free and purely Swedish nation" and when the question was put to the vote, the majority rejected the proposed rescue action. As long as the Germans were victorious after the outbreak of war, the ideological conflict in the student body remained. But more and more students were now away from the town for long periods on military service and the discussions petered out. In addition, there were the object lessons presented by the many student refugees from Norway and Denmark, who were hospitably received in Uppsala and who testified eloquently to the ravages of Hitlerism. The closure of the University of Oslo by the Germans in December 1943 led to one of the largest spontaneous demonstrations in the history of the Students' Union.

As an organization, the Students' Union mostly fulfilled only its old representative function up to the early 1920s. The President made speeches and called for the cheering. From the 1870s onwards, the Union arranged spring celebrations in the Botanicum. The great question which engaged the Union's attention during the first few decades of the century concerned, characteristically enough, a national memorial—the Sten Sture monument. Its erection caused endless complications. The Union had already collected the money during the 1870s, two competitions were announced about 1900 and the commission was finally awarded to the young Carl Milles. Altogether 17 Sten Sture Monument Committees had succeeded each other and several proposals about the siting of the monument had been submitted before it was at last erected in 1925, in Milles's final, austere design, on the Kronåsen ridge outside Uppsala.

By this time, however, the student body had begun to turn its attention to new activities. Student life was no longer as easy as it had been formerly. Study debts and future jobs were anxiously discussed and the old talk about the risk of creating an academic proletariat was heard again. During the 1920s, the students became politically and socially conscious. The Students' Union, which in 1921, together with the other Students' Unions in the country, formed the National Swedish Union of Students (SFS), found it natural to intervene in matters affecting students and to take on responsibility for them. It concentrated, in the first place, on the building

80. *Demonstration outside the University building in support of the Norwegian students, after the University of Oslo had been closed by the Germans in December 1943.*

of student housing at a reasonable cost. In 1930, it had the first student accommodation built on Övre Slottsgatan. Somewhat later, the Stiftelse Uppsala Studentbostäder (Uppsala Student-Housing Foundation) was formed and towards the end of the 1930s, new buildings were completed on Skolgatan (what was popularly known as the "Closet Palace") and on St. Johannesgatan (the "Parthenon", for women students). Now the individual nations also began to build housing for their own members' needs, the Värmland and the Södermanland-Närke nations being the first. This concentration on housing policy meant altering previously cherished plans in the Students' Union. Already during the heyday of Scandinavism in the 1850s, a Union building fund had been created and was soon supplemented by funds derived from the triumphal tours made by Allmänna Sången. What was envisaged, in the spirit of that time, was an official building with a spacious hall for festivities and banquets, a restaurant, a library, etc. These plans came to nothing, but the necessary building sites were purchased in the 1870s in the Ubbo quarter near Odinslund and the matter was kept alive for some decades to come. When the Students' Union actually began the building work about 1930, a new and more materialistic spirit prevailed; the necessities of student life rather than the public ceremonies were given priority. However, neither the resources nor

237

the interest sufficed to provide a student restaurant or *convictorium*, although the question was discussed several times. The contrast with Lund is striking; there the Akademiska Förening was open to all and the *convictorium* to the hungry.

Other welfare facilities came into existence during the 1930s—the period of breakthrough for social-welfare work in the Students' Union. The first student medical officer was appointed in 1934 (the first student chaplain not until 1943), a new indoor tennis court was opened in 1937 and somewhat later the Union acquired open-air recreation centres for the students at Norredatorp and Vårdsätra. Now the Union opened its own, extremely modest office, in which the main tasks were arranging employment and accommodation. The Uppsala student newspaper, *Ergo,* which had been run privately since its inception in 1924 and was, as far as its resources permitted, a cultural organ with many amusing features, was taken over by the Union in 1941, which did not by any means promote its quality in the long run.

The financial conditions of the students had hardly undergone any decisive change by this time. Many of them (about 1930 considerably over half) were still in receipt of regular contributions from their parents. This applied chiefly to the medical and law students, who came from more prosperous homes, while the theologians were the poorest, as always. The indebtedness to the banks peculiar to Swedish student life was still rife in the 1930s, pretty much as before, but the bill-jobbing never reached the same reckless heights in Uppsala as it did in Lund. However, there were other possibilities of raising money, as signs of a new age. Interest-free study loans from the government were available from 1919 onwards, and soon the nations started their own lending businesses, offering favourable terms to their needy fellow-countrymen, while in 1930 the Students' Union Credit Society came into existence for the same purpose. In addition, there were the countless scholarship funds, large and small, which had been donated to the nations or to the University and which were sheet-anchors in times of need for many students. Towards the end of the 1930s, the State finally realised, as it had done 300 years before, its full responsibility for student financing and set up a limited number of State scholarships (free board and lodging), which at least represented a step forward.

Student life at work and play went on essentially in the old forms. Even at the end of the 1930s, many students were living under extremely Spartan conditions, with wood-stoves for heating and outside privies; at night, the water froze in their jugs. There were special student barracks, chiefly the legendary Imperfectum, but otherwise the student quarter was Luthagen, where in the 1880s hideous wooden houses began to be built,

238

81. Two legendary dwelling-houses for students on Västra Ågatan: on the left, Olympen, and next to the Västgöta foot-bridge, Imperfectum.

in which rooms could be rented cheaply. Individual students had for a long time full board and lodging, but after the turn of the century it became the custom to take meals in groups, either at the table of some good housewife who was a skilled cook or at one of the many eating-places which sprang up at this time. The importance of these groups, which met for meals and in which students of different faculties and nations gathered round the table, as regards the students' comfort and intellectual improvement, can hardly be exaggerated. The amount of time spent in the taverns of an evening gradually showed a tendency to diminish. The period of glory was in the 1880s and 1890s, when Flustret, Gästis, Gillet, Phoenix, Rullan and the much-celebrated Taddis existed and offered all manner of refreshments to the thirsty. Later, Gillet and Gästis became the students' chief haunts.

As time went by, the nations strengthened their positions. Towards the end of the 19th century, one after another moved into new, spacious buildings with magnificent staircases, banqueting halls, club-rooms and libraries. The Renaissance palace built for the Norrland nation on Västra

Ågatan at the beginning of the 1880s was the most impressive example; the Gästrike-Hälsinge and Östgöta nations had already erected their buildings in Trädgårdsgatan. Within the walls of the new nation houses, social life took on increasingly exuberant forms, with May dinners, spring balls, Martinmas dinners, Lucia celebrations, and more or less improvised parties (long known as *zwyckar*) at all times, when, after a simple meal, bottles were placed on the long table in the banqueting hall and the nation members contributed to the entertainment in whatever way they could. Manners became softer as the years went by, especially after women students appeared in the 1920s and Venus, in the spirit of jazz, began to supersede Bacchus. Now the Saturday-night "hop" was introduced, in which the same tendency was even more obvious. Community singing round the table had been popular since the beginning of the century, and printed nation songbooks, including drinking songs and regional ballads, were issued, the first in 1910.

In addition, there were the stage shows peculiar to Swedish student life called *spex* (from the Latin word *spectaculum*)—burlesques, usually on a historical theme, with topical allusions and crazy anachronisms. The student *spex* was born in Uppsala, in the 1860s. For a long time, it was confined to the nations, of which Stockholm and Södermanland-Närke were at first the most assiduous in this line. Some of the very first productions, such as the opera parody entitled "Mohrens sista suck" (The Moor's Last Gasp), have retained their popularity down to the present day. The Västgöta *spex* entitled "Napoleon" (1928) was an enormous success and was performed on tours around the country; as late as 1957, the Juvenal Order was able to draw large audiences throughout Sweden with its *spex* entitled "Gustaf III". This Order, which was revived in 1907 (cf. above, p. 182), preserved the Uppsala *spex* tradition with tender care and also became a stronghold of academic humour in other respects. Today, as a private men's club alongside the nations, it flourishes more than ever.

Students devoted themselves to physical exercises in other connections. The Philochoros society (1880) performed strenuous folk dances in provincial costume with great success. Of the old "noble exercises", riding retained its position best. In the 1870s and 1880s, the nations competed in boat races on the English model ("in white gloves") on the River Fyris. The year 1909 was a memorable year, when the Students' Institute of Gymnastics and Athletics and the sports ground to the south of it were brought into use. The following decade was a golden age for student athletics, but later the interest waned. The new Musicum, which was completed in 1930 near the Observatory, was an academic institute of a very special kind. Hugo Alfvén, who had been an incomparable *director musices* for 20 years, moved there from the old Linnaeanum; he was the

82. A scene from the highly successful Västgöta spex *entitled "Napoleon" (1928). This scene is from a production by the Västgöta nation in 1931.*

composer of many beautiful cantatas and festival works and the conductor of both Orphei Drängar and Allmänna Sången.

The social origins of the Uppsala students did not show any essential changes during the first half of the 20th century. The great majority of them still came from the more or less well-to-do middle class and to a great extent from the families of university graduates. The advance of the working class under the banners of Social Democracy had little effect on the recruitment of students to higher education. The available investigations of the subject give a clear idea of the situation. In the 1880s, no less than a good 90% of all students came from the upper and middle classes and the rest were the sons of industrial workers, farmers, etc. The figures then remained largely unchanged for a long time and even showed a slight decline for the working class from the turn of the century. It is clear that in the early 1900s Uppsala was more of an upper-class university than Lund. It was only during and after the First World War that the lower classes began to increase their share somewhat—to climb above the 10% mark in the mid 1920s and then to slowly increase. It is estimated that in the 1930s (at *all* the Swedish universities and independent colleges) the proportion of students from the vaguely defined lowest class was 18–20%, though with a falling curve (18% in 1943). At any event, it is clear that university education in this period had only to a small extent been opened to new categories of citizens.

The students' choices of faculty and professional specialization underwent few drastic changes. The theologians were perhaps the most sensitive to the general economic conditions; they reached a peak (16% of all students) during the shortage of parish ministers in the 1920s and 1930s, but later their number decreased steeply. The fact that the medical students became fewer towards the end of the period was due entirely to the profession's recruitment policy. While the number of natural scientists gradually decreased up to the Second World War, the number of students reading the arts subjects showed a corresponding increase.

This was essentially due to the entry of the women students (see above, p. 212). They came, on the average, from somewhat more affluent homes than their male colleagues and were chiefly attracted to the arts subjects. As early as the mid 1930s, nearly 30% of the students in the arts section were women, and 10 years later the number was over 40%. This development had not proceeded without difficulty. Well into the 20th century, the woman student in Uppsala still faced isolation and discrimination in several respects. Elsa Eschelsson, the first woman teacher at the University (she was *docent* in civil law), encountered ruthless opposition and her life ended tragically. But the women students organized themselves; they had a forum in the Uppsala Women Students' Association (formed in 1892) and in the 1920s things became easier, as we have seen. The first student marriages took place and became common occurrences in time —perhaps not always beneficially to intensive concentration on study.

CHAPTER VII

The University Transformed

After the end of the Second World War, in the mid 1940s, everything was still more or less as usual in Uppsala. There were only a few thousand students, those who were roughly of the same age were to a large extent acquainted with each other, and almost all of them could be placed by the nation to which they belonged and the group in which they ate their meals. The odd "perpetual student" still walked the streets or could be found in the back room at Gillet. The University teachers were not so many as to make it difficult to keep track of them, even across the faculty boundaries. The professors dominated the worlds of the individual students, taught them from the first day, decided their fates and duly allowed them to address them informally at nation parties or post-seminars.

Nevertheless, it was obvious that everything could not go on as before. The number of professors and professorial chairs was grossly insufficient. For decades, the government authorities (cf. above, p. 213) had thrown cold water on all ideas of a systematic development of the Swedish universities. There was a crying need for improvements. The war was hardly over before a University Commission was set up in 1945 for the purpose of remedying the deficiencies. It took up the most burning question of the moment—the teaching posts and the training of research workers. The work bore fruit and the period of stagnation came to an end. A small number of academic teachers of a kind that was to some extent new —assistant teachers for elementary instruction and better-qualified "preceptors" (associate professors)—were assigned to the universities. But the chief thing was to increase the number of professors in accordance with modern demands. As far as the University of Uppsala was concerned, this meant that 15 new professorships were instituted in the latter half of the 1940s—the greatest improvement in this field since the days of Gustavus Adolphus. The Faculties of Medicine and of Arts derived all the benefit. The humanists were allotted nine new chairs and the Faculties of Science and of Medicine received three each. Among the subjects which now acquired professors of their own were musicology, ethnology, human geography and Egyptology in the humanities section, together with the new subject of sociology. The sciences were finally enriched with a chair

243

of zoophysiology; the new subjects of entomology and limnology were entrusted to associate professors. The medical men, who had complained for several years about the dire state of medical research in Sweden, had not yet obtained what they wanted. But, on the whole, these vigorous measures, which also applied to the University of Lund, seemed to have achieved their purpose, which was—in the words of the Commission—to remove the dangers "to education and scientific standards" in Sweden.

The 1950s saw the beginning of a development which soon confounded all the estimates and made the increased resources illusory. At all the Swedish universities, the numbers of students began to rise steeply, until finally, in a veritable explosion in the 1960s, they reached figures which had scarcely been believed possible. The universities, and principally the arts faculties, were exposed to enormous stresses. In contrast to the total of 5,500 *new enrolments* at all the arts faculties in the country in 1960–1, there were 23,500 new enrolments in 1968–9; only then was saturation achieved and the figures were reduced. The authorities did not know which way to turn; the government and the Office of the Chancellor were forced to work unceasingly on reforms, in order to cope with the onset. This occurred in a context in which society's demands on the universities were becoming more and more importunate, while at the same time the growing masses of students were demanding that they should be given power and influence on the decision-making processes. A series of government commissions on the universities were appointed, and one partial reform after another was carried out from the late 1950s onwards. It was obvious that the old university structure was creaking at the joints; State educational factories of a new type were looming on the horizon.

As far as Uppsala was concerned, this development meant that the number of students increased from a total of 4,380 at the end of the Second World War to well over 20,000 about 1970. These are gross figures. The difference between them and the number of students actually attending the University (active students) was considerable, as before (see above, p. 210). The accompanying diagram indicates the progress of the increases from 1955 to 1975 in the numbers of students actually attending the University. They show how the figures leapt after 1960 (1960, 8,320 students; 1965, 14,000; 1970, 21,290). The background of this increased hunger for education in the 1950s and 1960s will not be examined in detail here. The essential factor was unquestionably the general increase in the country's prosperity, accompanied by good prospects for graduates on the labour market; in addition, there was the availability of study loans and other welfare benefits for students. There is also the inevitable question, to what extent a greater influx of students from the lower social classes contributed to the total increase. No separate figures are available from

244

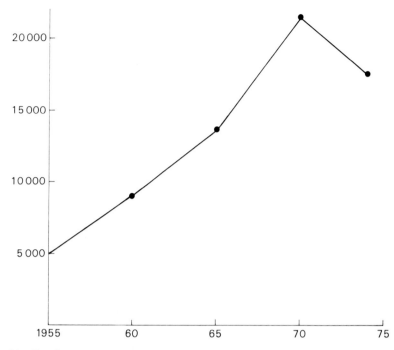

83. This diagram illustrates the "explosion" in the number of students attending the University during the 1950s and 1960s.

Uppsala, only general and not entirely consistent estimates concerning all the Swedish universities and colleges, together with some figures for Lund. At any rate, they show that the democratization of university education proceeded very slowly (cf. above, p. 241). The 12% of students who were reckoned to have come from working-class homes in the mid 1950s had risen to only 14% at the beginning of the 1960s; the total number of newly enrolled students from the working class was estimated to be 21% at the end of the 1960s. There are grounds for suspecting that Uppsala was below the national average. Thus, a certain amount of social levelling has occurred, but the working class is still seriously under-represented in higher education. One of the main goals of the university reforms carried out since the 1940s has been to remedy this state of affairs and to give every Swedish citizen the same opportunities of studying at a university. These reforms have largely failed. It is worth while to reflect that in the feudal society of the 17th century, when the clergy hand-picked gifted peasant boys, about the same percentage of students from

245

the lower classes probably attended the University of Uppsala as in the middle of the 20th century (cf. above, p. 83). The comparative lack of success of the modern democratic policy with regard to the universities is primarily due to deficiencies in the preparatory training given by the schools, which has not led to the intended goals and has hardly even succeeded in reducing the antagonism between manual workers and intellectuals in Swedish society.

On the other hand, the inflow of women students played an important part. It increased continuously, from 1,123 or 25% of the student body in 1945 to almost 7,000 or 42% in 1965 and has since remained at about that level. But, for well-known reasons, the women graduates are still only at the beginning of their climb to the higher university posts; there are only four women professors in Uppsala today.

The new and disquieting situation which already confronted the university authorities in the mid 1950s called for rapid steps to be taken. The main task of the University Commission appointed in 1955 was to cope with the increased influx of students and its consequences, chiefly as regarded the open-entry faculties, to which most of the students went. In these faculties, the periods of study at the lower stages had become far too long and the drop-outs too frequent; the instruction needed to be thoroughly reformed. The solution was found in elementary classroom or group instruction, conducted by a new type of teacher—the university lecturer. The number of lecturers, who had to hold the doctorate and to be skilled teachers, was, like other resources, to be calculated automatically, according to the number of groups studying the subject, as they were expressed in special syllabuses. The Riksdag approved of the scheme and in 1959 Uppsala received its first university lecturers. Their number was soon increased and today the lecturers are responsible for most of the basic instruction, at least in the arts faculties. This means that the professors and *docenter* have been relieved of this type of instruction and can concentrate on the training of postgraduate students. The freshmen now meet with a system similar to that of an ordinary school, with lessons in groups and frequent written tests. But this is, in principle, nothing new; the lectures from the lectern and the *collegia* or tutorials in the 17th and 18th centuries were equally elementary.

Ten years later, when the concourse of students had reached its peak, the time was ripe for the next step. The pace of study at the over-full institutes (what was called "the flow-through rate") was found to be still unsatisfactory. In the spring of 1969, the current degree regulations for the arts faculties were therefore revoked and replaced by a new ordinance, the notorious PUKAS. This provoked violent opposition from the conservative academics and the radical Left-wing students in an unholy alliance. The new system meant organizing the basic studies in the arts faculties according to a rigid timetable adapted to the needs of the labour market. All instruction was divided into 17 "general training lines", each with three sections comprising a certain number of study courses. A standard syllabus was devised for each course and was to be in force throughout the country but with some variations at different universities. The ancient grades (*approbatur* etc.) were abolished and instead the results were marked according to a points system, in which the courses passed in one academic year were assessed as meriting 40 points; 120 points were required for a complete degree. A student who did not keep up the prescribed pace was to be threatened with suspension. However, it was possible for those who did not wish to follow the general training lines, with their fixed combinations to choose a "special" line, which they could compose themselves. Now the 60-year-old Master of Arts degree also disappeared. All the fixed training lines were intended to be equally vocationally orientated and led to the Bachelor of Arts or more specialized degrees (Bachelor of Economics, Bachelor of Social Science, Secretarial diploma, etc.).

The new system introduced in 1969 signified a complete revolution in the arts courses. The training was tailored to fit the needs of society. The pendulum had swung to the other extreme; no greater contrast was conceivable with the vision of the 19th-century romantics of the universities as the strongholds of the spirit, where prospective public officials were trained in the eternal truths. Yet similar and in some ways even more radical lines of thought had, as will be remembered, been put forward by the Education Commission in the Age of Freedom. At that time, they were rejected in Uppsala as a deadly threat to academic freedom and scholarly thoroughness and were not carried into effect. The controversy over PUKAS, which was carried on with some of the same arguments, was also focussed on the prevailing government pressure on the universities, which were being made to conform, by continual re-organizations, to the pattern prescribed by the ruling Social Democratic ideology for what was called "post-gymnasial education". The antagonism between the universities and the government and its departments has, on the whole, hardened in the last 10–15 years. Part of the trouble is that the University Chancellor, who is now the head of an extensive official body, has since 1964 no longer been the universities' freely chosen representative but a politician appointed by the government. In this new situation, the universities have regarded it as a vital necessity to safeguard certain basic values in education and research. In this connection, their interests in relation to the State have been represented, above all, by Torgny T. Segerstedt, who has been the Rector of the University of Uppsala since 1955 and has consequently held this office for longer than any other man in the history of the University. The new study system also gave grounds for suspicion and criticism. It was soon found to be impossible to apply in its original rigour and after two years it had in practice for the most part ceased to operate. Even in 1972, no less than 75% of the newly enrolled students in the arts faculties preferred to study subjects of their own choice in a special training line.

The influx of students in the 1960s also meant that the old framework of Swedish university organization was broken. A fifth State university had already been founded in Umeå in 1963. At first, it consisted only of a Faculty of Medicine but was gradually expanded to include a Faculty of Arts; it absorbed thousands of students from Norrland who would otherwise have gone south to Uppsala or elsewhere. The foundation of Umeå was soon followed by that of a number of "branch universities" in southern and central Sweden, which were intended to relieve the pressure on the older universities. There were four of these "branches"—at Karlstad, Örebro, Linköping and Växjö—and the University of Uppsala assumed responsibility for Örebro. The educational work there, which began in the summer of 1967 and is devoted to basic training in the arts faculties, was subordinated in all respects to the University of Uppsala. To complete the picture, it must be mentioned that Gothenburg *Högskola,* which, like Stockholm *Högskola,* has now been raised to the status of a university, was substantially developed in the 1950s and 1960s by the addition of new subjects and institutes and thus kept the students of western Sweden, especially those reading medicine, in their home district.

The accommodation of the growing numbers of students presented difficult problems. Private lodgings and the few student halls of residence that existed were grossly inadequate. Consequently, an intensive programme of State-subsidized house-building was started through the agency of the Students' Union. From the beginning of the 1950s onwards, an extensive "student quarter" grew up at Rackarbacken, to the west of Uppsala. By the middle of the 1960s, there were considerably over 4,000 student rooms in Uppsala but far more were needed and about 1970 land even further to the west was acquired and new blocks of houses were built in Flogsta —too precipitately, as it turned out, for the inflow of students then diminished and many of the houses were left untenanted.

The educational reforms were not confined to the elementary instruction in the arts faculties. The courses in the other faculties were also transformed and streamlined. The old, thorough-going Bachelor of Divinity degree was finally abolished in 1973 and was succeeded by a new study system, in which Greek and Hebrew were set aside. Medical studies had already been squeezed into a period of 5½ years in 1969. But the training of postgraduate students was also recast in the general transformation. No one disputed that the old system, or lack of system, had obvious defects. Candidates for the licentiate or doctorate at Swedish universities struggled single-handed with extensive literature courses and heavy work on their theses, more or less absent-mindedly supervised by their professors. Only in the most fortunate cases was the doctoral thesis subjected to a thorough examination at his seminars. Year after year went by before it was finished, at least in the humanities and theology, and the scope and the printing costs increased accordingly. The Postgraduate Students Commission appointed in 1963 discussed the problem and its report was published in 1966 (*Forskarutbildning och forskarkarriär*, Postgraduate Training and Careers in Research). Three years later, in the borderline year of 1969, the proposals were implemented in the current regulations governing the training of postgraduate students in arts subjects in Sweden. The Commission had proceeded without prejudice. The almost-a-century-old licentiate degree was abolished. Instead, after a formal admission procedure, the postgraduate student proceeds directly to what is now designated the new doctoral degree; thus the traditional doctoral degree has disappeared, in all likelihood for ever. According to the programme, the new doctoral degree in arts subjects must be passed in four years and comprises, on the one hand, certain courses of study arranged in accordance with a fixed syllabus and, on the other, a doctoral thesis with a fairly limited scope, written under the constant supervision of a tutor, who need not be the professor. The public defence of the thesis has been simplified and made less ceremonious (dress-suits are not worn). However, the solemn conferment of doctorates is still held in the University Aula. The old scale of graded marks, which caused so many painful deliberations in the assessment of the theses, has been replaced by a simple "Pass" or "Fail" mark. The external form of the doctoral thesis may vary within wide limits; theses produced by stencil duplicating or office-offset printing are just as acceptable as those printed by letterpress or ordinary offset. The author himself now takes no financial risk. Ever since the University of Uppsala was re-established, the poor candidates for the doctorate had to defray the costs of their theses themselves and this became a heavy financial burden with the enormous increase in the number of pages in the present century. Moreover, the candidate had to pay for the dinner that followed the disputation. It was not until 1943 that the State stepped in and refunded 75% of the printing costs; under the present system, this is increased to 100% for a work of at most 160 pages. Candidates for the doctorate also enjoy a certain amount of financial support in other respects during their training. Even about 1940, a few scholarships for students working for the licentiate or the doctorate were awarded to students of law and medicine; some years later, they were awarded to students in all faculties and became increasingly numerous later on. However, they have by no means kept pace with developments and today are grossly insufficient in both numbers and amounts.

The career of research scholar has long been poorly remunerated and still is. This has been the Achilles' heel of Swedish university policy ever since the 17th century, when poverty-stricken *adjunkter* struggled for their places in the sun. Later, the *docenter* came into existence as the up-and-coming scholars, but the *docent* posts were few in number and limited in point of time; the institution has often been condemned but still survives. The Postgraduate Students Commission of 1963, like the academic bodies which it consulted, fretted over the problem of how the gap between the doctoral examination and the professorship should be bridged. The choice lay between security of employment, on the one hand, and mobility, on the other. The result was a career ladder that looked well on paper: the new doctoral degree, research assistant, *docent* and then professor. Almost everything depended on the new type of post entitled "research assistant", which had already been introduced into other faculties and was now (1969) extended to the humanists. These posts, which, like the *docent* posts, were limited to a three-year period with possibilities of an extension, would give promising new doctors opportunities to acquire further qualifications on their way to *docent* posts. But the research-assistant posts are too few in number and the arrangement may be likened to a bottle-neck, through which infrequent drops trickle, i.e. only a few doctors manage to continue in academic life and gain a secure livelihood. Here the national research councils must also be mentioned. They grew up towards the end of the 1940s and in recent years have purposely invested funds in research and research posts within the framework of the universities. This has benefited scholars at all levels. Young candidates for the doctorate have been recruited for scholarly projects financed by the councils and directed by experienced research workers, temporary research posts have been established, and, in addition, individual scholars have been appointed to personal professorships by the councils.

The improvement of the permanent, higher, research posts after the Second World War was rendered insufficient by the great invasion of students. The 90 professors in Uppsala in 1950 were unable to cope successfully with the four times as many students 20 years later, even though the elementary instruction had been placed in other hands. The professorial body was gradually expanded from the latter half of the 1950s onwards. The number of permanent professors reached exactly 100 in 1960 and 115 five years later; thereafter the growth was even more rapid (145 professors in 1970 and 155 in 1975). In addition, there is now a number of assistant professors, previously known as senior lecturers in science, preceptors, etc. But the allocation of new professorships has been regrettably uneven. Hardly surprisingly, the Faculties of Medicine and Science have been favoured as being particularly prestigious and advantageous to society. A total of 60% of the increase (15 and 18 chairs respectively) was allocated to medicine and the natural sciences, together with eight professorships of pharmacy in connection with the transfer of pharmaceutical training to Uppsala. During the entire period, the theologians acquired only one new professor and the lawyers three. The humanists, excepting the social scientists, gained only five new chairs during the same period and consequently—a typical sign of the present age—no longer constituted the largest faculty, being left behind by both the doctors of medicine and the natural scientists. It is more remarkable that the popular social scientists, who formed their own faculty in 1964, were not favoured with new top posts to any great extent either; there were eight in 1960 and no more than 13 in 1975. Considering that it was the Faculties of Arts and Social Sciences which were especially affected by the explosive influx of students in the 1960s, this miserliness in the establishment of new professorial posts meant, and still means, that these faculties are working under stringent conditions, particularly as regards research and the training of research workers.

On the whole, it may be asked what consequences the expansion of the University and the new structures introduced in recent years have had, as regards scientific life in Uppsala. They have hardly been particularly beneficial. The total production of scientific literature would certainly seem to have increased. The bulk of it consists of the doctoral theses, but in their new reduced form they are mostly to be regarded as test pieces and cannot be compared with the old theses *pro gradu,* which often represented 7–8 years or more of hard work. The many university lecturers are wholly absorbed in their educational duties and can keep up with new developments in their own subjects only at a pinch. The professors, who should be showing the way, are snowed under with meetings and administrative duties, especially when they are also the heads of unwieldy institutes or when the candidates for the doctorate gather in denser throngs. A Henrik Schück, who as professor and *rector magnificus* published a never-ceasing stream of scholarly works, would be an inconceivable phenomenon today. It remains for the professors, who should, in the nature of things, be the best-qualified research workers in their subjects, to sacrifice themselves for others and to direct the scholarly work of their pupils, which is being carried on more and more often in the form of team-work, in which the contribution of one member of the team can hardly be distinguished from that of another.

The University was, of course, also extended in a purely literal sense. The old institutes were becoming increasingly cramped for space and were replaced by new ones equipped with all modern conveniences. Even the humanists, who were accustomed to living in shabby accommodations, acquired new and lavishly fitted-out quarters. In January 1976, the "Humanist Centre" was inaugurated—an extensive complex of buildings containing the institutes for the philologists, the literary historians and the social scientists, together with a central library and a spacious restaurant. Other humanists remained without a murmur in their old quarters. But, of course, it is chiefly the medical men and the natural scientists who have needed improved working conditions. The quarter devoted to housing natural-science research activities has continued to grow on the field beyond the Zoologicum. During the 1950s and 1960s, a building, including a geomorphological laboratory, was erected there for the Institutes of Geography and Geology jointly, together with institute buildings for the new subjects of zoophysiology and limnology. For some years, it has been possible to take the Master of Engineering degree in technical physics at the newly built Teknikum on Villavägen. But the continued expansion, at an accelerated pace, has compelled the University planners to move further south, to the former Artillery Field on the old Stockholm road. There, during the last 10 years, large complexes of institute buildings have been created; they are unconventional in that there research and instruction in medicine and the natural sciences have been co-ordinated into a whole to an extent that was previously unknown. The scientists in the Wallenberg Laboratory work in flexible forms in the boundary areas between different sciences. The still incomplete Biomedical Centre—a whole modern research and training community in itself—houses most of the preclinical medical subjects (which have consequently left their antiquated premises in the town), together with the entire Faculty of Pharmacy. During the same period, the University Hospital was extended to the south with its new wards and blocks, so that now it has accommodation for almost 1,500 patients in all (compared with about 50 in Hwasser's time). The University Computer Centre, which is frequently used also by humanists and social scientists, is situated in Sysslomansgatan in the town. It is in the nature of things that, in the increasingly trying conditions, the resources of the University Library have been strained to the utmost, but with the aid of extensions—a new reading-room, a new office and underground book-stores—the Carolina Rediviva has managed to get the situation pretty well under control.

The incessant changes during the 1960s also affected the organization and administration of the University. The new statutes issued in 1956 offered few innovations. The change of direction came in 1964, when a

84. The "Humanist Centre" in Kyrkogårdsgatan, into which the arts and social-sciences institutes moved at New Year 1976, after having previously been housed in various premises scattered about in the town.

new university ordinance was issued, as a result of the University Commission's deliberations and conclusions. This gave the University administration increased concentration and powers. An administrative director (the University Counsellor) was placed alongside the Rector and was made responsible under the Senate for the University's finances and central administration and, together with the Rector, constituted the Rector's Office. Thus, the traditional post of the University Bursar disappeared for ever. The Council and the Finance Committee were abolished. The Senate, to which all matters were submitted, was reduced in size; its membership consisted only of the Rector, the Pro-Rector, the University Counsellor and the Deans. In 1956, the two sections of the old Faculty of Arts and Sciences—the humanities section and the natural-sciences section—had split up and formed separate faculties. Now the long-discussed idea of detaching the social sciences from the humanities

253

and creating a faculty of social sciences was implemented, while the Faculty of Sciences was divided into three sections. Since a Faculty of Pharmaceutics has now come into existence (1969) and the training of pharmacists has gradually been transferred from Stockholm to Uppsala, the University of Uppsala has seven faculties. To supervise their activities in the long run, "Faculty Planning Boards" were appointed in 1964 in the Office of the Chancellor; their task was to draw up long-term plans for the expansion of the faculties, but they have hardly accomplished what was expected of them. The fact that in recent years, despite some simplification of the organization, the University has been burdened with an ever-increasing administrative apparatus is inherent in the nature of growth and bureaucracy. The figures are eloquent. In 1945, 21 persons in the University Office, the Bursary, etc. were responsible for the whole of the University's administration; in 1975, the corresponding figure had reached 189, i.e. its growth was far greater than the influx of students would seem to have required. In 15–20 years, the University administration has been transformed into a complex civil-service department, whose routines are carried on far above the heads of the individual students.

In recent years, the professors have lost most of their former sovereignty and are no longer all-powerful in the faculties and sections, in which the university lecturers are almost equally numerous. This does not by any means imply that the post of professor has lost its attraction. The disputes about promotion to vacant chairs have raged as bitterly as ever right down to the present day, although printed protests—the most peculiar of Swedish academic literary genres—are no longer set before the enlightened public. But the traditional, centuries-old procedure in the appointments of professors has now been abandoned. Since 1975, it has not been the professors assembled in faculty or section sessions who have decided on the applicants' order of merit but a special appointments committee, which includes, in addition to the experts and a few professors, representatives of the students and the non-academic staff.

This is one sign, among many others, of yet another change which the University has undergone during the last few hectic decades—the growth of student power or academic democracy. This is, of course, only one special instance of the general democratization process that has been going on in Sweden and the western industrialized countries during the same period. Co-determination and contributory influence were demanded not only in the sphere of political power but also in the external conditions of individual life, with no restrictions. These demands for freedom found violent expression in the student revolutions in 1968, when extreme Left-wing students at universities in Europe and America attacked the established academic system and, with the vision of a socialist

85. *During the last few years, a whole "research community", the "Biomedical Centre", has grown up on the Artillery Field, south of the town. It contains all the institutes devoted to the preclinical medical subjects and the entire Faculty of Pharmaceutics.*

future before their eyes, clamoured for the power to change it. The unrest reached the Swedish universities in the spring of 1968. In Uppsala, it never rose to the same heights of revolutionary frenzy as in Lund or Stockholm, where the students occupied their own Union building for a few bewildering days. But it was inevitable that the Uppsala students should also be caught up by the political currents of the day. In the autumn, there were meetings in the Aula at which excited students demanded a new order of things and an unpleasant disturbance outside the closed doors of the Senate Hall, which were, however, found to be solid enough. Distrust between students and professors was nothing new in the history of the University; during the Caroline period, it could take the form of violent demonstrations. But these were directed against individual disagreeable teachers and not, as in the 1960s, against the entire professorial body as a collection of obscurantists and oppressors who were plotting the students' ruin. But this mood did not last. The revolutionary group was never more than a small minority of the student body and it soon returned to its studies. Of course, extreme Left-wing sympathies have remained alive, especially in the social-science institutes, and the Vietnam debate provided them with a channel through which they could be expressed. But, in the main, the prevailing mood now is one of relaxed political tension, unlike that at the "Red" University of Umeå, where the social recruitment of the students displays a different structure. Thus, it is a remarkable fact that Marxist ideas are not at all or only to a minor extent characteristic of humanistic and social-scientific research in Uppsala today.

That the crisis of confidence was overcome was due, of course, not least to the fact that the radical students' demands were to a large extent satisfied. In recent years, the students have been given, to an extent which would have been unthinkable only a generation ago, statutory means of influencing their own situation. This applies as much to the content of their studies and the forms of instruction as to the general aims of university education.

The reforms were begun as early as the mid 1950s. Up to the end of the previous century, the individual student had been at the mercy of his professor's arbitrary decisions. As the examiner, the professor had dictatorial control over the set books and the requirements as regarded knowledge. The syllabuses and students' guides which appeared at this time (see above, p. 209) represented a step towards inspection and insight. But the students were never consulted. When the first teaching committees were set up at the universities in 1941, they were pure faculty bodies, and students were not included. In this respect, the university statutes of 1956 brought about a decisive change: the teaching committees in the faculties and sections, which prepared and scrutinized all questions concerning academic education, were to include three members appointed by the Students' Union. The teaching committee—now called the training committee—gained additional stability in the university statutes of 1964, and later on a training supervisor was attached to each committee as the person mainly responsible for its entire field of action. In the training committees, teachers and students have co-operated, almost always in mutual confidence, to improve the instruction and to find solutions for educational problems. Over the years, the committees have taken on more and more of the duties previously performed by the faculties and sections, which means that the gap between instruction and research has been widened still further.

At the same time, the students obtained influence over their own immediate environment. From 1964 onwards, there was at each large institute a

86. The doctoral disputation has now been shorn of its former dramatic features. Both the respondent and the opponents now appear in simple, everyday clothes.

collegium, which included the teachers and, for some matters, assistants and two student representatives. This half-hearted idea was gradually replaced by a new provisional order of a very ambitious nature. Administrative bodies were set up at the institutes, according to different models, but all with a strong student element and, in extreme cases, having the right to decide also on questions of staff appointments. At this time, the students, together with representatives of the administrative staff, the *docenter* and the assistants, also gained entry to the University's highest decision-making authority, the Senate, although this also was only by way of experiment for the time being. The students are now entitled to vote in the election of the Rector and the Pro-Rector.

The democratic principles which form the essence of the social order in Sweden have been implemented on the academic level also by making it easier to gain admission to the universities. The gates have been opened to students who do not come from the *gymnasium* in the traditional way. This process began in the mid 1960s with the elementary-school teachers; then the welcome was extended, on certain conditions and in certain subjects, to all persons over the age of 25 who have five years' experience in their profession or trade. As a result of these and other measures, the age distribution of the students at Uppsala and elsewhere has changed;

young freshmen are being increasingly mixed with adult students. It is undeniable that this development has helped to increase the number of students from the lower social classes (see above, p. 245). A precondition for any expansion of recruitment—and for the enormous influx of students on the whole—are the social-welfare measures for the benefit of students introduced by the government authorities. The age of borrowing and bank loans is past or at least should be. Every student who fulfils certain conditions receives a government grant of a fixed annual amount, the greater part of which, however, has to be repaid on unfavourable terms.

The daily life of the students and the Students' Union as an organization cannot be the same in the overcrowded educational industry in Uppsala today as it was 20–25 years ago. The Students' Union, which has to take care of the interests of its members in an increasingly complex society, has grown into a ramified bureaucracy with a number of committees, directed by an assembly of 41 elected representatives and a board of 11, headed by the President. Alongside this bureaucracy, there is a local committee which organizes and directs the student health services, keep-fit training and athletics. In the last decade, strong, though now somewhat subdued antagonisms have manifested themselves in the Uppsala Students' Union. They have a political basis and are accentuated by the fact that the annual elections to the Union Council are held on more or less markedly party-political lines. Radical Left-wing students campaign against Conservatives, and at Council meetings an uninhibited and capricious parliamentarianism is practised which may bewilder an outsider. The centre of all the activities of the student body is the new Union building on Övre Slottsgatan, erected on the old Ubbo site, which came into the possession of the Union 100 years ago. The changes of Union politics probably make little difference to the great majority of the students. But the nations have also declined in importance. The manifold increase in the number of students meant that the nation premises could not accommodate them all; many students have refused to enrol in any of the 13 traditional nations, and the discussion of their continued existence or abolition flares up now and then. Nevertheless, the old rituals and ceremonies are still kept alive in Uppsala. The freshmen's party, the Lucia celebration, Walpurgis-night, May Day and the spring ball even today mark the rhythm of academic life in a changed world, at least for most of the students. Life as a student in an old university town has not entirely ceased to be a way of life with a distinctive character. But it is no longer a guarantee of continued success and happiness in life. The increased influx of students to the universities has created a proletariat of indebted graduates, for which the labour market is not adapted; many graduates, even after they have defended a doctoral thesis, seek in vain for a livelihood that accords with their qualifications or are forced to work in industrial jobs while awaiting better times.

In the course of a few years, the University of Uppsala had undergone a great transformation. One might think that it would then be allowed to reflect on its circumstances and to continue its work in peace and quiet. But the government has had other ideas. Even in the spring of 1968, before the new educational reform had been carried out, a large commission was appointed to examine and make plans for the entire system of higher education in Sweden. It worked with extraordinary conscientiousness and freedom from prejudice and published its report in 1973. The universities were not enthusiastic about this report. The commission expressed a radically new way of thinking, in which the old universities lost a large part of their independence and time-honoured character. Modern bureaucratic and ideological strategies determined the aims in general and the practical application. All higher education after the *gymnasium* should be co-ordinated, should, in the interests of equality, be given the name and status of college training (*högskoleutbildning*) and should be divided into 19 college areas, grouped in their turn into six educational regions. A college board, including representatives of various interests in the community, should plan and direct the activities in each college area, which should provide a more or less complete range of equivalent, fixed training lines. As far as the University of Uppsala was concerned, the commission proposed that it should be amalgamated with the nursery-school-teachers' training colleges and teacher-training colleges in Uppsala and Gävle and the domestic-science college in Uppsala. This unit, under a joint board, should be called "Uppsala *Högskola*". The Swedish educational system was on the way into a new age.

In the spring of 1975, the Riksdag decided that the proposed general reform should be carried out in all essentials and at the time of writing (in 1976) organizing committees are engaged in working out proposals concerning the forms it is to take in the different regions. In the new, enlarged *Högskola* in Uppsala, which will probably be allowed to retain the designation of "university", a large number of elementary training lines will be offered—for teachers of child welfare and languages, for financial managers, for cultural communicators, for teachers of textile handicrafts and for chemists. The curricula in these lines, which have been completely geared to the needs of the labour market, seem to be just as rigid as in the original educational reform in 1969; many traditional academic subjects will not be compulsory in any line. For each of these lines, a committee of about 10 persons will be responsible; a certain proportion of them will come from non-academic commercial life. The academic teachers will not be in the majority on the "Uppsala *Högskola* Board"

259

which will replace the 350-year-old Senate; representatives of commercial life, the administrative staff and the students altogether will probably be more than twice as numerous. The faculties and sections will remain in being. But they and the professors will have less and less power and will probably be able to influence only research and the training of research workers. There will no longer be any intellectual bond between the basic education and the scientific research. It is not self-evident that there should be such a bond. In 17th-century Uppsala, only elementary instruction by lectures was officially given, and it was actually vouchsafed to the bourgeois idealism of the 19th century to allow lectures and seminars to be imbued with the latest advances in science and, at best, the personality of the professor. It is this fruitful interplay which has been eliminated stage by stage—with the handing over of basic training to lecturers, with the strictly vocationally-orientated training lines, and with the impending division of the University into two halves on different levels, one devoted to research and the other—which has wiped out the old concept of a University—to the acquisition of professional knowledge. But research and the training of research workers is finally envisaged, according to the new College Act now in preparation, as also being placed at the service of the public good and the labour market. In accordance with this programme, the Swedish universities and colleges, bureaucratically controlled and regulated by the political powers and the interests of the community, will exist primarily to promote the country's welfare and the growth of democracy.

The great educational reform is to come into force in the summer of 1977. It is an irony of fate that this will be taking place at the same time as the University of Uppsala is celebrating its 500th anniversary. The University has never undergone so great a change before. It was founded some time towards the end of the Middle Ages as a free and independent intellectual corporation and has remained so through all the vicissitudes of the centuries. It now faces a future in which its freedom will be drastically cut down. When Johannes Rudbeckius paid tribute to the still infant university in Uppsala some time during the first few years of the 17th century, he referred to it as the abode of Apollo and the Muses, where the beauty, loftiness and glory of the sciences were revealed. We can hardly use such high-flown language today. But without a free academic life, independent of all considerations of short-term political and economic interest, no university worthy of the name can exist. Linnaeus knew that, and so did Geijer. The future continuance of the University of Uppsala is not sufficient. It must also be filled with an inquiring spirit of research which knows no bounds and will not be subservient to the temporary powers of the age.